Modern Cryptography Primer

Czesław Kościelny · Mirosław Kurkowski ·
Marian Srebrny

Modern Cryptography Primer

Theoretical Foundations and Practical Applications

Springer

Czesław Kościelny
Faculty of Information Technology
Wrocław School of Information Technology
Wrocław, Poland

Mirosław Kurkowski
Inst. of Computer and Information Sciences
Czestochowa University of Technology
Czestochowa, Poland

and

European University of Information
Technology and Economics
Warsaw, Poland

Marian Srebrny
Institute of Computer Science
Polish Academy of Sciences
Warsaw, Poland

and

Section of Informatics
University of Commerce
Kielce, Poland

ISBN 978-3-662-52453-4   ISBN 978-3-642-41386-5 (eBook)
DOI 10.1007/978-3-642-41386-5
Springer Heidelberg New York Dordrecht London

Printed on acid-free paper

Springer is part of Springer Science+Business Media (www.springer.com)

Preface

For centuries, the need to ensure confidentiality of some gathered or transmitted information got a lot of attention in various political or military contexts. Nowadays, in the era of a general necessity for privacy, and the conscious awareness of one's rights to it, cryptography is found useful in a wide range of practical applications. For the most part, it is used for securing confidentiality in interpersonal computerized communication. The turn of the 21st century is sometimes called the Internet age, computer era; communication takes place instantly and without hindrance. Obviously, no one can imagine the functioning of various types of communication and telecommunication networks without the appropriate security measures against undesirable listening in on our information.

Modern cryptography would not exist without solid mathematical foundations, especially in number theory. The recent and most advanced security algorithms are built on such arithmetic constructs as integer arithmetic divisibility, modulo operations, prime numbers, or the Euler function.

Today's societies depend to a large extent on computers which process huge amounts of information, often transferred via telecommunication networks, and stored in databases. This information often needs adequate security protection against being read by unauthorized users of computer systems and networks, particularly illegal users. Cryptography provides economical means that enable this protection. The experts in cryptography work on more and more efficient methods of ensuring the secrecy of information and electronic documents which require it. Striking advances in the proliferation of electronic data storage, linkage, and transmission have created significant new challenges in maintaining confidentiality and developing adequate methods of authentication. The ambition of cryptanalysis and cryptanalysts is to break the security codes and forge encrypted messages in such a way that they look authentic.

Until quite recently, cryptography was applied only in the area of military forces and diplomacy. This is also why cryptographers usually worked in agencies dealing with state security, and all research work concerning cryptography, as well as cryptanalysis, was classified. It was not until the late 1960s that a multinational group of scholars, who were not controlled by security agencies, became interested in the problems of cryptology and started to publish their research papers on this subject, thanks to which cryptographic data protection was found useful also in various civilian fields. The new paradigm requires that the cryptographic algorithms be publicly known, whereas only the private keys must be secret. Nowadays, the public access to the algorithms is treated as a safeguard of their security, assurance that there are no flaws due either to poor, unprofessional work by their designers or to deliberate insertion of so-called hidden backdoors (e.g., collecting copies of private keys).

Cryptographic methods are the most efficient ways of secure protection of modern telecommunication network users against computer break-ins, which have by now become a plague. That is why business promotes the use of cryptography since a basic requirement for worldwide economic growth is the development of secure worldwide computer networks underlying the information society economic infrastructure. In this context, possible administrative limitations on the use of cryptography are considered responsible for a substantial decline in a country's attractiveness in the eyes of foreign investors. Cryptographic security means are inevitable in order to improve trading and legal proceedings in the electronic economy, as well as to ensure at least the minimum of civil privacy and freedom.

The aim of this book is to introduce the currently most interesting and most important issues of modern applied cryptography in the technological practice of telecommunication networks, along with the necessary basic mathematics. Cryptography is an area on the edge of mathematics and practical software engineering. Like no other, it combines immense, challenging unsolved mathematical problems with the issues of authentic use in practical security tools in currently deployed vital data communication systems.

We present all the best known and most often used technologies, algorithms and protocols, and methods of their design and analysis. The algorithms are presented in readable pseudocode; i.e., written in English with some mathematical or programming symbols, or simple graphics and diagrams. We will not go into details on finding implementation bugs or methods of program engineering depending on the features of a particular programming environment, specification and implementation in any favorite programming language.

We bring particular attention in this book to performance analysis of the presented algorithms and protocols because since the late 1980s efficiency has essentially become the central concept to understanding modern cryptographic mechanisms, their usage, and many related problems, especially the problems of breaking the codes.

There are many very good publications on the market devoted to cryptography and/or its usage. However, only very few of them can serve as course textbooks. The material they present seems to us either extensively broad or too narrow for a graduate course, often too mathematical, and therefore very difficult for the majority of student readers with no deep mathematical background.

This book is written at the level of a graduate lecture course textbook for students of any technical university in the European Union or North America. As prerequisites it requires only some very basic elementary mathematical experience in algebra, number theory, probability, data structures, as well as the design and efficient analysis of algorithms. The material presented in the book can constitute a one-year graduate course, as well as providing material for shorter courses on selected topics to be used without the need to search other parts of the book. Each chapter contains all the necessary background information concerning the problems being discussed. Selected chapters can constitute a reasonable basis for further studies of the subject, e.g., in the form of seminar or term credit papers, etc. The references provided will definitely be of help in completing such tasks. For the same reason, this book can be treated as a useful source of information in the field of data and network transactions security for practitioners and researchers just after their studies.

Today's cryptography is a very broad and lively field. We are aware that many areas need much broader treatment. For example, the elliptic curve algorithms, quantum cryptography, secret sharing, and various cryptanalytic techniques. Cryptographic hash algorithms are limited in this book to signaling the basic approaches and challenges, with no coverage of the most recent very interesting advances. These areas have got a lot of attention in the last few years, with many different methods and their own challenges. These topics will be covered in full detail in our follow-up textbook to appear soon.

This book consists of nine chapters discussing today's actual practice in applied cryptography from the very basics to strong state-of-the-art security algorithms and protocols.

The first chapter introduces the basic concepts of cryptography. The general diagram of encryption/decryption, as well as the notion of a cryptographic algorithm and the definition of cryptographic keys are discussed. The rules for building strong cryptographic codes are introduced. The chapter also presents the fundamental notions of theoretical and practical computational complexity, and discusses its meaning for determining the difficulty of breaking cryptosystems. Next, we introduce codes known from history such as Caesar's ancient code, and Playfair and Enigma, which were applied during the World Wars.

Modern cryptography would not exist without solid mathematical foundations, therefore in Chap. 2 we recollect and present mathematical concepts and properties required for continuing the course. Elements of the theory of algebraic structures, as well as elements of number theory, are presented. Also, we present simple arithmetic algorithms applied in cryptography. The chapter ends with a discussion on currently applied algorithms for testing integer primality, and computationally hard problems in number theory.

In Chap. 3 the most important symmetric ciphers are presented, among them the standards of symmetric encryption applied in widespread practice today. The DES (Data Encryption Standard) algorithm, its modifications and modes of operation are given and discussed in detail. A lot of attention is focused on the most recent American standard for symmetric cipher, the AES (Advanced Encryption Standard) algorithm. The IDEA algorithm, as well as the algorithms of the RC family are presented. As an interesting detail illustrating the resistance of encryption algorithms against attempts to break them, we present the process of the global competition in breaking RC algorithms, and the results.

In Chap. 4 the reader will find exact descriptions of asymmetric algorithms, beginning with the Diffie-Hellman scheme, through the ElGamal algorithm. Next, the well known RSA algorithm, and various issues concerning unceasing attempts to break it are discussed. An interesting detail is the discussion on the results of the RSA factorization challenge, illustrating the cryptographic power of the RSA code.

Chapter 5 presents one of the most important modern applications of cryptography, namely the electronic signature. The general scheme, as well as several of the currently most essential and most interesting applied algorithms for generation and verification of the validity of e-signature are covered. We present various algorithms of digital signature and hash functions. We discuss the current issues concerning the usage of these functions, and their security.

In Chap. 6 the reader will find the exact description of the popular cryptosystem PGP (Pretty Good Privacy). The overall scheme of the system and the algorithms used in it are surveyed. The installation and the usage of PGP are described, encryption and signing documents (messages, e-mails, files) among others. In this chapter, the authors introduce other, non-commercial solutions enabling the application of strong cryptography by any computer user.

Chapter 7 is devoted to the public key infrastructure as a solution enabling application of the electronic signature for business and legal proceedings in the form required by legislation in most countries. The role of the so-called trusted third party in contemporary solutions, as well as the issues concerning certification of cryptographic keys, are presented.

Another important feature of cryptography in day-to-day reality is the cryptographic protocols applied often in mass scale in all kinds of communication via computer networks, especially for entity authentication and preventing identity theft. The goals to be achieved by the cryptographic protocols, as well as their examples, are presented. Issues and problems of their specification, design and application, methods of complexity analysis as well as methods of verification of correctness, and the security of cryptographic protocols are introduced and covered more broadly than in any other textbook available so far.

In Chap. 9 the remaining aspects of the application of cryptography in data and transaction security are taken up. The problems and solutions of preserving the secrecy and privacy of electronic mail, as well as secure exchange of documents in electronic form are discussed. The commonly applied SSH (Secure SHell) and SSL (Secure Socket Layer) protocols are also studied.

Like every book, ours is surely not flawless. In case of any errors, mistakes or inaccuracies in this publication, we would appreciate if the reader could kindly submit them to us via e-mail at cryptobook@icis.pcz.pl. Any feedback will be appreciated. In return, we promise an up-to-date list of corrections, a constantly revised corrigendum.

Our thanks for help and support in various stages of the process of writing and editing this book are due to many of our friends and collaborators, as well as our students, audience and participants in lectures and seminars given by each of us. Our special thanks must be given to Professor Leonard Bolc (1934–2013) of the Institute of Computer Science of the Polish Academy of Sciences, without whose kind and gentle but tenaciously ongoing systematic encouragement this book would most definitely never have come into existence. Very special acknowledgments go to Professor Andrzej Borzyszkowski for his fruitful cooperation on the early versions of the materials for the chapter on the security protocols, their specification and verification of correctness. Similarly to Maciej Orzechowski. The third author gratefully acknowledges many useful conversations and discussions with Professors Paweł Morawiecki, Stanisław Spież, and Jerzy Urbanowicz (1951–2012). The latter was entirely responsible for dragging the third author in a friendly manner into the world of cryptologic research and practice, and for educating him on the field's special beauty and problems, splendors and shadows. The first author acknowledges support from Wrocław School of Information Technology. The second author acknowledges support from Czestochowa University of Technology and the European University of Information Technology and Economics, Warsaw. We would also like to thank Kasia Grygiel, Gosia Berezowska, Ewelina Gajek and Janek Jay Halicki for their help in the preparation of the English version of our book. Last but not least, the authors thank the copyeditor for his excellent careful work, and Springer's Ronan Nugent for successfully and nicely driving us through the whole editorial and production process.

Poland   Czesław Kościelny
August 2013   Mirosław Kurkowski
                                                                      Marian Srebrny

Contents

Chapter 1
Basic Concepts and Historical Overview

1.1 Introduction

Cryptography is the science of transforming, or encoding, information into a form non-comprehensible for anyone who does not know an appropriate key. In such forms information can be securely transferred via any communication channel or stored in data archives with its access restricted or even forbidden (for one reason or another). Cryptography is a part of a broader discipline called *cryptology*, which includes also so-called *cryptanalysis*—the art of breaking codes (ciphers), i.e., regaining the content of encrypted messages without an authorized access to the decryption keys.

1.1.1 Encryption

Cryptography is the art of providing confidentiality of information (messages, documents) through encryption, whenever required, together with means of information security, data integrity, entity and data authentication.

Let us suppose someone (a sender) wishes to deliver some information to someone else (a receiver) via a public channel, e.g., the Internet. Moreover, the sender would like to make sure that no one else, but the intended receiver, can get the content being transmitted. The sender can do so by hiding the information content according to the following scheme. The information content being transferred is called a *plaintext*, or a *cleartext*. The procedure of hiding the content is called *encryption*, and the encrypted message is called its *ciphertext* or *cryptogram*. The reverse procedure of recapturing the content from its cryptogram is called *decryption*. The encryption and decryption algorithms together form a *cipher*. These concepts are illustrated in Fig. 1.1.

Depending on the encryption algorithm, a plaintext can be any information formulated in any way as a sequence of bits, text file, sequence of voice samples, digital video, et cetera. The examples listed come from the pervasive digital world, but

C. Kościelny et al., *Modern Cryptography Primer*,
DOI 10.1007/978-3-642-41386-5_1, © Springer-Verlag Berlin Heidelberg 2013

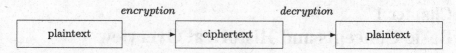

Fig. 1.1 Encryption and decryption

clearly in general one can encrypt information presented in any form whatsoever—it requires only an encryption algorithm to be applied or designed for this purpose. In this book a cipher's input is considered as binary data.

We usually denote a plaintext message by the letter M and its ciphertext by C. Computer output ciphertext is a binary data sequence as well, often of the same size as M, sometimes longer. (In the case of combining encryption with compression, C may turn out smaller than M; encryption itself does not give this effect, usually.) One can view encryption as a function E associating with each given plaintext data its ciphertext data. The encryption procedure can then be written as the mathematical formula:

$$E(M) = C.$$

Similarly, the decryption procedure can be thought of as the function

$$D(C) = M,$$

which takes a cipher text C and outputs its plaintext M.

The goal of decrypting an encrypted message is to recapture the input plaintext; hence the following is required:

$$D(E(M)) = M.$$

1.1.2 Algorithms and Keys

Historically, the security offered by a cipher was to a large extent based on keeping secret its encryption/decryption algorithm. Modern cryptography considers that such ciphers do not provide an adequate level of security. For instance, they cannot be used by a larger group of users. A problem arises when someone would like to leave the group, the others would have to change the algorithm. A similar procedure would apply when someone reveals the algorithm. Another serious concern and source of doubt about secret ciphers is due to the impossibility of having the quality of the algorithms, their standardization and implementations, checked by external experts.

A secret cipher algorithm would have to be uniquely designed for each group of users, which excludes the possibility of ready-to-use software or hardware implementations. Otherwise, an adversary would be able to purchase an identical product and run the same encryption/decryption algorithms. Each group of users would have to design and implement their own cipher. If in such a group there was no good cryptographer and cryptanalyst, the group would not know if its cipher was reliable enough.

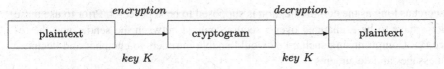

Fig. 1.2 Encryption and decryption with one key

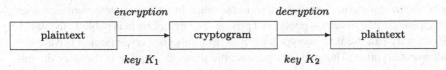

Fig. 1.3 Encryption and decryption with two keys

Modern cryptography solves the above security concerns in such a way that usually the cipher used is publicly known but its encryption/decryption execution uses an extra private piece of information, called a cryptographic key, which is another input parameter. A key is usually denoted by the letter K. It can take one of a wide range or *keyspace* of possible values, usually numbers.

The central idea is that both encryption and decryption functions use a key, and their outputs depend on the keys used, with the following formulae:

$$E(K, M) = C \quad \text{and} \quad D(K, C) = M.$$

In the literature often the following notation appears:

$$E_K(M) = C \quad \text{and} \quad D_K(C) = M$$

where the subscripts indicate the key. Note the following property (see Fig. 1.2):

$$D_K(E_K(M)) = M.$$

Some ciphers use different encryption and decryption keys (Fig. 1.3). This means that the encryption key K_1 is different from the corresponding decryption key K_2. In this case we have the following properties:

$$E_{K_1}(M) = C, \qquad D_{K_2}(C) = M, \qquad D_{K_2}(E_{K_1}(M)) = M.$$

As pointed out above, the security of good ciphers is based on the secrecy of the keys. The algorithms are publicly known and can be analyzed by the best experts. Software and hardware implementations or partial components of the ciphers can be produced and distributed on an industrial scale. Any potential intruder can have access to the algorithms. As long as she does not know our private key and the cipher is good enough, she will not be able to read our cryptograms.

By a cipher or *cryptosystem* we shall mean the two algorithms of encryption and decryption together with (the space of) all the possible plaintexts, cryptograms and keys. There are two general types of ciphers which use keys: symmetric ciphers and public-key ciphers.

Symmetric ciphers, often also called traditional ciphers, *secret-key ciphers*, *single-key algorithms* or *one-key algorithms*, use the same key for encryption and decryption. Here, the same means that each of the two keys can be practically determined (computed) from the other. The keys used in such ciphers have to be kept secret as long as the communication is supposed to be kept secret. Prior to use these keys have to be exchanged over a secure channel between the sender and the receiver. Compromising such a key would enable intruders to encipher and decipher messages and documents.

The basic idea of public key cryptographic algorithms is that encryption and decryption use two different keys, matched in such a way that it is not possible in practice to reconstruct one of them from the other. In such a cryptosystem each user has a unique pair of keys—public and private. The first of them is publicly available. Everybody can use it to encrypt messages. But only the corresponding private key allows decryption. Thus the only person able to run decryption is the one who has the private key.

1.1.3 Strong Cryptosystems Design Principles

An encryption procedure transforms a given *plaintext* document into its enciphered form (*cryptogram*). An encryption algorithm input consists of a plaintext and a key. It outputs the cryptogram. The associated decryption algorithm input consists of a cryptogram and a key, and it outputs the original plaintext.

The basic step in any cryptosystem design is a kind of evaluation of the level of security offered by the resulting system. It can be measured in terms of the computational resources required to break—by any known or foreseeable method—the ciphertexts generated by the system. In the course of many years of research the following conditions have been developed as basic requirements on a strong cryptographic algorithm:

- it should be infeasible to find the plaintext from its cryptogram without knowing the key used;
- reconstructing the secret key should be infeasible.

A good cipher should meet the above criteria also when the cryptanalyst trying to break it has access to some relatively large number of sample plaintexts together with their corresponding cryptograms and knows all the details of the cipher algorithm. It is generally assumed that the cryptanalyst has all the resources (space, devices, technology) feasible currently and in the foreseeable future. Given these assumptions, it should be emphasized strongly that a strong cryptographic system's robustness is based on the secrecy of the private keys.

We do not require that there does not exist a way to break such a cryptosystem. We only require that there is no currently known feasible method to do so. The strong cryptographic algorithms that correspond to the above definition could theoretically be broken, although in practice it happens very rarely.

The most important rules to date for constructing difficult-to-crack cryptographic code systems were formulated by Claude Elwood Shannon [94] in 1949 (Fig. 1.4). He defined breaking a cipher as finding a method to determine the key and/or cleartext on the basis of its cryptogram. The cryptanalyst can obtain great help from information about certain statistical characteristics of the possible plaintexts such as

Fig. 1.4 Claude E. Shannon

the frequency of occurrences of various characters. On this basis one can determine whether the plaintext is a program written in C, a fragment of prose in Japanese, or an audio file. In each of these cases in every plaintext there is an apparent redundancy of information which can greatly facilitate cryptanalysis. By now many statistical tests based on information theory have been developed, which effectively help in the breaking of ciphers whenever the plaintext statistics parameters are known.

According to Shannon a cryptographic system that allows *excellent protection against unauthorized access* must not provide any statistical information about the encrypted plaintext at all. Shannon proved that this is the case when the number of cryptographic keys is at least as large as the number of possible plaintexts. The key should therefore be of roughly the same or more bits, characters or bytes as the plaintext, with the assumption that no key can be used twice. Shannon's perfect encryption system is called the *single-key system* or *one-time pad*.

According to Shannon to define a mathematical model of a reliable system of strong cryptography it is necessary to be able to reduce the redundancy of plaintext information, so that the redundancy is not carried into the cryptograms. Shannon proposed techniques of *diffusion* and *confusion*, which in practice have been reduced by many crypto designers to some kind of alternation of combining block cipher components with substitutions and permutations.

Claude Elwood Shannon (30 April 1916–24 February 2001) was an eminent American mathematician, founder of information theory, one of the many scholars working during World War II with US military and government agencies as a consultant in the field of cryptology.

1.1.4 Computational Complexity of Algorithms

In this section we introduce the basic concepts of theoretical and practical computational complexity, to the minimum extent that is necessary to understand modern cryptography and the next chapters of this book.[1]

---

[1] For more on this background topic the reader is referred to [27, 68].

Modern cryptography uses publicly known algorithms. Before their deployment they are subject to objective analysis by independent experts. The private keys are the closely guarded secrets, not the algorithms. Without knowing the appropriate keys no one can encrypt/decrypt documents in any good cryptosystem. According to Shannon's principles the algorithms must be designed in such a way that the complexity of the two tasks previously described as infeasible makes breaking the ciphers practically impossible. Often, however, the high complexity is an estimated upper bound on the performance of one algorithm, with the additional argument that *currently no efficient cipher-breaking algorithm is known.*

An important part of the analysis of encryption and decryption algorithms, and algorithms in general, is their computational complexity, the efficiency of calculations and of solving algorithmic and computational problems and problem instances. In this context, by a computational problem we mean a function of the input data into the output data, that we want to calculate using the analyzed algorithm.

As motivating examples, consider the problem of computing the determinant of an integer-valued matrix and the problem of integer factorization. A given matrix or an integer are called *instances* of these problems, respectively. The bigger the matrix or integer, the more computational resources are needed to calculate the determinant or the prime factors. In general, the bigger the size of the input data, the more resources (time, space, processors) are needed to compute such a problem instance. The complexity of an algorithm is a function of the instance input data size.

One can define the complexity of an algorithm in various ways, however in general it expresses the amount of resources needed by a machine (computer) to perform the algorithm. The resources considered most often are *time* and *space*. For obvious reasons, the amount of these resources can differ greatly from instance to instance depending on several parameters. The time complexity of an algorithm is a function that indicates how much time is needed for its execution. The time here is not measured in seconds or minutes, but in the number of calculation steps, or of bit operations. How many seconds it takes, depends largely on the equipment on which the calculations are performed. Independently from equipment and from the rapid development of computing devices, the complexity of an algorithm is defined as a function expressing how many elementary operations on individual bits have to be performed, in the course of each run of the algorithm, depending on the size of the input data. The time complexity of a given computational problem is the function of the input data size expressing the time complexity of the best algorithm solving the problem.

The time complexity of a given algorithm is defined as the number of elementary operations on input data during one run of the algorithm. By the elementary operations one usually understands the simplest nondecomposable instructions in a certain programming language or in a certain abstract model of computation; e.g., a Turing machine or a (single-core) *Random Access Machine*, RAM. It does not matter what language it is, because what matters is just the proportional order of magnitude of the number of operations, up to a possible (finite) constant multiplicative factor. Without loss of generality, it can be the language Java. Alternatively, one can treat the single instructions (lines) of the algorithm's pseudocode as the elementary operations. In this book we do not refer to anything like that, nor to any abstract machine model. Instead, as elementary we define the arithmetic bit-operations of primary school addition and subtraction of the binary representations of nonnegative integers.

The addition of binary numbers is calculated in the same way as traditional column addition of decimal numbers. You do it by writing one number below the other and adding one column at a time: add up the digits (binary, bits), then write down the resulting 0 or 1, and write down the carry to the next column on the left. Subtraction is calculated just as addition, but instead of adding the binary digits you deduct one bit from the other, and instead of the carry operation you take a *borrow* from the next column.

Multiplication can be done using only the above elementary bit operations. The school division algorithm is much more complicated, but it also refers only to the same elementary operations on single bits. Just add the divisor to some extra parameter (initialized to zero) until it gets bigger than the dividend. Then the number of additions made so far (minus one) makes the resulting quotient of the division, while the dividend minus the final value of the extra parameter (minus the divisor) makes the resulting remainder left over.

In computer architecture the elementary bit operations are implemented in a special section of the central processing unit called the arithmetic logic unit, ALU.

In complexity analysis of a given algorithm it suffices to care about the time of the dominating operation only. That is, the operation performed much longer than all the other operations of the algorithm taken together. In this book, indeed in cryptography in general, the multiplication of two integers is dominating in almost all cases. Sometimes it is integer addition, subtraction, or division. In cryptography, these four basic arithmetic operations can be taken as elementary, the more so as more and more often these operations get hardware implementations in the arithmetic and logical processors, and each of them can be executed in a single clock tick.

Computational complexity is thus a kind of device-independent simplification, an approximation that allows comparisons of the hardness of algorithms (programs) regardless of the machines that can run them. It also neglects a lot of details such as, for instance, the generally much shorter time required for a variety of auxiliary actions, for example, memory register access operations, (sub)procedure calls, passing parameters, etc. It omits all the technical features of the computer on which the calculations are performed. It is generally accepted that the algorithm execution time is proportional to the number of elementary operations performed on the input bits.

Adding two integers m and n written as $|m|$ and $|n|$ binary digits (bits zero or one), respectively, can be done in $\max(|m|, |n|)$ bit-operations. Subtraction has the same estimate. The primary-school multiplication of two $|n|$-bit integers requires at most $|n|^2$ elementary bit-operations. Dividing an $|m|$-bit integer by an $|n|$-bit integer requires at most $|m| \cdot |n|$ time.

In general, the larger the input data, the more resources needed for their processing. However, an analyzed algorithm can do this in a nonuniform, not necessarily monotone, way. The time and space it needs can vary considerably on different input instances of the same size. We distinguish: pessimistic complexity, that is the case of input data on which the analyzed algorithm requires the most resources over all data of that size; expected, or average complexity; and asymptotic complexity, i.e., the limit of the complexity function values on arbitrarily large inputs.

Space complexity refers to how much space on the computer is required. Space complexity of an algorithm (program) is a measure of the amount of memory needed, for example, the number of cells visited on a Turing machine tape. In this book, indeed in modern cryptography in general, the required space is expressed in bits—as the maximum number of bits simultaneously written down (stored) in the course of the analyzed algorithm run.

It is generally considered that a superpolynomial performance of an algorithm, i.e., expressed by a function with asymptotic growth faster than all polynomials with integer coefficients, is infeasible (or intractable) on sufficiently large input data. For example, when we say that there is no known feasible algorithm for integer factorization, we usually mean: no algorithm running in polynomial time.

Theoretical polynomial complexity is not a sufficient criterion for practicality. For example, in 2002 [4] published a polynomial time algorithm checking whether a given natural number is prime (that is, divisible only by 1 and itself). However, the degree of this polynomial is too high for practical use in testing primality of numbers of the size currently interesting in practical applications. These are approximately 1000-bit integers.

One more concept of computational complexity is often called *practical complexity* and measured in seconds on currently available computers and on input data of the size of current interest. Algorithm AKS, mentioned above, has too high practical complexity. Similarly, the currently (August 2012) best attacks on the SHA-1 hash function standard are treated as merely theoretical, because the best of them gives a chance of finding a collision (i.e., two different messages with the same hash) in time corresponding to over 2^{60} SHA-1 evaluations. Nobody can have that much time on currently available computers (without very high extra financial and organizational effort).

The concepts introduced above have been extensively studied in computational complexity theory. The standard reference textbooks are [27, 77].

In modern cryptology the strength of a cipher (in general, a cryptosystem) is usually expressed in terms of the computational complexity of the problem of breaking the analyzed cipher—how much time or space is required to find the secret key or recover the plaintext from its encrypted version with no prior knowledge of the appropriate secret key, even when the cryptanalyst has possibly a large number of pairs plaintext/ciphertext. *How much time is required* refers to the fastest currently known algorithm performing this task. Cryptography can be called cryptocomplexity.

Similarly to time complexity, space complexity is defined as the amount of space required for running an algorithm. It can be measured either by the maximum number of cells in an abstract machine model of the algorithm execution or by the size of actual physical memory space expressed in bits or bytes.

A specific big-oh notation has been introduced for comparison of the rate of growth of functions describing the computational complexity of algorithms. The expression

$$f(n) \in O(g(n))$$

is read and defined as: *function f is at most of order g if and only if there exist positive real c and natural n_o such that for every n greater than or equal to n_o, the value $f(n)$ is at most equal to the product $c \cdot g(n)$.* In symbols it can be written as follows:

$$f(n) = O(g(n)) \Leftrightarrow \exists_{c \in \mathbf{R}_+} \exists_{n_0 \in \mathbf{N}} (n \geq n_0 \Rightarrow f(n) \leq c \cdot g(n)).$$

By way of a simple illustration, we give an estimate of the time cost (computational time complexity) of the algorithms for grade-school addition and multiplication of binary integers.

Consider two binary numbers x and y of bit-length k. Adding these binary numbers is usually realized as k additions of single bits. So, the time complexity is $O(k)$. Multiplying x by y is in the worst case (when y has all ones in the binary notation) $k - 1$ additions of x to x shifted by one bit to the left each time. It requires $(k - 1) \cdot k = k^2 - k$ additions of single bits. So, the time complexity of integer multiplication is $O(k^2)$, i.e., quadratic.[2]

Basic Complexity Classes

- $O(1)$—constant complexity—the algorithm performs a constant number of steps no matter what size its input data is.
- $O(n)$—linear complexity—for each input data size $|n|$, the algorithm performs a number of steps proportional to $|n|$. The growth rate of the running time is linear w.r.t. the input data size.
- $O(n^2)$—quadratic complexity—the algorithm's running time is proportional to the square of the input data size $|n|$.
- $O(n^3), O(n^4), \ldots$—polynomial time complexity.
- $O(\log n)$—logarithmic complexity.
- $O(2^n)$—exponential complexity—the algorithm performs a constant number of operations for every subset of the size n input data.
- $O(n!)$—the algorithm performs a constant number of steps on each permutation of the size n input data.

Algorithms of exponential or higher complexity are infeasible. Their running time grows rapidly with increasing n. On large input data size, their running time gets monstrously, inconceivably long. If we imagine that we have two computers, one of which can perform a million operations per second, and the second is a million times faster (which gives the performance of 10^{12} operations per second), the time required by an exponential algorithm (with time complexity $O(2^n)$) is shown in Table 1.1.

---

[2]See Table 2.1 in [68].

Table 1.1 Running time of an algorithm of class $O(2^n)$

Input size n	20	50	100
10^6 op./s	roughly 1 s	about 35 years	about $4 \cdot 10^{16}$ years
10^{12} op./s	about 10^{-6} s	about 18.5 min	about $4 \cdot 10^{10}$ years

Table 1.2 Enumerating letters of the Latin alphabet

A	B	C	D	...	W	X	Y	Z
↓	↓	↓	↓	...	↓	↓	↓	↓
1	2	3	4	...	23	24	25	26

The table clearly shows that even a big increase of hardware computational power cannot beat the device-independent complexity of an algorithm. The time required for its execution can become unimaginably large. For example, for $n = 100$, in both cases probably we would never see the results.

Here we are talking about asymptotic complexity bounds. This does not exclude the possibility of particular input data instances of even very large size that can be computed very fast by an exponential time complexity algorithm. In practice an algorithm's running time, measured in seconds, behaves irregularly, with many downs and ups. Over the last decade or two a whole domain of research has arisen with significant successful real-life applications of some asymptotic exponential time algorithms, often on some industrial-scale input sizes.

1.2 Simple Stream Ciphers

1.2.1 Caesar Cipher

One of the simplest encryption algorithms is the so-called Caesar cipher, already used by the Roman army.[3] Let us assume that the texts we want to encrypt are written in the 26-letter Latin alphabet excluding capitalization. We assign consecutive positive integers to symbols of the alphabet (see Table 1.2).

The idea of the algorithm consists in replacing each symbol of a plaintext with the symbol whose number is greater by three computing modulo 26 (the last three letters of the alphabet X, Y, Z are replaced with, respectively, A, B, C). If we denote the integer assigned to a letter x by L_x, then we can write the replacement operation mathematically in the following way (addition is performed modulo 26, however we do not replace 26 with 0):

$$C(L_x) = L_x + 3.$$

---

[3]One can find comprehensive information about this and many other ciphers used in the past in [54]. The history of contemporary cryptography is well discussed in [29]. See also Sect. 7.3 in [68].

An important feature of the Caesar cipher is the distributivity of encryption over the sequence of symbols that forms a plaintext. Formally, we can present it as follows:

$$C(xy) = C(x)C(y).$$

Obviously, it is easy to notice that the algorithm can be modified by changing the number of positions by which symbols are shifted.

Although very simple, the Caesar cipher is a symmetric key algorithm. The key in the original version of the Caesar cipher is equal to 3 (the shift parameter). In the next section we will generalize Caesar's method to all possible permutations of the alphabet.

What is interesting is that the Caesar cipher was used even during World War I by the Russian army. The applied shift parameter was equal to 13.

From the theoretical point of view the cost of encrypting a k-bit ciphertext is linear—it equals $O(k)$. Of course, nowadays it is very easy to break the Caesar cipher even with an unknown shift parameter. Actually, it can be broken without using a computer—a piece of paper and a pen are enough.

1.2.2 XOR Encryption (Vernam Cipher)

Now we are going to present an encryption algorithm known in the literature as the Vernam cipher or simply *XOR*. This algorithm, which requires some mathematical knowledge, uses the *XOR* function. Formally, the latter is a Boolean function (i.e., a function $f : \{0, 1\} \times \{0, 1\} \to \{0, 1\}$) that satisfies the following conditions:

$$f(0, 0) = f(1, 1) = 0 \quad \text{and} \quad f(0, 1) = f(1, 0) = 1.$$

One can easily notice some of its properties. For arbitrary $x, y, z \in \{0, 1\}$ the following equations hold:

1. $f(x, y) = f(y, x)$ (commutativity),
2. $f(x, x) = 0$,
3. $f(x, 0) = x$ (0 is a neutral element of f).
   It can be proved that the function is associative, i.e.,
4. $f(x, f(y, z)) = f(f(x, y), z)$.

When we consider the function *XOR* as an operation defined on the set $\{0, 1\}$, then the above equations can be expressed as follows:

(a) $0 \, XOR \, 0 = 1 \, XOR \, 1 = 0$,
(b) $0 \, XOR \, 1 = 1 \, XOR \, 0 = 1$,
(c) $x \, XOR \, y = y \, XOR \, x$,
(d) $x \, XOR \, x = 0$,
(e) $x \, XOR \, 0 = x$,
(f) $(x \, XOR \, (y \, XOR \, z)) = ((x \, XOR \, y) \, XOR \, z)$.

If we take two sequences of bits $X = (x_1, x_2, \ldots, x_n)$ and $Y = (y_1, y_2, \ldots, y_n)$, then by $X\ XOR\ Y$ we mean the sequence of values of the XOR operation on consecutive entries of sequences X and Y:

$$X\ XOR\ Y = (x_1, x_2, \ldots, x_n)\ XOR\ (y_1, y_2, \ldots, y_n)$$
$$= (x_1\ XOR\ y_1, x_2\ XOR\ y_2, \ldots, x_n\ XOR\ y_n).$$

The above properties allow us to execute the following encryption algorithm. In order to encrypt a k-bit sequence we divide it into blocks with n elements each (in case there are not enough bits for the last block, we fill it with, e.g., zeroes). As a key we take an arbitrary (random) bit sequence of length n: $K = (k_1, k_2, \ldots, k_n)$. The ciphertext for a block $A = (a_1, a_2, \ldots, a_n)$ is simply expressed by:

$$C = K\ XOR\ A = (k_1\ XOR\ a_1, k_2\ XOR\ a_2, \ldots, k_n\ XOR\ a_n)$$
$$= (c_1, c_2, \ldots, c_n).$$

The above-mentioned features of the XOR operation enable us to specify the method by which the ciphertext is decrypted. In order to reconstruct the block A it is sufficient simply to execute:

$$K\ XOR\ C = K\ XOR\ (K\ XOR\ A) = A.$$

Indeed, for any entry of the ciphertext c_i $(i = 1, \ldots, n)$ we have:

$$k_i\ XOR\ c_i = k_i\ XOR\ (k_i\ XOR\ a_i) = (k_i\ XOR\ k_i)\ XOR\ a_i$$
$$= 0\ XOR\ a_i = a_i.$$

The second equation in the above notation follows from the associativity of XOR, while the third and the fourth ones follow from properties 2 and 3, respectively.

The cost of this encryption is very low and, as in the case of the Caesar cipher, is equal to $O(k)$ for a k-bit ciphertext. Let us notice that if the key applied is appropriately long (for instance of several bits), then the cipher provides a high security level. Due to its construction it is not vulnerable to any known attacks but the brute force technique. The latter, however, is actually unfeasible in the case of long keys because of its time complexity. Moreover, if the key length is as long as the length of the ciphertext and the key is used only once, then the Vernam cipher turns out to be an ideal cipher that cannot be broken. It can easily be seen that one can adjust a key for a ciphertext of a given length and any plaintext of the same length. The complexity of the brute force method for breaking encryption with a k-bit key equals $O(2^k)$.

Despite its simplicity, the Vernam cipher is still applied: WordPerfect, a very popular text editor, uses it in an only slightly modified version. This encryption scheme is used in many other ciphers, e.g., DES and AES, as well. It is also applied in secure communication with the use of the first quantum communication networks.

1.3 Simple Block Ciphers

1.3.1 Permutations

The Caesar cipher is one of the simplest substitution ciphers. Replacing each alphabet letter with another one is performed in a regular manner—it depends on the alphabetical order. One can easily see that this assignment may be done arbitrarily.

Let us now recall some elementary mathematical facts. Given a finite set X, any one-to-one function $f : X \to X$ is called a permutation.

If the cardinality of X is equal to n, then there are $n!$ permutations (one-to-one functions) on X.

The Caesar cipher can be generalized to all possible permutations of the alphabet. In this situation a key is given by a 26-element non-repetitive sequence of integers from 1 to 26. Such a sequence determines the substitution that has to be applied in order to encrypt a message.

It can be seen that for an alphabet with 26 characters the number of all permutations equals 26!, which amounts to about $4 \cdot 10^{26}$, a number that is large even for modern computers. Verification of all possible keys (sequences) would take a great deal of time.

It turns out, however, that substitution ciphers can easily be broken using so-called frequency analysis. Certain letters and combinations of letters occur more often than others. Therefore, it is easy to check which symbols appear in a given ciphertext and with what frequency (for obvious reasons it is better to work with suitably long ciphertext messages).

1.3.2 Transpositions

Another simple method of encryption consists of inserting a plaintext in adequately defined (e.g., as geometrical shapes) blocks. Such a block may be represented as an array with a given number of rows and columns. A plaintext is placed in the matrix row-wise. Then the matrix is transposed (rows are replaced with columns). The ciphertext should be read row-wise after such a transposition.

Example 1.1 Let us consider the following plaintext: *ITISASIMPLEEXAMPLE*. If we decide to encrypt the message with a simple transposition cipher using, for instance, a 3×6-matrix, then we obtain the matrix with the plaintext (Table 1.3).

After performing the transposition, we get the matrix presented in Table 1.4:

Finally, we get the ciphertext: *ISILXPTAMEALISPEME*.

In this system, the key is given by the matrix dimensions. For example, in the case of a 6×3-matrix the ciphertext is as follows: *IIXTMAIPMSLPAELSEE*.

Table 1.3 Matrix with the
plaintext

I	T	I
S	A	S
I	M	P
L	E	E
X	A	M
P	L	E

Table 1.4 Transposition

I	S	I	L	X	P
T	A	M	E	A	L
I	S	P	E	M	E

Table 1.5 Table for
constructing encryption
templates

0	1	1	2	3	3	0	3
1	3	2	2	3	0	0	3
3	0	3	2	0	1	0	3
2	1	0	2	1	2	3	2
1	2	1	1	0	3	1	2
2	1	0	1	0	0	2	3

1.3.3 *Example of a Simple Transposition Cipher*

We are going to explain the principle of constructing such a cipher by a simple,
however non-trivial, example. Now, a plaintext and a ciphertext are expressed over
a 32-symbol alphabet:

$$ABCDEFGHIJKLMNOPQRSTUVWXYZ.:,;-$$

which consists of 26 capital letters of the Latin alphabet, a space, a period, a colon,
a comma, a semicolon, and a hyphen. We assume that a block of a plaintext contains
48 symbols from the above alphabet which are arranged in 6 rows. Given these
assumptions, we can apply the following encryption algorithm for a transposition
cipher:

1. Create a table with 6 rows and 8 columns and fill it with integers 0, 1, 2 and
   3 in such a way that the number of zeroes, ones, twos and threes is the same
   and equals 12. At the same time, try to minimize the number of adjacent cells
   containing the same integers. These conditions are satisfied in Table 1.5. Such a
   table can easily be found, for instance by means of the following program written
   in Pascal:

```
var i, k, r: Byte;
    l: array[0..3] of Byte;
begin
  repeat
    Randomize;
```

Table 1.6 Block of the
plaintext

A	D	I	U	N	K	T	-
L	E	C	T	U	R	E	R
A	F	O	R	Y	Z	M	-
A	P	H	O	R	I	S	M
A	K	T	O	R	K	A	-
A	C	T	R	E	S	S	.

```
        for i:=0 to 3 do l[i]:=0;
        for i:=1 to 6 do
        begin
           for k:=1 to 8 do
           begin
              r:=Random(4); Inc(l[r]);
              Write(r:2);
           end;
           WriteLn
        end;
        WriteLn;
     until (l[0]=l[1]) and (l[0]=l[2]) and(l[0]=l[3])
  end.
```

2. Cut four rectangular pieces of paper that have the same size as the tables from the first step of the algorithm. Then create four templates, numbered 0, 1, 2 and 3. In each template cut 12 holes covering the cells which contain the number of the template.
3. The cryptogram will be written on a blank piece of paper that is exactly the size of the template. Put this piece of paper consecutively against the templates prepared in the second step and insert 48 letters of the plaintext into empty cells (4 times 12 letters).

The decryption algorithm is easier and consists of only one step:

1. Put the templates consecutively against the ciphertext and read the symbols of the plaintext from the holes and write them down in the matrix of six rows and eight columns.

Let us take the part of the Polish-English dictionary shown in Table 1.6 as a plaintext. After encrypting this text according to the algorithm we obtain the cryptogram given in Table 1.7. It can easily be verified that by decrypting this ciphertext according to the algorithm presented above one obtains the proper plaintext.

The just-described substitution block cipher, whose keys are given by encryption templates and the order of their use, can be specified in a more formal manner. If we enumerate 48 symbols of a plaintext consecutively, then the encryption process obtained by applying templates takes the form of the table presented in Table 1.8, from which it follows that the first symbol of the ciphertext corresponds to the first symbol of the plaintext, the second symbol corresponds to the 13th symbol of the

Table 1.7 Block of the cryptogram of the transposition cipher

A	U	R	A	R	K	D	A
E	-	P	H	A	I	U	C
T	N	R	O	K	R	T	E
R	A	-	I	F	S	S	M
O	A	R	Y	L	S	Z	K
T	M	E	-	C	T	O	.

Table 1.8 Encryption permutation

1	13	14	25	37	38	2	39
15	40	26	27	41	3	4	42
43	5	44	28	6	16	7	45
29	17	8	30	18	31	46	32
19	33	20	21	9	47	22	34
35	23	10	24	11	12	36	48

Table 1.9 Decryption permutation

1	7	14	15	18	21	23	27
37	43	45	46	2	3	9	22
26	29	33	35	36	39	42	44
4	11	12	20	25	28	30	32
34	40	41	47	5	6	8	10
13	16	17	19	24	31	38	48

plaintext, the third to the 14th, etc. Using this table, which represents a permutation of the set $\{1, 2, \ldots, 48\}$, one may thus determine the encryption procedure more precisely than by means of encryption templates. What is more, considering this permutation as an encryption key, it is possible to specify the exact number of all possible keys for the above cipher, which is equal to

$$48! = 12413915592536072670862289047373375038521486354677760000000000,$$

which amounts to about $1.241391559 \cdot 10^{62}$. Not a small number, especially when compared to the number of all atoms on our planet which is estimated to be 10^{51}.

In order to decrypt ciphertexts of the cipher in question one has to apply the permutation that is inverse to the encryption permutation presented in Table 1.9. At first sight it seems that the cipher may be broken by trying 48! permutations one by one. Assuming that we would be able to test a million permutations per second (even such an assumption is too optimistic for the current state of technology), it would take around 10^{47} years to break a ciphertext. On the other hand, the age of the universe is estimated to be 10^{11} years. However, if cryptanalysts apply statistical tests, then breaking such a cipher takes them just a couple of seconds.

Table 1.10 Symbols of the plaintext and corresponding symbols of the cryptogram

A	B	C	D	E	F	G	H	I	J	K	L	M	N	O	P
X	H	Y	U	Z	R	.	V	Q	A	:	W	T	,	B	C

Q	R	S	T	U	V	W	X	Y	Z		.	:	,	;	-
S	D	;	E	I	G	L	F	J	K	-	M	P	N	0	

Table 1.11 Table with ciphertext symbols and plaintext symbols corresponding to them

A	B	C	D	E	F	G	H	I	J	K	L	M	N	O	P
J	O	P	R	T	X	V	B	U	Y	Z	W	.	,	;	:

Q	R	S	T	U	V	W	X	Y	Z		.	:	,	;	-
I	F	Q	M	D	H	L	A	C	E	-	G	K	N	S	

Table 1.12 The block of the substitution cipher cryptogram obtained using Table 1.10 which corresponds to the block of the plaintext presented in Table 1.6

```
X U Q I , : E
W Z Y E I D Z D
X R B D J K T
X C V B D Q ; T
X : E B D : X
X Y E D Z ; ; M
```

1.3.4 Example of a Substitution Block Cipher

In the easiest case the operation of substitution block ciphers consists in replacing symbols of a plaintext with other symbols one by one. Hence, when performing the encryption algorithm we have to apply a table which contains the rule of this substitution, i.e., the table represents some permutation of the alphabet. Of course, in order to decrypt messages one uses the inverse permutation.

Let us assume that in the considered case the same alphabet as in the example of a transposition cipher is used, the 48-symbol block of a plaintext is the same as previously, and the substitution table presented in Table 1.10 is applied during encryption. Then one obtains immediately a table for use during decryption (Table 1.11).

Now, we can illustrate the process of creating a cryptogram using the substitution cipher. If the plaintext is given by the block presented in Table 1.6, then, after applying Table 1.10 and executing 48 symbol substitution operations, one gets the cryptogram shown in Table 1.12. The obtained cryptogram may yet be easily decrypted since its symbols occur in the same order as the corresponding symbols in the plaintext. For this reason cryptanalysts break substitution ciphers very quickly.

1.3.5 Example of a Product Cipher

A product cipher applies two encryption algorithms sequentially: it starts by encrypting a plaintext by means of the first algorithm, then the obtained cryptogram

Table 1.13 Block of the
product cipher cryptogram
obtained by encrypting a
block of the plaintext by
means of the substitution
cipher and then using the
transposition cipher

X	I	D	X	D	:	U X
Z		C	V	X	Q	I Y
E	,	D	B	:	D	E Z
D	X		Q	Q	;	; T
B	X	D	J	W	;	K :
E	T	Z		Y	E	B M

is encrypted with the second one, which results in the ciphertext of the product cipher. This method can be explained by encrypting the plaintext given in Table 1.6
with the use of the substitution cipher described above and then by considering the
resulting ciphertext (Table 1.7) as an input for the transposition cipher encryption
algorithm. The cryptogram obtained in this way is presented in Table 1.13. One may
easily check that decryption of the ciphertext presented in Table 1.13 should be performed in the reverse order to the encryption process: the decryption algorithm for
the substitution cipher followed by the decryption algorithm for the transposition
cipher have to be executed.

Although the product encryption algorithm presented above consists of two weak
ciphers, breaking it is a non-trivial task—even for an advanced cryptanalyst.

As indicated by Claude Shannon, such an alternate use of transposition and substitution ciphers results in break-resistant ciphers. A slight modification of this principle is applied in many practically used cryptographic block encryption systems
operating on a two-element alphabet, such as *DES*, *IDEA* or *AES*.

1.3.6 Generalized Substitutions—Bigrams

Simple substitution ciphers, which apply single symbols of an alphabet, can easily
be generalized to ciphers that apply substitutions of blocks (sequences) of symbols.

Instead of permutations $f : X \to X$ (where X is a set of alphabet symbols), one
can consider, in the simplest case, permutations $f : X \times X \to X \times X$ ($f : X^2 \to X^2$) or, more generally, $f : X^n \to X^n$. Of course, the number of possible keys
significantly increases in this approach. Indeed, in the simplest case when $n = 2$ the
number of permutations reaches 676!, while for an arbitrary n it increases to $(26^n)!$.

A problem for the cryptographer is to represent a key (a permutation)—let us
notice that even in the simplest case when $n = 2$ we have 676 values of the given
permutation. For the sake of simplicity, geometric methods are used in order to
represent the key.

The *Playfair* cipher, used by British forces during World War I, is an example of
such systems. It uses a 25-symbol alphabet (the letter J is substituted by the letter I).
A key is given by an arbitrary expression contained in a square matrix of size 5×5.

We demonstrate execution of the algorithm by the following example.

Example 1.2 Let us consider as a key the following phrase: *CRYPTOGRAPHY-
ISOK*. Now, let us construct a square matrix of size 5×5 filling it in with letters

of the key without repetitions. The empty entries of the matrix are filled with the remaining letters of the alphabet (i.e., those that do not appear in the key).

We obtain the following matrix:

C	R	Y	P	T
O	G	A	H	I
S	K	B	D	E
F	L	M	N	Q
U	V	W	X	Z

The cryptogram is created from a plaintext by appropriate, i.e., with respect to the matrix, substitutions of pairs of letters (if the text has an odd number of symbols, then it is completed with any symbol).

Let us consider the following plaintext: *ENCRYPTIONKEYS*. At the first stage of encryption, the sequence of letters is divided into pairs *EN CR YP TI ON KE YS*. Each pair is transformed with respect to the rectangle contained in the matrix determined by the letters that form the pair (according to the row-wise order). For instance, the pair *EN* is converted to the pair *QD* (as these two letters form the two remaining corners of the rectangle defined by the digraph *EN*). If encrypted letters are placed in the same row/column or they are equal, then we choose the symbols to their right, e.g., *AW* is converted to *HX*, while *FL* is converted to *LM*.

D	E
N	Q

A	H
B	D
M	N
W	X

The whole ciphertext is as follows: *QDRYPTCOFHBSBC*.

Let us present another example of a bigram system.

Example 1.3 Keys are given by two independent permutations of a 25-letter alphabet. We place them in two square matrices (of dimension 5 × 5).

A	K	N	Y	E		E	R	T	B	O
R	D	U	O	I		W	I	U	M	K
Q	S	W	B	G		N	D	A	S	F
H	C	X	T	Z		Q	X	G	Z	V
V	M	L	P	F		H	Y	P	L	C

A plaintext, for instance *TODAYISABEAUTIFULDAY*, is divided into several rows of a fixed length:

T	O	D	A	Y	I	S	A	B	E
A	U	T	I	F	U	L	D	A	Y

The encryption process consists in replacing columns of the plaintext with entries of matrices (keys) that are determined by the corresponding rectangle, similarly to the Playfair system. The upper symbol of the bigram is marked in the left matrix and the lower symbol in the right one. Thus, in our example, the bigram *TA* is replaced with *BG*, and so on.

The whole plaintext is transformed into the following cryptogram:

$$BG\ IM\ KU\ RR\ BO\ RM\ MS\ QR\ GS\ FR.$$

Both systems presented above are substitution block ciphers. Let us recall that cryptanalysis of simple substitutions is hindered by the fact that now all operations are performed on blocks of letters. The number of functions that map blocks into blocks is very much greater than the number of functions that map single symbols. Applying statistical methods is much more complex, as well.

1.3.7 Polyalphabetic Substitutions

Besides frequency analysis, a successful attack on simple or complex substitutions can be carried out due to invertibility of applied transformations. It is easy to notice that letters or blocks of letters of a plaintext correspond to fixed letters or blocks of letters in the ciphertext, regardless of their positions. This causes specific patterns to be preserved and, with the additional use of statistical methods that are easy to apply nowadays, facilitates breaking ciphers.

The idea of polyalphabetic substitutions is based on applying substitution rules that depend on the current position in the text. Pioneering ideas were developed already in the second half of the fifteenth century. Let us now present probably the best-known example of a polyalphabetic cipher: the *Vigenère cipher*.

1.3.8 Vigenère Cipher

In order to present one of the simplest methods using polyalphabetic substitutions, let us recall the Caesar cipher. Each symbol (encoded as an integer in the range 1 to 26) is mapped into one fixed value. Let us assume that a plaintext is divided into blocks of four letters. Polyalphabetic encryption may be defined as a transformation of consecutive letters of each block by different (but fixed) values. For instance, the first letter of a block is shifted by 2, the second by 4, the third by 3 and the fourth by 10 (remember that each shift is executed modulo 26). In this system, the key is given as the length of a block and values of all shifts.

And so, with the assumed data, the plaintext: *OLDHABITSDIEHARD* is transformed into the cryptogram: *QPGRCFLDUHLOJEUN*. The encryption process is shown in Table 1.14. When using blocks of length n, the above algorithm is nothing else but an n-fold convolution of the Caesar cipher. It is clear that the same letters

Table 1.14 Example of applying the Vigenère cipher

Plain text	O	L	D	H	A	B	I	T	S	D	I	E	H	A	R	D
Letter numbers	11	20	15	16	25	20	1	14	9	5	2	12	1	4	26	9
Key	2	4	3	10	2	4	3	10	2	4	3	10	2	4	3	10
Cipher numbers	13	24	18	26	1	24	4	24	11	9	5	22	3	8	3	19
Cipher	Q	P	G	R	C	F	L	D	U	H	L	O	J	E	U	N

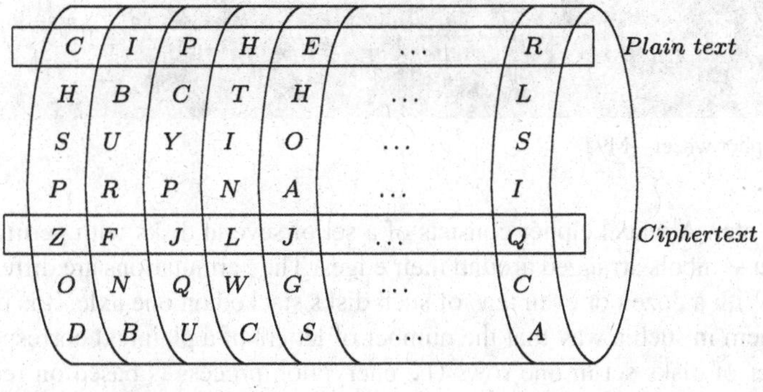

Fig. 1.5 Idea of wheel cipher

of a plaintext are not necessarily mapped into the same symbols in a cryptogram. In general, this hinders cryptanalysis that applies statistical methods.

However, even this cipher is not very hard to break. If only the length of blocks is known, then given cryptograms that are sufficiently long one can focus on each n-th symbol and analyze the obtained set with the use of statistical methods. In case the parameter n is not known, the problem is a bit more complex, nonetheless, it is still not very difficult to solve. It is enough to analyze the text for consecutive values of the parameter n, starting with 2. Applying computers the cipher may quickly be broken.

1.4 Wheel Cipher and Rotor Machines

1.4.1 Wheel Cipher

Upon the development of computers, the substitution and polyalphabetic ciphers described in previous sections were no longer difficult for cryptanalysts to break. As long as encryption using these methods was done manually, they were considered an extremely hard problem of cryptanalysis.

The invention of the wheel cipher constituted an upgrade of polyalphabetic methods (Fig. 1.5).

The cipher was introduced by Thomas Jefferson in 1795, however at this time it did not become well known. It was independently discovered by Étienne Bazeries

Fig. 1.6 Cipher wheel—M94

a century later. A wheel cipher consists of a set of several disks with permutations of alphabet symbols arranged around their edges. The permutations are different for all disks. With a dozen or even tens of such disks stacked on one axle, it is possible to place them in such a way that the number of letters of a plaintext corresponds to the number of disks set in one row. The encryption process is based on reading a text placed one or more rows above or below. A person decrypting the text arranges consecutive letters of the cryptogram in one row of the wheel and reads the plaintext from the appropriate row (for instance, in the case of 30 disks it gives 30!, i.e., about $2.6 \cdot 10^{32}$ possibilities).

According to current criteria, this method does not provide a sufficient security level. An intruder may come into possession of the device used for encryption. They could then quite easily find the appropriate arrangement of disks.

A wheel cipher known as the M-94 [54] was used by the United States Army from 1923 until 1942 (Fig. 1.6).

1.4.2 Rotor Machines

Rotor machines were a step forward with respect to cipher cylinders—they were the first encryption devices that used electricity. Below, we present how they work.

Let us consider a disk containing an alphabet permutation. A simplified version of this situation (for a 4-letter alphabet) is depicted in Fig. 1.7.

Encryption by means of such a disk corresponds to a simple substitution cipher, thus its encryption power is not very impressive. Let us notice, however, that this disk may rotate around its axis in a specific way during the encryption process. The cipher obtained in this way constitutes the Vigenère cipher described before.

Now, let us consider several disks containing different alphabet permutations stacked on one axle (Fig. 1.8). Composing the appropriate number of such disks (permutations) gives a unique permutation, however, it turns out that such a scheme allows us to rotate all disks during encryption. This increases the encryption power significantly and complicates analysis of ciphertexts.

Fig. 1.7 Permutation

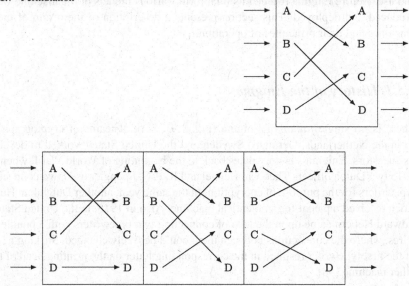

Fig. 1.8 Idea of rotor machines

The algorithm for rotating the disks has to be specified precisely and both parties exchanging messages need to know it, as well as how to arrange the disks to form the whole device. The cipher key is given by the output positions and the order of disks (the initial configuration of the machine).

Machines constructed in this way are called rotor machines. Patents for such machines were filed around 1920 by several inventors concurrently. Disks of these machines are called drums or *rotors*.

Physically, rotors were thick disks made of an insulator. Every disk had 26 contacts equidistant and symmetric from the center on both its sides. Each contact on the left side was connected to exactly one contact on the right side—the pattern of connection (some permutation of the alphabet) was of course to be kept secret. There were 26 circuit terminals (corresponding to letters of the alphabet) adjacent to each side of the disk. If voltage is applied to one of the terminals, then the current flows through one of the contacts on the right side and lights one of 26 bulbs. In this way, the machine performs the afore mentioned permutation of the alphabet.

The most famous machine of this type was Enigma, developed in Germany and used before and during the World War II by the Axis powers.

1.5 Enigma

The name Enigma comes from Greek and literally means *secret*. The designation *Enigma* was used to name a number of encryption machines with the same root and use. Before Enigma reached its final form, various models of the machine were produced and deployed. This section presents a description of the origin of these machines and their principles of operation.

1.5.1 History of the Enigma

There is no single *father* of Enigma (Fig. 1.9). Several teams of cryptographers from the Netherlands, Germany, Sweden and the United States worked to develop its ancestors. Enigma's history dates back to the beginning of World War I, when in 1915 two Dutch officers Theo van Hengel and R. P. C. Spengler used two connected typewriters for the purpose of encryption. In the same year, another Dutchman Hugo Koch received a patent for an identical machine. Also in 1915, in the United States, Edward Hebern came upon the idea of connecting two typewriters with a bundle of wires, where the connections between them could be freely changed. Striking a key of the first typewriter resulted in the corresponding letter on the printing head of the other machine [48].

A set of machines connected in this way, or later with radio or microwave connection, realized a simple monoalphabetic substitution cipher, thus implementing one of the many permutations of the alphabet used. It was not a great invention, of course, from the point of view of today's cryptography. It must be emphasized, however, that the encryption was running in a completely automatic manner. The ability to change the wiring in the unit was then expanded to include a rotor (a wheel with electrical wires) between the keyboard and the printer, just as in the rotor machines described in the previous section. From here, it was a short way to the application of multiple rotors. Also added was the idea of simultaneous turning of the rotors by different angles during the machine's operation. Each particular position of the rotors provides an electrical path through all of the rotors. The current passes through the interconnections, defined by a relative position arrangement of the rotors, to a printer at the other end and outputs the ciphertext letter substituting an input plaintext letter. This realized a polyalphabetic substitution cipher, of possibly very high complexity. Frequency analysis no longer works for cryptanalysis of such a cipher.

Soon after the Hebern inventions, the idea of a cipher machine was developed in Europe by a Swede, Arvid Gerhard Damm, and a German, Arthur Scherbius. The company they founded developed and promoted the first machine to be given the working name *Enigma*. This ancestor of the whole subsequent family of encryption machines was equipped with four rotors placed on a common spindle in a fixed order. The fact that each of the rotors could turn through a different angle, when the machine was in operation, was an additional obstacle to potential cryptanalysis of the implemented cipher [48].

In 1926, the company released a version designated by the letter C, which had two important innovations. The typewriter was abandoned, because it was cumbersome to use when operating the machine, though the keyboard remained part of the machine. Instead, Enigma C was equipped with a board for a set of light bulbs of

Fig. 1.9 Enigma

number corresponding to the number of characters of the alphabet used. Pressing a key would cause the corresponding light to come on.

An equally important innovation introduced in the C model was an idea from one of the designers of the team, Willi Korn. He suggested additional equipment for Enigma, a special drum, called the *reflector* (Fig. 1.11). It was designed in such a way that it would send each signal back through the rotors. When an electrical signal reached it, after negotiating three movable rotors, the reflector sent it back through all three rotors in the same position. Thus, if, for example, letter G was converted to letter P, then using the reflector and the same rotor arrangement, letter P would be mapped back to G. Note that in this way the transition path through the rotors' contacts was doubled in length. The reason for the introduction of the reflector was an issue in Enigma decryption. Until that time, separate keys had been needed for encryption and decryption. Indeed, it had been necessary to reverse the rotor mounting to decrypt the ciphertext. In this way, the decryption process could be carried out without rotor reversal. It turned out that this seemingly wonderful idea made it easier for analysts to break the Enigma code, since the introduction of the reflector meant that no letter could be mapped to itself. This information became very helpful later on in cracking the cipher.

In 1927, Enigma model D was developed. In this version, the reflector did not rotate during operation of the machine and it could be assembled in any of the possible positions. In 1925, the German navy purchased several of these machines. Over the subsequent years, Enigma kept evolving. A version was created for the German army (*Wehrmacht*), and for the Navy (*Kriegsmarine*). The Enigma system was also made available to Japan, which built its cipher machines based on it. In February 1942, the German navy introduced a version of Enigma with a fourth rotor for messages to and from Atlantic U-boats. In this way the number of possible settings was multiplied by 26. This necessitated 26 times greater cryptanalytic effort. In mid-1942 a much bigger 12-rotor version, called Lorenz, was introduced for messages between the German High Command and field commanders. In the Lorenz cipher each letter of the alphabet was represented by five electrical impulses. Messages were enciphered by combining randomly generated letters with the original text using a variant of the XOR function, character by character. At the receiving end Lorenz applied exactly the same obscuring letters back to the ciphertext to recover the plaintext.

In its time, Enigma undoubtedly presented a significant technological advance in the field of encryption. The machine had a very large key space, and thus, at that time, it was not possible to break the code by brute force. However, as safe as Enigma would seem before the war, it was effectively broken, first by Polish intelligence, and then in later versions by the Allied intelligence services. This fact significantly influenced the result of World War II.

1.5.2 Construction of the Enigma

Below, we present the construction and operation of the most popular version of the Enigma machine—the so-called *Wehrmacht Enigma* model, widely used during WWII by the German land forces and the air force (*Luftwaffe*).

As indicated above, the starting point for the construction of the Enigmas was an electric typewriter. Pressing a key would close the electric circuit, and then the flow of the electric current would cause the corresponding letter printing and advancement of the print head by one position on the printing machine. In the first version of the device, Hebern connected two typewriters with a bundle of 26 cables. This machine, of course, generated a simple permutation cipher code. One could complicate its function by introducing additional encryption rotors.

The introduction of the stationary rotor between the contacts leading to the keyboard and the print head does not increase the strength of the cipher, which remains a simple permutation. However, the same mechanism which is used to move the print head can also turn the rotor on its spindle by one position. In this case, each additional letter of the cryptogram will be encrypted by a different substitution (permutation). After encrypting 26 letters, the machine returns to the initial substitution, and the cycle of the used permutations is repeated. One can, of course, introduce between the keyboard and the print head not one but several rotors mounted on a common spindle and equipped with hooks, which will cause the turning of the next rotor by one position each time the previous rotor makes a full turn. The same mechanism is used by car odometers to show distance driven.

Consider an Enigma model with three movable rotors. The total cycle length of all encrypting rotors causes the cipher substitution to repeat itself after $26 \cdot 26 \cdot 26 = 17576$ characters. Let's look at encryption operations performed by a simplified three rotor machine, whose coded alphabet contains only characters A, B, C and D (Fig. 1.11). In our simplified Enigma the first rotor replaces letter A by C, B by B, etc., realizing the joint permutation described as (AC, BB, CA, DD). The second rotor performs the permutation (AB, BD, CA, DC), the third (AB, BA, CD, DC).

As the figure above shows, the three rotors together implement the permutation (AB, BC, CA, DD), which is the composition of the permutations equivalent to the

Fig. 1.10 Rotors

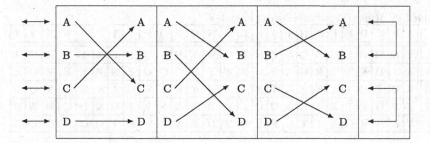

Fig. 1.11 Three rotors with reflector

actions of the first, second and third rotor, respectively. Taken together with the application of the reflector application, the machine thus implements the permutation (AC, BD, CA, DB). After encrypting the first letter, the first (leftmost) rotor turns by one position, changing the permutation implemented jointly by the rotors to (AA, BC, CD, DB). As one can see from the figure, the reflector plays the role of an extra encrypting element as well as an element allowing decryption of messages without changing the order of the rotors.

In reality, the *Wehrmacht Enigma* utilized three different rotors (Fig. 1.10). They were placed on a common spindle in the order determined by the cipher key. Rotors were identified by Roman numerals; from the moment it was put into use, the Enigma machine was equipped with rotors I, II and III, rotors IV and V were added at the end of 1938 (see Table 1.15).

A plugboard (Fig. 1.12) was also added to the discussed structure to perform one more initial permutation. Enigma's switchboard looked like an analog telephone switchboard. The user would set the connections manually by inserting cable plugs into plugboard sockets. Enigma was also equipped with a so-called initial rotor directly connected to the plugboard, which could perform one more permutation. However, in military machines the drum was used only to relay the signal and transmit letters without any changes.

Fig. 1.12 Plugboard

Table 1.15 Wiring Diagram of Enigma's rotors I–V

	A	B	C	D	E	F	G	H	I	J	K	L	M	N	O	P	Q	R	S	T	U	V	W	X	Y	Z
I	E	K	M	F	L	G	D	Q	V	Z	N	T	O	W	Y	H	X	U	S	P	A	I	B	R	C	J
II	A	J	D	K	S	I	R	U	X	B	L	H	W	T	M	C	Q	G	Z	N	P	Y	F	V	O	E
III	B	D	F	H	J	L	C	P	R	T	X	V	Z	N	Y	E	I	W	G	A	K	M	U	S	Q	O
IV	E	S	O	V	P	Z	J	A	Y	Q	U	I	R	H	X	L	N	F	T	G	K	D	C	M	W	B
V	V	Z	B	R	G	I	T	Y	U	P	S	D	N	H	L	X	A	W	M	J	Q	O	F	E	C	K

Enigma cipher key elements need to be divided into those available to the regular signalman operating the device and those reserved for authorized officers only. The encrypting rotors' starting position belonged to the second category, however the cryptographer operating the Enigma needed to have the possibility of positioning the rotors. It was therefore necessary to separate the real location of the rotor from the description visible on the outside of the machine. Paul Bernstein suggested covering the rotor with a moving ring which hid the actual configuration. Then the officer would set the position of the rings on the rotors, and the cryptographer would position the rotors in the machine according to the rings.

An Enigma key contained the following data:

1. the cable plugboard setting—the wiring plugs on the plugboard,
2. the selection of rotors—three of the available five were chosen (or eight in the Kriegsmarine machine),
3. the sequence of selected rotors,
4. the starting position of the rotors—chosen by the operator, different for each message,
5. in later versions, the wiring of the reversing drum.

Keys were typically valid for a specified period of time, usually one day, but rotors were set individually for every message to be encrypted. During World War II, the Enigma coding books contained only the information about the collection of rotors, and their mutual positioning, without data relating to the daily keys.

Before sending each message, a cryptographer would himself decide the initial rotor positioning, such as *ADE*, and the key for that message, e.g., *PQH*. After the Enigma rotors were positioned in the *ADE* configuration, the cryptographer typed the message key *PQH* resulting, for example, in the string *KLR*.

Consequently, the machine rotors were set in the *PQH* configuration and the rest of the information was encoded. The transmitted cipher text began with characters describing the initial *ADE* setting, followed by the encoded message key *KLR*, and the actual content of the ciphertext. The operator receiving the message performed the same actions in the reversed order: he first positioned rotors in the *ADE* configuration to decode the *KLR* message key from the cipher text, that is *PQH*. Then he configured the machine in accordance with the *PQH* key, to decipher the message.

The military Enigma used a 26-letter alphabet. Punctuation marks were replaced by certain rare strings of letters. Space was usually ignored or replaced by the letter X, which was also used as a dot. Some characters were used differently by different forces. The Wehrmacht and Luftwaffe used ZZ instead of a comma, a string FRAQ or FRAGE instead of a question mark. The Navy, in turn, used the letter Y instead of a comma and UD instead of a question mark. The letters CH, as in the word Acht (eight) or Richtung (direction) were replaced by Q (AQT, RIQTUNG). Two, three or four zeros were replaced by, respectively, CENTA, MILLE and MYRIA.

1.5.3 Enigma Operation

We will now describe the exact function and operations of the *Wehrmacht Enigma* machine. Suppose that an analyst knows the principle of operation of the machine, but does not know how the rotors are connected inside the device. This corresponds to the situation in which the cryptoanalysts trying to attack the Enigma found themselves [48].

Each of the Enigma rotors has 26 pairs of terminals that can be connected together in 26! ways. Choosing a permutation for the first rotor eliminates one of the theoretically possible combinations, so the number of possible combinations for how the second rotor could be connected is equal to $26! - 1$ thus the number of possible connections for the second rotor is equal to $26! - 1$.

Similarly, the third rotor adds $26! - 2$ capabilities. In the same way, the number of possible permutations of the input cylinder is $26! - 3$. To summarize, the total number of possible combinations of how the rotors can be connected is the product of the above numbers and is equal to:

264530715874844359665653831541878252695965874756791441686294391112
09842955552229117170256864719821864960000000.

Regardless of how the rotors are chosen from all the possible combinations, the selected rotors can be ordered in $3! = 6$ ways. The reflector has 13 connections between the pairs of pins. Connecting a cable to the first pin allows the other end of the cable to be connected to one of the remaining 25 pins. After selecting the first

Table 1.16 The number of plugboard combinations

Value p	Number of combinations	Value p	Number of combinations
0	1	7	1305093289500
1	325	8	10767019638375
2	44850	9	53835098191875
3	3453450	10	150738274937250
4	164038875	11	205552193096250
5	5019589575	12	102776096548125
6	100391791500	13	7905853580625

end of the second wire there is a choice from the remaining 23 contacts, the third—from 21, etc. The total number of possible combinations of reflector connections is equal to $25 \cdot 23 \cdot 21 \cdots 1$, that is 7905853580625.

A ring on each of the Enigma rotors can be set in one of 26 positions. Positioning the rings over the first and second rotors affects the number of available states, because it determines the state in which another rotor is moved to the next position. The third rotor is followed by a stationary reflector, so the position of its ring does not affect the number of states. As a result, ring settings make $26 \cdot 26$ states, or 676.

Before the work is started, each of the Enigma rotors is set in one of the 26 possible locations, which translates into 26^3 combinations, i.e., 17576.

The last element of the Enigma that contributes to the number of possible states is a plugboard. The number of connected letter pairs (we denote it by p) can vary from 0 to 13. On 26 plugboard sockets, selection of connected letter groups can be made in $26/2p$ ways. The number of possible connections within a selected group of sockets is similar to the number of possible pairs of connections in the reflector; when the first socket is selected, the location at which the wire will be connected can be chosen from $2p - 1$ possibilities. Selection of further sockets gives $2p - 3, 2p - 5, \ldots, 1$ possible states. The total number of possible letter pair connections is $(26/2p) \cdot (2p - 1) \cdot (2p - 3) \cdots 1$.

Table 1.16 shows the number of possible combinations, depending on the value of p.

Putting together the partial results, we get the number of possible Enigma states (assuming $p = 11$), equal to:

3064537774667781245162783206916868949205691845820125435032225270994269522075900473712575645083889591356267102713648819347298713600000000000000,

or approximately $3 \cdot 10^{114}$.

These estimates are for the case when no details are known about Enigma settings and wiring. In real war conditions the rotors and wiring were known from captured equipment. In this case, the number of possible Enigma operating conditions is 619953965349522804000000 (about $6 \cdot 10^{23}$) [48]. Such a number does not

Fig. 1.13 Marian Rejewski in 1932

shock today's reader who has a fast computer at his disposal. For an average computer, code breaking by brute force would not take a lot of time. However, during World War II, that was a huge number preventing brute force attacks. The Enigma code was broken by other techniques, mentioned below.

1.5.4 Breaking the Enigma Cipher

The first attempts to break the Enigma cipher were undertaken by the French, British and Polish intelligence services in the late 1920s. However, the first attempts were unsuccessful. The main problem was that the Enigma cipher was polyalphabetic, a breakthrough for those times. That is a cipher in which the plaintext letters are encrypted using various permutations of the alphabet. As we know, this hides linguistic properties and precludes the use of statistical cryptanalysis.

So far, the most important role in code breaking had been played by specialist linguists who tried to capture specific language features, such as the frequency of repetition of letters or words, or their lengths, etc. In the case of a mechanical encryption machine, linguistic analysis did not bring any results. Poland's military Cipher Bureau offered to employ professional mathematicians. The selected young candidates knew the German language very well. They had been recruited from areas in proximity to the German-Polish border, where knowledge of German was a universal skill. Three of the brightest math students were hired: Marian Rejewski (Fig. 1.13), Henryk Zygalski and Jerzy Różycki (Fig. 1.14).

From 1930, they worked with Poland's intelligence service on cracking the Enigma code. The Poles took advantage of Enigma machine engineering plans made available to them by the French intelligence service, gained around 1931 by a French agent, Hans-Thilo Schmidt (aka *Asche*).

In December 1932 Rejewski and his colleagues first broke the Enigma codes. Soon after, in February 1933, they ordered an exact copy of the German cipher machine to be manufactured by the AVA Radio Engineering Plant. After that time,

Fig. 1.14 Henryk Zygalski and Jerzy Różycki

the Poles could read German correspondence, despite the fact that the Germans continued to improve both the machine and the encryption method [84].

The Poles developed very effective methods of breaking ciphers, in fact they developed a way of discovering Enigma's work settings. For that purpose they applied mathematical theories of combinatorial cycles and transpositions. To determine the permutation cycles used by the Enigma rotors, so called cyclometer and special data characteristics sheets were developed by Rejewski. In September 1938, using these tools it took only about 15 minutes to determine the daily key. Then the Germans changed the parameters of the machine.

At the end of 1938 Rejewski developed plans for another tool, this time an electromechanical device that could search by brute force through all 17576 possible positions. He called the machine a *cryptologic bomb* [84].

The bomb would find the daily settings of the Enigma machines on the various German military communication networks, e.g., the set of rotors in use and their positions, and the rotor start positions for a particular message (the message key). The purpose of this machine was to crack the Enigma cipher through the use of a specially developed theory of cycles. The cryptologic bomb consisted of six copies of the Polish Enigma coupled together and powered by an electric motor. In mid-November of the same year six such bombs were built in Warsaw. They were used only for decoding twice-encrypted daily keys, never to decode the ciphertexts. Those were decoded using perforated Zygalski sheets, developed in order to find the proper positions of the Enigma rotors. One cryptologic bomb made it possible to decode a daily key in a couple of hours and did the work of about 100 people.

In 1939, Germany once again changed their encryption scheme, which created the need to build an additional 54 cryptologic bombs (for a total of 60) and for the development of 60 labor-intensive sets of Zygalski sheets (one set consisted of 26 sheets). Such investment far exceeded the financial capabilities of Poland's intelligence service at that time. For this reason, and because of the threat of war, it was decided to present the Polish Enigma to the British and the French intelligence services—countries which at that time were associated with Poland through a mili-

Fig. 1.15   Alan Turing

tary alliance. Each of them received a replica of the Polish Enigma machine together with all the documentation. The transfer took place on July 25, 1939 at Pyry near Warsaw, where the Polish cryptanalytic center was located [38].

In particular, the Poles passed all of their information over to two mathematicians working at Bletchley Park, Alan Turing (Fig. 1.15) and Gordon Welchman, who were able to build on this research to develop their substantially enhanced *bombe* machine. Following Rejewski's precedent, Turing called their new device a *bombe* (an improvement after the original Polish *bomba kryptologiczna*. (The whole family lineage became referred to as *bombes* at Bletchley Park and then in the US throughout WWII, and in the following reports.) Soon after, at the Bletchley Park cryptanalytic center, the UK's main decryption establishment—the Government Code and Cypher School (GC&CS), mathematicians headed by Alan Turing and with intelligence experts began the complex and urgent task of cracking the enemy military and naval Enigma radio communications, with the help of primitive early computers. They devised and modified cryptologic bombes, based on the equipment and materials provided by the Poles. Bletchley Park also hired a number of promising mathematicians, among them Hugh Alexander, Peter Hilton, and Max Newman [26].

After the outbreak of WWII, Poland's Cipher Bureau personnel were evacuated through Romania, to the French cryptanalytic center codenamed Bruno in the Château de Bois-Vignolles in the village of Gretz-Armainvilliers, 40 km from Paris. They continued cracking the Enigma traffic in close inter-Allied collaboration with the French. Jerzy Różycki perished in 1942 in the Mediterranean Sea, near the Balearic Islands, in unclear circumstances. Rejewski and Zygalski arrived in the UK in August 1943. They immediately began working in the radio unit of the Chief of Staff of the Polish Armed Forces in Boxmoor near London, where they remained until the end of the war.

Bletchley Park is known mainly for cracking messages enciphered on the Enigma cipher machine, and its greatest cryptographic achievement was the breaking of the advanced teleprinter Lorenz version of the Enigma cipher. The most important Bletchley Park machine was the highly advanced Colossus (Fig. 1.16) of which the first started working in December 1943, and a total of ten were in use by WWII's

Fig. 1.16 Colossus

end. They were the world's first electronic digital computers. Colossus's parameters could be changed through plugboards and jumper cables. Colossus compared two data streams, counting each match. The encrypted message was read from a paper tape. The other stream was an internally generated electronic simulation of the Lorenz machine at various trial settings. If the match count for a setting was above a certain threshold, it was sent as output. The Colossus was used to find possible key setting combinations for the rotors, realizing the basic idea of a cryptographic bombe. The Colossus decrypted Enigma and Lorenz traffic containing the most vital secrets of the German High Command.

Bletchley Park produced modified bombes (Fig. 1.17), but it was through the success of UK and US intelligence cooperation that a US Navy bombe was soon designed and produced as well. The US Navy's signals intelligence and cryptanalysis group started investigating designs for a Navy bombe, based on the full blueprint and wiring diagrams received from Bletchley Park in mid-1942. Turing travelled to the US in November 1942 for five months and worked with US Navy cryptanalysts on the naval four-rotor Enigma and the bombe construction in Naval Communications in Washington, DC, and in the Computing Machine Laboratory in Dayton, Ohio [49].

In May 1943 two prototype bombes were ready, named Adam and Eve. In 1943 and 1944 many more bombe machines arrived from Dayton and worked in Naval Communications in Washington, DC, bringing tremendous success for the Allied navies over the German U-boats. Throughout the remainder of the war, as the Germans altered their Enigmas, the US Navy kept pace. The four-rotor problem fell exclusively to the US. A total of 121 Navy bombes were assembled at the US Naval Computing Machine Laboratory in Dayton, at a cost of about six million dollars, see [101].

Like the Polish and British bombes, the American machines required pieces of unencrypted text from intercepted messages, either assumed or known to appear in the message. The text corresponded to the cipher and created the daily settings key for the bombe. With the daily key, all the current day's communication could be

Fig. 1.17 Turing-Welchman
Bombe

read. The text pieces could come through a variety of intelligence and cryptanalysis
methods. Some came from errors made by the German operators themselves. One
frequent German mistake was to use standardized messages. For example, a shore
weather station in the Bay of Biscay sent out a message every day at 7:00 a.m. which
began, *The weather in the Bay of Biscay will be....* Knowing the exact wording of a
message was a great help for the Allies, so it became a high priority to intercept the
daily message from this weather station. Also, the initial rotor setting changed with
every message. Since the German cipher clerk determined the initial rotor settings,
they had to be sent to the intended recipient in the clear, that is, unencrypted. The
first three letters of the code group, sent unenciphered, told the receiver where to set
the rotors. But the clerk made up his own six-letter settings, and the cryptanalysts
could occasionally guess the settings. For example, if the first three letters were HIT,
the cryptanalysts could guess that it was followed by LER, spelling out HITLER.
BER was usually followed by the ciphers of LIN. One particular German code clerk
continually used his girlfriend's name, Cillie, for his messages (see [103]).

Through the work of the Polish cryptographers, and later the British in Bletchley
Park and the US Navy and US Army, as well as thanks to the Enigma machines
and codes which were captured in the meantime, at the end of the war almost all
Enigma traffic, nearly thousands of encrypted messages each day, was being read
by the Allies. During the Normandy landings, Bletchley Park was deciphering over
18000 messages each day. On average, one or two days were enough to decrypt a
German message [89, 95, 96].

Chapter 2
Mathematical Foundations of Cryptography

This chapter introduces some basic mathematical concepts necessary to understand the design of modern cryptographic algorithms and protocols. It begins with definitions of such algebraic structures as groups, rings, and finite fields, followed by some of their applications. This part also includes fundamental number theoretic definitions and properties playing an important role in cryptographic applications: the integer divisibility relation, the greatest common divisor, the least common multiple, the prime numbers, Euler's totient function, the congruence relation, and their basic properties.[1]

Throughout this book the set of natural numbers will be well ordered by the relation *less than*. This means that every subset of the natural numbers has the least element. Also it will be assumed throughout that zero is a natural number. Thus **N** will denote the set of all natural numbers with zero. To denote the set of positive integers $\mathbf{N}_+$ will be used.

2.1 Basic Concepts in the Theory of Algebraic Structures

Let S denote a nonempty set and let $S \times S$ denote the Cartesian product of S with itself (the Cartesian square of S), i.e., the set of all ordered pairs (x, y) such that $x \in S$ and $y \in S$. Every mapping $f : S \times S \to S$ of the Cartesian square of S into S is called an operation defined on the set S. The operation f is thus given by the function $f(x, y) = z$, where the element $z \in S$ is called the result of f on the pair of elements x and y. In practice, operations are usually not denoted by letters but by operation symbols, e.g. $+, \star, \cdot, -, \odot$, etc. When using operation symbols, the result of an operation on elements x and y is denoted in the same way as when performing standard arithmetic operations on numbers: $x + y$, $x \star y$, $x \cdot y$, etc. It is important to note that according to the definition above not all operations on numbers are

---

[1] Further background on mathematical structures in cryptography can be found in [27, 92], and [68].

C. Kościelny et al., *Modern Cryptography Primer*,
DOI 10.1007/978-3-642-41386-5_2, © Springer-Verlag Berlin Heidelberg 2013

operations. For example, division is not an operation on the set of integers $\mathbf{Z}$ (the result is not necessarily an integer) and subtraction is not an operation on the set of natural numbers $\mathbf{N}$ (which does not contain negative integers). However, addition and multiplication are well-defined operations on those sets.

We will also use the notion of an algebraic structure which is defined as a set S together with operations defined on this set. Usually structures will contain either one operation, in which case they will be denoted by $\langle S, + \rangle$, or two operations when we will denote them by $\langle S, +, \cdot \rangle$.

2.1.1 Groups

Definition 2.1 An algebraic structure $\langle G, \bullet \rangle$ is called a *group* if the following conditions are satisfied:

1. The operation $\bullet$ is associative, i.e.,

$$\forall_{a,b,c \in G} \big[a \bullet (b \bullet c) = (a \bullet b) \bullet c \big].$$

Thanks to associativity an expression $x_1 \bullet x_2 \bullet \ldots \bullet x_k$, where $x_i \in G$ and $1 \le i \le k$, always has the same value, irrespective of the order of operations performed on elements x_i.

2. There exists an identity element $e \in G$ which is neutral with respect to the operation $\bullet$, i.e.

$$\exists_{e \in G} \forall_{a \in G} [a \bullet e = e \bullet a = a].$$

3. For every element $a \in G$ there exists an element $\tilde{a} \in G$ satisfying the following property:

$$\forall_{a \in G} \exists_{\tilde{a} \in G} [a \bullet \tilde{a} = \tilde{a} \bullet a = e].$$

If the operation in a group has the symbol $+$, then it is called addition and the group is called additive. In this case the element $\tilde{a}$ is denoted by $-a$ and called the inverse element of a. The identity element of an additive group is called the zero of the group and is denoted by 0. In a multiplicative group the operation is called multiplication and is denoted by a dot $\cdot$, which is often neglected in the notation, analogously as in the case of multiplying numbers. In this case the inverse element of a is denoted by a^{-1}. The identity element in a multiplicative group has the symbol 1 and is called the unit of the group.

4. Additionally, if the group operation is commutative, i.e.,

$$\forall_{a,b \in G} [a \bullet b = b \bullet a],$$

then the group is called commutative or Abelian (in honor of the Norwegian mathematician N.H. Abel).

Although a group is an algebraic structure consisting of a set and an operation, we will often write just the set symbol to denote the group.

On the basis of the axioms above, it is easy to prove that there exists only one identity element and that for every element of a group there exists a unique inverse element.

In order to simplify expressions in which an operation is performed many times on the same element from an additive (multiplicative) group $a \in G$, the following notation and rules will be used:

$$
\begin{array}{ll}
\text{Additive group} & \text{Multiplicative group} \\[4pt]
ma = \underbrace{a + a + \ldots + a}_{m \text{ arguments}} & a^m = \underbrace{aaa \cdots a}_{m \text{ arguments}} \\[16pt]
(-n)a = n(-a) & a^{-n} = (a^{-1})^n \\
na + ma = (n + m)a & a^n a^m = a^{n+m} \\
m(na) = (mn)a & (a^n)^m = a^{nm} \\
0a = 0 & a^0 = 1
\end{array}
$$

where $m, n, 0, 1 \in \mathbf{Z}$ and the symbols 0 and 1 denote identity elements for operations in additive and multiplicative groups, respectively. Thus, in a multiplicative group powers of elements exist. In an additive group multiples of elements are their analogs.

Definition 2.2   Let G be a group consisting of a finite number of elements. We call G a *finite group* and the number of its elements the *order* of G. The order of a group G is denoted by $|G|$ or card G.

Definition 2.3   A multiplicative group G is called *cyclic* iff

$$
\exists_{g \in G} \forall_{a \in G} \exists_{j \in N} \left[a = g^j \right].
$$

The element g is called a *generator* of the cyclic group, since each element of G can be represented as some power of g. We denote this fact by $G = \langle g \rangle$. It follows from this definition that every cyclic group is commutative ($\forall_{x,y \in \mathbf{Z}}[g^x g^y = g^{x+y}]$, and because $x + y = y + x$, we have $g^{y+x} = g^y g^x = g^x g^y = g^{x+y}$) and $g^{|G|} = 1$ (where 1 is the unit of the group).

Definition 2.4   Let G be a finite multiplicative group. The *multiplicative order s* of an element $a \in G$ is defined in the following way:

$$
s = \min\{m \in \mathbf{N} : a^m = 1\}, \quad \text{where 1 is the unit of } G.
$$

Such s divides the order of G, i.e., $s \mid \operatorname{card} G$. For instance, if card $G = 63$, then G contains elements of order $1, 3, 7, 9, 21$ and 63.

Definition 2.5   Let G be a group and let H be a subset of G. An algebraic structure $\langle H, \bullet \rangle$, consisting of a set H and an operation $\bullet$ defined on G, is called a *subgroup* of the group G, denoted by $H \subset G$, if it fulfills the axioms of a group (Definition 2.1). Alternatively, a subgroup may be defined as a structure that satisfies:

$$\forall_{a,b \in H} \begin{cases} a \bullet (-b) \in H & \text{for an additive group,} \\ a \bullet b^{-1} \in H & \text{for a multiplicative group.} \end{cases}$$

There are two trivial subgroups of G: an algebraic structure $\langle e, \bullet \rangle$ and the group G itself. Therefore, if card $H \notin \{1, \text{card} \, G\}$, then a subgroup H of G is called *non-trivial*.

2.1.2 Rings and Fields

Definition 2.6   An algebraic structure $\langle R, +, \cdot \rangle$ is called a *ring* if the following axioms are satisfied:

1. the structure $\langle R, + \rangle$ is an Abelian group;
2. the operation $\cdot$ is associative, i.e., $\forall_{a,b,c \in R}[(a \cdot b) \cdot c = a \cdot (b \cdot c)]$.
3. the operation $\cdot$ is distributive over $+$, i.e.,

$$\forall_{a,b,c \in R}\big([a \cdot (b+c) = a \cdot b + a \cdot c] \wedge [(b+c) \cdot a = b \cdot a + c \cdot a] \big).$$

Operations $+$ and $\cdot$ are usually called addition and multiplication, however, they are not necessarily these commonly understood number operations. A neutral element of a structure $\langle R, + \rangle$ is denoted by 0 and the inverse element of an element $a \in R$ by $-a$. For the sake of simplicity, we commonly use the following convention: $a + (-b) = a - b$, $a \cdot b = ab$. On the basis of the definition of a ring, we get that $\forall_{a \in R}[a0 = 0]$, since $a0 = a(b - b) = ab - ab = 0$. Similarly, it can be proven that $\forall_{a,b \in R}[(-a)b = a(-b) = -ab]$.

Depending on the properties of multiplication, we can classify rings as follows:

1. If $\exists_{e \in R}\forall_{a \in R}[ae = ea]$, then a ring R is called a *ring with a unit*.
2. If multiplication in a ring is commutative, then such a ring is called *commutative*.
3. If a ring is commutative and additionally it contains a neutral element of multiplication $e \neq 0$ and $ab = 0 \Rightarrow (a = 0) \vee (b = 0)$, then it is called an *integral domain* or an *integral ring*. A neutral element of multiplication is usually denoted by 1. It follows from the definition that an integral domain does not contain *zero divisors*.
4. Let R be an integral domain. We call it a *Euclidean ring* if there exists a function $\nu : R \setminus \{0\} \to \mathbf{N} \cup \{0\}$, called a *norm* of R, such that

$$\forall_{a,b \neq 0 \in R}\exists_{q,r \in R}\big[(a = bq + r) \wedge (\nu(r) < \nu(b) \vee r = 0) \big].$$

Here element $r \in R$ is called a *remainder*, 0 is the zero of the ring R, and 0 is an integer.

Table 2.1 Addition table for
GF(16)

+	0 1 2 3 4 5 6 7 8 9 a b c d e f
0	0 1 2 3 4 5 6 7 8 9 a b c d e f
1	1 0 3 2 5 4 7 6 9 8 b a d c f e
2	2 3 0 1 6 7 4 5 a b 8 9 e f c d
3	3 2 1 0 7 6 5 4 b a 9 8 f e d c
4	4 5 6 7 0 1 2 3 c d e f 8 9 a b
5	5 4 7 6 1 0 3 2 d c f e 9 8 b a
6	6 7 4 5 2 3 0 1 e f c d a b 8 9
7	7 6 5 4 3 2 1 0 f e d c b a 9 8
8	8 9 a b c d e f 0 1 2 3 4 5 6 7
9	9 8 b a d c f e 1 0 3 2 5 4 7 6
a	a b 8 9 e f c d 2 3 0 1 6 7 4 5
b	b a 9 8 f e d c 3 2 1 0 7 6 5 4
c	c d e f 8 9 a b 4 5 6 7 0 1 2 3
d	d c f e 9 8 b a 5 4 7 6 1 0 3 2
e	e f c d a b 8 9 6 7 4 5 2 3 0 1
f	f e d c b a 9 8 7 6 5 4 3 2 1 0

5. If an algebraic structure $\langle R \setminus \{0\}, \cdot \rangle$ is a group, then the ring R is called a *division ring*.
6. A commutative division ring is called a *field*.

Thus, a field can be defined in the following way:

Definition 2.7   A structure $\langle F, +, \cdot \rangle$ is called a *field* iff

1. the structure $\langle F, + \rangle$ is a commutative group with a neutral element denoted by 0;
2. the structure $\langle F \setminus \{0\}, \cdot \rangle$ is a commutative group with a neutral element denoted by 1;
3. multiplication is distributive over addition, i.e., the following condition is satisfied:

$$\forall_{a,b,c \in F} \left(\left[a(b+c) = ab + ac \right] \wedge \left[(b+c)a = ba + ca \right] \right).$$

The number of elements of a field is either infinite or equal to a power of some prime. A field with a finite number of elements is called a finite field or a Galois field and is denoted by $GF(q)$.

Example 2.1   A Galois field $GF(16)$ is a structure $\langle F_{16}, +, \cdot \rangle$ consisting of a set $F_{16} = \{0, 1, 2, \ldots, 9, 10, a, b, \ldots, f\}$ and operations of addition and multiplication defined as in Tables 2.1 and 2.2:
One can verify that this structure satisfies all axioms of a field.

Definition 2.8   An algebraic structure $\langle S, +, \cdot \rangle$, where $S \subset R$, is called a *subring* of a ring $\langle R, +, \cdot \rangle$ if it satisfies all axioms of a ring.

Table 2.2 Multiplication table for $GF(16)$

·	0	1	2	3	4	5	6	7	8	9	a	b	c	d	e	f
0	0	0	0	0	0	0	0	0	0	0	0	0	0	0	0	0
1	0	1	2	3	4	5	6	7	8	9	a	b	c	d	e	f
2	0	2	4	6	8	a	c	e	3	1	7	5	b	9	f	d
3	0	3	6	5	c	f	a	9	b	8	d	e	7	4	1	2
4	0	4	8	c	3	7	b	f	6	2	e	a	5	1	d	9
5	0	5	a	f	7	2	d	8	e	b	4	1	9	c	3	6
6	0	6	c	a	b	d	7	1	5	3	9	f	e	8	2	4
7	0	7	e	9	f	8	1	6	d	a	3	4	2	5	c	b
8	0	8	3	b	6	e	5	d	c	4	f	7	a	2	9	1
9	0	9	1	8	2	b	3	a	4	d	5	c	6	f	7	e
a	0	a	7	d	e	4	9	3	f	5	8	2	1	b	6	c
b	0	b	5	e	a	1	f	4	7	c	2	9	d	6	8	3
c	0	c	b	7	5	9	e	2	a	6	1	d	f	3	4	8
d	0	d	9	4	1	c	8	5	2	f	b	6	3	e	a	7
e	0	e	f	1	d	3	2	c	9	7	6	8	4	a	b	5
f	0	f	d	2	9	6	4	b	1	e	c	3	8	7	5	a

Definition 2.9 An algebraic structure $\langle I, +, \cdot \rangle$, where $I \subset R$, is called an *ideal* of a ring $\langle R, +, \cdot \rangle$ if this structure is a subring of R and $\forall_{a \in I} \forall_{r \in R} [ar \in I \wedge ra \in I]$.

Definition 2.10 An ideal $\langle I, +, \cdot \rangle$ is called *principal* if there exists an element $a \in R$ such that $I = (a)$, where (a) stands for the set Ra. Then we say that a is a generator of an ideal (a). If every ideal $\langle I, +, \cdot \rangle$ of a ring $\langle R, +, \cdot \rangle$ is principal, then the ring $\langle R, +, \cdot \rangle$ is called a *principal ring*.

A structure $\langle I, + \rangle$, where $I = \{0, a_1, a_2, \ldots, \}$, is a subgroup of a group $\langle R, + \rangle$; therefore a ring, similarly to a group, can be decomposed into cosets with respect to an ideal:

$$
\begin{matrix}
0 & a_1 & a_2 & a_3 \ldots, & a_m \ldots, \\
r_1 & r_1 + a_1 & r_1 + a_2 & r_1 + a_3 \ldots, & r_1 + a_m \ldots, \\
r_2 & r_2 + a_1 & r_2 + a_2 & r_2 + a_3 \ldots, & r_2 + a_m \ldots, \\
\vdots & \vdots & \vdots & \vdots \quad \vdots & \vdots \ldots,
\end{matrix}
$$

The first row of the table depicting the decomposition of the ring into cosets represents an ideal of the ring and the cosets are called *remainder classes*. Elements of the ring located in the first column of the table are representatives of remainder classes. Addition and multiplication of cosets are defined in the following way:

$$[r_i] \oplus [r_j] = [r_i + r_j], \qquad [r_i] \odot [r_j] = [r_i r_j],$$

where $[r_s]$ denotes the remainder class to which an element r_s of the ring belongs. Both operations are associative and multiplication of remainder classes is distribu-

Table 2.3 Addition and multiplication tables for $\mathbf{Z}/(4)$

Addition table for the ring $\langle \mathbf{Z}/(4), \oplus, \odot \rangle$					Multiplication table for the ring $\langle \mathbf{Z}/(4), \oplus, \odot \rangle$				
$\oplus$	[0]	[1]	[2]	[3]	$\odot$	[0]	[1]	[2]	[3]
[0]	[0]	[1]	[2]	[3]	[0]	[0]	[0]	[0]	[0]
[1]	[1]	[2]	[3]	[0]	[1]	[0]	[1]	[2]	[3]
[2]	[2]	[3]	[0]	[1]	[2]	[0]	[2]	[0]	[2]
[3]	[3]	[0]	[1]	[2]	[3]	[0]	[3]	[2]	[1]

tive over addition. In this way, from a ring $\langle R, +, \cdot \rangle$ and its ideal $\langle I, +, \cdot \rangle$, we obtain a *remainder class ring*, denoted by R/I.

Example 2.2 The set of integers $\mathbf{Z}$ together with the arithmetical operations of addition and multiplication forms a ring. Let (4) denote the set of all multiples of 4:

$$(4) = [\dots, -20, -16, -12, -8, -4, 0, 4, 8, 16, \dots].$$

It is easy to prove that the structure $\langle (4), +, \cdot \rangle$ is an ideal of the ring $\langle \mathbf{Z}, +, \cdot \rangle$. Thus, this ring can be decomposed into remainder classes with respect to the ideal (4):

$$[0] = 0 + (4) \quad [1] = 1 + (4) \quad [2] = 2 + (4) \quad [3] = 3 + (4).$$

The structure $\langle \mathbf{Z}/(4), \oplus, \odot \rangle$ is a ring with the following operation tables (Table 2.3):

In this ring $[2] \odot [2] = [0]$, thus the remainder class $[2]$ is a zero divisor.

The ring $\langle \mathbf{Z}/(n), \oplus, \odot \rangle$ exists for any positive integer n and is isomorphic to the ring $\langle \mathbf{Z}_n, \oplus, \odot \rangle$, i.e., the set $[0, 1, \dots, n-1]$ in which addition and multiplication are performed modulo n.

Theorem 2.1 *A ring $\langle \mathbf{Z}/(p), \oplus, \odot \rangle$ is a finite field if and only if p is a prime.*

Definition 2.11 Let p be a prime. Additionally, let

$$GF(p) = \langle F_p, \oplus, \odot \rangle, \qquad F_p = [0, 1, \dots, p-1].$$

Then a finite field $GF(p)$ is called a *Galois field* with p elements. Thus, we can write: $GF(p) = \langle \mathbf{Z}_p, \oplus, \odot \rangle$. Addition and multiplication in this field are performed modulo p.

Definition 2.12 Let $\langle R, +, \cdot \rangle$ be a ring. If

$$\exists_{n \in \mathbf{N}} \forall_{r \in R} [nr = 0],$$

then the least integer n fulfilling this condition is called the *characteristic* of R. If such an integer does not exist, the ring R has characteristic equal to 0.

Table 2.4 Addition and multiplication tables for $GF(2)$

Addition in $GF(2)$				Multiplication in $GF(2)$		
$+$	0	1		$\cdot$	0	1
0	0	1		0	0	0
1	1	0		1	0	1

Theorem 2.2 *The characteristic of a ring* $\langle R, +, \cdot \rangle$ *with a unit, where* $\mid R \mid \neq 0$, *and with no zero divisors is equal to some prime* p. *Moreover, the following condition is satisfied in such a ring:*

$$\forall_{a,b \in R} \forall_{n \in \mathbf{N}} \left[(a \pm b)^{p^n} = a^{p^n} \pm b^{p^n} \right].$$

Example 2.3 The characteristic of the Galois field from Example 1 is equal to 2, since $\forall_{a \in GF(16)} [a + a = 0]$.

2.1.3 Finite Fields

We have already mentioned that a structure $\langle F, +, \cdot \rangle$ is a finite field provided the cardinality of F is a power of some prime. As an example of a finite field we can give the algebraic structure $\langle \{0, 1\}, +, \cdot \rangle$ in which operations of addition and multiplication are defined in Table 2.4.

This is the two-element field $GF(2)$. One can easily verify that the field axioms are satisfied: the structure $\langle \{0, 1\}, + \rangle$ is a commutative group with 0 as a neutral element and the unit as its own inverse element. The structure $\langle \{1\}, \cdot \rangle$ is a typical multiplicative group and multiplication is distributive over addition. As another example of a finite field one can give the structure $\langle \{0, 1, 2, 3, 4, 5, 6\}, \oplus, \odot \rangle$ with operations of multiplication and addition modulo 7. We denote this field by $GF(7)$. One can check that the multiplicative group $GF(7)$ has elements of order 1, 2, 3. Thus, there exist two- and three-element subgroups of the group $\langle \{1, 2, \ldots, 6\}, \odot \rangle$.

By considering finite fields $GF(q)$, it can easily be seen that due to the closure property of addition, the sums $\sum_{i=1}^{k} 1$, where $k = 1, 2, \ldots$, cannot be different for all k, since the result of the operation has to be an element of the field. Therefore, there exist two integers m, n, where $m < n$ such that $\sum_{i=1}^{n} 1 = \sum_{i=1}^{m} 1$, which implies that $\sum_{i=1}^{n-m} = 0$. This means that there exists the least prime p such that $\sum_{i=1}^{p} 1 = 0$. Such a prime is called the characteristic of the finite field.

Theorem 2.3 *The characteristic* p *of a finite field is a prime.*

Now let a denote a nonzero element from $GF(q)$. Since the field $GF(q)$ is closed under multiplication then consecutive powers of a

$$a^1 = a, \quad a^2 = a \cdot a, \quad a^3 = a \cdot a \cdot a, \quad \ldots$$

are elements of the field. As in the case of addition, subsequent powers of a cannot be all different, i.e.,

$$\exists_{m,k}\left[m > k \wedge a^k = a^m\right].$$

If we denote the multiplicative inverse element of a by a^{-1}, then the element $(a^{-1})^k = a^{-k}$ is the multiplicative inverse element of a^k. Multiplying both sides of the equation $a^k = a^m$ by a^{-k} we obtain $1 = a^{m-k}$. Hence, there exists a least positive integer n such that $a^n = 1$. As we already know, such n is the multiplicative order of a. Thus, the sequence of elements

$$a^1, a^2, a^3, \dots, a^n, a^{n+1} = a \dots$$

repeats after the element a^n, and powers $a^1, a^2, a^3, \dots, a^{n-1}, a^n = 1$ are all pairwise different. Therefore, if $i + j < n$, then

$$a^i \cdot a^j = a^{i+j}.$$

On the other hand, if $i + j > n$, then $i + j = n + r, 0 \leq r < n$, and

$$a^i \cdot a^j = a^n \cdot a^r = a^r.$$

Theorem 2.4 *Let a be a nonzero element of order n from the finite field $GF(q)$. Then n is a divisor of $(q - 1)$.*

2.1.4 Polynomial Ring

Let $\langle R, +, \cdot \rangle$ be a ring. A *polynomial* over this ring is an expression of the form

$$f(x) = \sum_{i=0}^{n} a_i x^i = a_0 + a_1 x + \cdots + a_n x^n,$$

where $n \in \mathbf{N}$. *The coefficients* of a polynomial are elements from the ring, i.e., $a_i \in R, 0 \leq i \leq n$, and the symbol x is called an *independent variable*. It is customary to omit a monomial $a_i x^i$ in the notation of a polynomial whenever $a_i = 0$. Verifying the equality of two polynomials consists of checking whether they have the same coefficients standing at corresponding powers of their independent variables.

Let

$$f(x) = \sum_{i=0}^{n} a_i x^i, \qquad g(x) = \sum_{i=0}^{m} b_i x^i, \qquad m \leq n.$$

If $n = m$, then the condition on the equivalence of two polynomials can be written as follows:

$$f(x) = g(x) \Leftrightarrow a_i = b_i, \quad 0 \leq i \leq n.$$

We define the sum and the product of two polynomials in the following way:

$$f(x) + g(x) = \sum_{i=0}^{n} (a_i + b_i)x^i,$$

$$f(x)g(x) = \sum_{k=0}^{n+m} c_k x^k, \qquad c_k = \sum_{i+j=k} a_i b_j, \quad 0 \leq i \leq n, \ 0 \leq j \leq m.$$

Definition 2.13 The set of all polynomials over a ring $\langle R, +, \cdot \rangle$ together with operations of polynomial addition and multiplication is called a *polynomial ring* and we denote it by $R[\mathrm{x}]$.

The zero polynomial, i.e., the polynomial with only zero coefficients, is the zero of $R[\mathrm{x}]$. We denote it by 0, thus by the same symbol as the element of R. Therefore, when considering a ring $R[\mathrm{x}]$ one has to be careful not to confuse the zero of the polynomial ring with the zero of the ring from which coefficients of polynomials are taken.

Definition 2.14 If

$$f(x) = \sum_{i=0}^{n} a_i x^i \in R[\mathrm{x}], \quad a_n \neq 0,$$

then n is called the *degree* of the polynomial $f(x)$, which is denoted by $\deg(f(x)) = n$, whereas a_n is the *leading coefficient* of the polynomial. If a ring R has a neutral multiplication element, denoted by 1, and the leading coefficient of a polynomial is equal to 1, then such a polynomial is called *monic*. If $\deg(f(x)) = 0$, then the polynomial $f(x)$ is called *constant*. The coefficient a_0 is called a *free term*. Conventionally, we assume that the degree of the zero polynomial is equal to $-\infty$. Constant polynomials are in fact elements of a ring R, therefore R is a subring of the ring $R[\mathrm{x}]$ and the latter inherits some properties of the ring R.

Usually we consider polynomial rings over a field F, i.e., structures denoted by $F[\mathrm{x}]$. Every polynomial ring is an integral domain, so if $f(x), g(x) \in F[\mathrm{x}]$, then

$$\deg(f(x) + g(x)) \leq \max(\deg(f(x)), \deg(g(x)))$$

and

$$\deg(f(x)g(x)) = \deg(f(x)) + \deg(g(x)).$$

Definition 2.15 Similarly to the case of division in the ring $\langle \mathbf{Z}, +, \cdot \rangle$, we say that polynomial $f(x)$ divides $g(x)$ ($f(x)$ is a divisor of $g(x)$) if and only if there exists a polynomial $h(x)$ such that $g(x) = f(x) \cdot h(x)$. We denote this property by $f(x) \mid g(x)$. In symbols:

$$f(x) \mid g(x) \Leftrightarrow \exists_{h(x) \in F[\mathrm{x}]} (g(x) = f(x) \cdot h(x)).$$

Theorem 2.5 *Let* $g(x) \neq 0, g(x) \in F[x]$. *Then*

$$\forall_{f(x) \in F[x]} \exists_{q(x), r(x) \in F[x]} [f(x) = q(x)g(x) + r(x)],$$
$$where \ \deg(r(x)) < \deg(g(x)).$$

The above theorem describes an algorithm for division in a polynomial ring. One can thus compute the greatest common divisor of two polynomials $f(x), g(x) \in F[x]$ by means of Euclid's algorithm,[2] repeating the algorithm for polynomial division in the following way:

$$
\begin{aligned}
f(x) &= q_1(x)g(x) & + r_1(x), & \quad \deg(r_1(x)) < \deg(g(x)), \\
g(x) &= q_2(x)r_1(x) & + r_2(x), & \quad \deg(r_2(x)) < \deg(r_1(x)), \\
r_1(x) &= q_3(x)r_2(x) & + r_3(x), & \quad \deg(r_3(x)) < \deg(r_2(x)), \\
&\vdots & \vdots & \quad \vdots \\
r_{k-1}(x) &= q_{k+1}(x)r_k(x) & + r_{k+1}(x), & \quad \deg(r_{k+1}(x)) < \deg(r_k(x)), \\
r_k(x) &= q_{k+2}(x)r_{k+1}(x), &
\end{aligned}
$$

until the remainder equals zero. If the leading coefficient of the polynomial $r_{k+1}(x) \in R[x]$ is equal to c, then $\gcd(f(x), g(x)) = c^{-1}r_{k+1}(x)$, since it has to be monic. Of course, Euclidean algorithm can be applied to compute the greatest common divisor of three or more polynomials, for instance: $\gcd(f_1(x), f_2(x), f_3(x)) = \gcd(\gcd(f_1(x), f_2(x)), f_3(x))$.

Theorem 2.6 *If* $\gcd(f(x), g(x)) = h(x)$, *then there exist polynomials* $u(x), v(x) \in R[x]$ *such that*

$$u(x)f(x) + v(x)g(x) = h(x).$$

Definition 2.16 A polynomial $f(x) \in F[x]$ is called *irreducible* over a field F if $\deg(f(x)) > 0$ and $f(x) = a(x)b(x), a(x), b(x) \in F[x]$, implies either $a(x)$ or $b(x)$ is constant, i.e., $(a(x) \in F) \vee (b(x) \in F)$.

In other words, an irreducible polynomial over F is divided only by itself and constant polynomials. If neither $a(x)$ nor $b(x)$ is a constant polynomial, then the polynomial $f(x)$ is reducible over F. Irreducible polynomials over F are crucial in constructing Galois fields.

Theorem 2.7 *Every polynomial* $f(x) \in F[x], \deg(f(x)) > 0$, *can be presented in the following form*:

$$f = a \prod_{i=1}^{k} (g_i(x))^{e_i},$$

---

[2]The detailed presentation of the algorithm can be found in Chap. 3.

where $a \in F, e_1, \ldots, e_k \in \mathbf{N}$ and $g_1(x), \ldots, g_k(x) \in F[x]$ are different monic polynomials. Such a decomposition is unique up to the order of the factors.

It can easily be checked that the set of all multiples of a polynomial $f(x) \in F[x]$ is an ideal in the ring $F[x]$, which can be denoted by $I = (f) = \{f(x)g(x) : g \in F[x]\}$. We say that the polynomial $f(x)$ generates the ideal (f).

Decomposition of the polynomial ring $F[x]$ into remainder classes with respect to an ideal generated by an irreducible polynomial plays an important role in applications of Galois fields.

Theorem 2.8 *Let $f(x) \in F[x]$. The ring of remainder classes $F[x]/(f)$ is a field if and only if $f(x)$ is irreducible over F.*

Definition 2.17 An element $b \in F$ is called a *root* or a *zero* of a polynomial $f(x) \in F[x]$ if $f(b) = 0$.

Theorem 2.9 *An element $b \in F$ is a root of a polynomial $f(x) \in F[x]$ if and only if $(x - b) \mid f(x)$.*

Theorem 2.10 *Let $f(x) \in GF(q)[x]$ be a nonzero polynomial of degree $m \geq 1$ and let $f(0) \neq 0$. Then there exists a positive integer $s \leq q^m - 1$ such that $f(x) \mid (x^s - 1)$.*

Definition 2.18 The least positive integer s satisfying the assumptions of the above theorem is called the *exponent* of the polynomial $f(x)$. If $f(x) = 0$, then $f(x) = x^a g(x), a \in \mathbf{N}, g(x) \in GF(q)[x], g(0) \neq 0$. In such a case we regard the exponent of $f(x)$ as the exponent of $g(x)$.

Example 2.4 The polynomial ring over the field $GF(3)$, denoted by $GF(3)[x]$, consists of polynomials of all degrees with coefficients taken from the set $\{0, 1, 2\}$. Now, we decompose this ring into remainder classes with respect to the ideal generated by the polynomial $f(x) = x^2 + x + 2$. Thus, the ideal constitutes the following set of polynomials:

$$(f) = \{0, f(x), 2f(x), xf(x), (1 + x)f(x), (2 + x)f(x), 2xf(x), \ldots\}$$

In this case we can create the following remainder classes:

$$
\begin{aligned}
\{0\} &= & 0 + (f), \\
\{1\} &= & 1 + (f), \\
\{\alpha\} &= & x + (f), \\
\{\beta\} &= 1 + 2x + (f), \\
\{\gamma\} &= 2 + 2x + (f), \\
\{\delta\} &= & 2 + (f), \\
\{\eta\} &= & 2x + (f), \\
\{\kappa\} &= 2 + x + (f), \\
\{\zeta\} &= 1 + x + (f).
\end{aligned}
$$

Table 2.5 Addition table for $GF(9)$

+	{0}	{1}	{α}	{β}	{γ}	{δ}	{η}	{κ}	{ζ}
{0}	{0}	{1}	{α}	{β}	{γ}	{δ}	{η}	{κ}	{ζ}
{1}	{1}	{δ}	{ζ}	{γ}	{η}	{0}	{β}	{α}	{κ}
{α}	{α}	{ζ}	{η}	{1}	{δ}	{κ}	{0}	{γ}	{β}
{β}	{β}	{γ}	{1}	{κ}	{α}	{η}	{ζ}	{0}	{δ}
{γ}	{γ}	{η}	{δ}	{α}	{ζ}	{β}	{κ}	{1}	{0}
{δ}	{δ}	{0}	{κ}	{η}	{β}	{1}	{γ}	{ζ}	{α}
{η}	{η}	{β}	{0}	{ζ}	{κ}	{γ}	{α}	{δ}	{1}
{κ}	{κ}	{α}	{γ}	{0}	{1}	{ζ}	{δ}	{β}	{η}
{ζ}	{ζ}	{κ}	{β}	{δ}	{0}	{α}	{1}	{η}	{γ}

Table 2.6 Multiplication table for $GF(9)$

·	{0}	{1}	{α}	{β}	{γ}	{δ}	{η}	{κ}	{ζ}
{0}	{0}	{0}	{0}	{0}	{0}	{0}	{0}	{0}	{0}
{1}	{0}	{1}	{α}	{β}	{γ}	{δ}	{η}	{κ}	{ζ}
{α}	{0}	{α}	{β}	{γ}	{δ}	{η}	{κ}	{ζ}	{1}
{β}	{0}	{β}	{γ}	{δ}	{η}	{κ}	{ζ}	{1}	{α}
{γ}	{0}	{γ}	{δ}	{η}	{κ}	{ζ}	{1}	{α}	{β}
{δ}	{0}	{δ}	{η}	{κ}	{ζ}	{1}	{α}	{β}	{γ}
{η}	{0}	{η}	{κ}	{ζ}	{1}	{α}	{β}	{γ}	{δ}
{κ}	{0}	{κ}	{ζ}	{1}	{α}	{β}	{γ}	{δ}	{η}
{ζ}	{0}	{ζ}	{1}	{α}	{β}	{γ}	{δ}	{η}	{κ}

The polynomial $f(x) = x^2 + x + 2$ is irreducible over $GF(3)$ since $f(0) \neq 0$, $f(1) \neq 0$, $f(2) \neq 0$, thus the ring of remainder classes $\langle F_9, +, \cdot \rangle$, where

$$F_9 = \big\{\{0\}, \{1\}, \{\alpha\}, \{\beta\}, \{\gamma\}, \{\delta\}, \{\eta\}, \{\kappa\}, \{\zeta\}\big\}$$

forms, according to Theorem 2.8, the field $GF(9)$ with operations defined as in Tables 2.5 and 2.6.

2.1.5 Applications of Galois Fields

Galois fields are mostly used as a mathematical tool applied in cryptography (e.g., in algorithms such as AES, IDEA, ElGamal) and in the theory of erasure codes. The latter constitutes the basis for designing devices used in many systems, for example in radar systems and systems of microwave links, mobile radio and satellite communications. Knowledge of Galois fields is essential when designing data recording systems with the use of magnetic tapes and disks and optical drives. Moreover, Galois fields are applied in designing self-checking arithmetic and logical circuits, high-speed semiconductor memories, digital television systems and Hi-Fi acoustic systems. Galois field arithmetic is applied in spread spectrum radio communication systems. Computation techniques in Galois fields are very useful in developing some types of radio and television antennas, and loudspeakers, and in cryptography and the synthesis of random number generators. Galois fields can also be applied in precise optical and acoustic measurements, in designing concert halls, and even in handicrafts and graphic design.

2.2 Elements of Number Theory

2.2.1 Divisibility

Let us consider two arbitrary natural numbers x and y ($x, y \in \mathbf{N}$).

Definition 2.19 We say that x divides y (x is a divisor of y) if and only if there exists a natural number z such that $y = x \cdot z$. We denote this property by $x \mid y$. In symbols,

$$x \mid y \iff \exists_{z \in \mathbf{N}}(y = x \cdot z).$$

Example 2.5 We have, of course, $2 \mid 4$, $3 \mid 27$, $1233 \mid 44388$, but the following relations do not hold: $2 \mid 5$, $3 \mid 26$ and $123 \mid 14287$.

The following properties of divisibility are valid:

Theorem 2.11 *For all* $x, y, z \in \mathbf{N}$ *we have*

1. $x \mid x$,
2. $(x \mid y \wedge y \mid z) \Rightarrow x \mid z$,
3. $(x \mid y \wedge y \mid x) \Rightarrow x = y$,
4. $(x \mid y \wedge x \mid z) \Rightarrow (y \geq z \Rightarrow x \mid (y - z))$,
5. $(x \mid y \wedge x \mid z) \Rightarrow \forall_{a,b \in \mathbf{N}}(x \mid (a \cdot y + b \cdot z))$.

Proof of 5 Let $x, y, z \in \mathbf{N}$. Additionally, let us assume that $x \mid y \wedge x \mid z$. It follows that for some natural numbers p, q we have $y = p \cdot x$ and $z = q \cdot x$. Then

$$a \cdot y + b \cdot z = a \cdot p \cdot x + b \cdot q \cdot x = x \cdot (a \cdot p + b \cdot q),$$

so

$$x \mid (a \cdot y + b \cdot z).$$

Let us recall that if $x, y \in \mathbf{N}$ and $y > 1$, then there exists exactly one pair of natural numbers p, r such that $x = p \cdot y + r \wedge r < y$.

This property is called the *unique factorization* of natural numbers (a similar law is valid for reals). The number p is simply the result of dividing y by x, while r is the remainder of this division.

Let us introduce the following notation: $r = x \bmod y$ and $p = x \operatorname{div} y$.

We say that x is a common divisor of y and z when $x \mid y$ and $x \mid z$.

The greatest common divisor of natural numbers y and z is defined as the natural number x such that

1. $x \mid y \wedge x \mid z$,
2. $(p \mid y \wedge p \mid z) \Rightarrow p \mid x$.

Let us notice that the first condition states that x is a common divisor, while the second determines that x is the greatest one.

If x is the greatest common divisor of y and z, then we write $x = \gcd(y, z)$.

Natural numbers x and y are called coprime if $\gcd(x, y) = 1$. This means that they have no common divisors but 1.

It is easy to observe the following fact.   □

Theorem 2.12 *If we divide two natural numbers by their greatest common divisor, then the obtained numbers are coprime. In symbols,*

$$\gcd\left(\frac{x}{\gcd(x, y)}, \frac{y}{\gcd(x, y)}\right) = 1.$$

Proof Let $z = \gcd(x, y)$. Then there exist two integers p, q such that $x = p \cdot z$ and $y = q \cdot z$ (then, of course, $p = \frac{x}{\gcd(x,y)}$ and $q = \frac{y}{\gcd(x,y)}$).

Unless p and q are coprime, then they have a common divisor greater than 1. Let us denote it by d. Then the number $z \cdot d$ is also a divisor of both x and y. Since $d > 1$, then it must be greater than z. We arrive at a contradiction.

We say that x is a common multiple of natural numbers y and z if $y \mid x$ and $z \mid x$.

The least common multiple of two natural numbers y and z is defined as the natural number x such that

1. $y \mid x \wedge z \mid x$,
2. $(y \mid p \wedge z \mid p) \Rightarrow x \mid p$.

We will denote the least common multiple of x and y by $\operatorname{lcm}(x, y)$.

The following interesting relation between the gcd and lcm of two natural numbers holds.   □

Theorem 2.13 *The product of two natural numbers x and y is equal to the product of the greatest common divisor and the least common multiple of these two numbers.*

In symbols,

$$x \cdot y = \gcd(x, y) \cdot \operatorname{lcm}(x, y).$$

Example 2.6 Let $x = 957$ and $y = 2117$. Then $\gcd(x, y) = \gcd(957, 2117) = 29$, while $\operatorname{lcm}(x, y) = \operatorname{lcm}(957, 2117) = 69861$.

Let us notice that $xy = 957 \cdot 2117 = 2025969$.

Furthermore, $\gcd(x, y) \cdot \operatorname{lcm}(x, y) = \gcd(957, 2117) \cdot \operatorname{lcm}(957, 2117) = 29 \cdot 69861 = 2025969$.

Corollary *If* $\gcd(x, y) = 1$, *then* $\operatorname{lcm}(x, y) = xy$.

2.2.2 Prime Numbers and Their Properties

Definition 2.20 A natural number $p > 1$ is called prime if it has exactly two divisors: 1 and p itself.[3]

The following theorems about prime numbers are valid.

Theorem 2.14 *Every integer greater than 1 has at least one prime divisor.*

Proof Let us consider an integer $x > 1$. This number has divisors greater than 1 (x itself is one of these divisors). Let us denote by q the least of these divisors. We will prove that q is prime. Let us assume, on the contrary, that there exists p greater than 1 and smaller than q that divides the latter. Then $1 < p < q$, $p \mid q$ and as $q \mid x$ we have that p is also a divisor of x. We get a contradiction with the assumption that q is the least divisor of x. Therefore, q is prime. $\qquad\square$

Theorem 2.15 *Every natural number larger than 1 can be uniquely, up to the order of factors, factorized into the product of primes. In symbols, for a natural number n we have*

$$n = p_1^{\alpha_1} \cdot p_2^{\alpha_2} \cdots p_k^{\alpha_k},$$

where the p_i (for $i = 1, \ldots, k$) are different primes.

Proof (sketch) Let us consider an integer x greater than 1. According to the previous theorem, x has at least one prime divisor. Let us denote it by q_1. Then we have $x = q_1 \cdot p_1$ for some p_1. As previously, p_1 has at least one prime divisor, which we denote by q_2. And so on. As a result we obtain a sequence of prime divisors of x. It is obvious that this sequence is finite and its last element is prime. Therefore, x can be represented as a product of primes. $\qquad\square$

---

[3] A comprehensive and interesting study on primes can be found in [85].

Theorem 2.16 *If* $n = p_1^{\alpha_1} \cdot p_2^{\alpha_2} \cdots p_k^{\alpha_k}$ *and* $m = p_1^{\beta_1} \cdot p_2^{\beta_2} \cdots p_k^{\beta_k}$, *then*

$$\gcd(n, m) = p_1^{\min(\alpha_1, \beta_1)} \cdot p_2^{\min(\alpha_2, \beta_2)} \cdots p_k^{\min(\alpha_k, \beta_k)}$$

and

$$\mathrm{lcm}(n, m) = p_1^{\max(\alpha_1, \beta_1)} \cdot p_2^{\max(\alpha_2, \beta_2)} \cdots p_k^{\max(\alpha_k, \beta_k)}.$$

It is easy to notice that natural numbers n and m are coprime if for all i ($i = 1, \ldots, k$) we have $\min(a_i, b_i) = 0$. Then, of course,

$$\gcd(n, m) = p_1^0 \cdot p_2^0 \cdots p_k^0 = 1.$$

Example 2.7 Let us factorize into primes $x = 10976$ and $y = 18772$.
We have $x = 10976 = 2^3 \cdot 7^1 \cdot 13^2$ and $y = 18772 = 2^2 \cdot 13^1 \cdot 19^2$.

$$p_1 = 2 \quad \alpha_1 = 3 \quad \beta_1 = 2$$
$$p_2 = 7 \quad \alpha_2 = 1 \quad \beta_2 = 0$$
$$p_3 = 13 \quad \alpha_3 = 2 \quad \beta_3 = 1$$
$$p_4 = 19 \quad \alpha_4 = 0 \quad \beta_4 = 2$$
$$\gcd(x, y) = \gcd(10976, 18772) = 2^2 \cdot 7^0 \cdot 13^1 \cdot 19^0 = 52,$$
$$\mathrm{lcm}(x, y) = \mathrm{lcm}(10976, 18772) = 2^3 \cdot 7^1 \cdot 13^2 \cdot 19^2 = 3963236.$$

Theorem 2.17 *There exist infinitely many prime numbers.*

Proof

- Euclid (5th century BC).
  Let us assume that there are finitely many prime numbers. Let $p_1, p_2, \ldots, p_k$ be all of them and let P denote their product increased by one: $P = p_1 \cdot p_2 \cdots p_k + 1$. As we have already shown, each natural number, including P, has at least one prime divisor. Let us denote a prime divisor of P by q. Now the question arises whether q is one of numbers $p_1, p_2, \ldots, p_k$. If it were, then we would have $q \mid p_1 \cdot p_2 \cdots p_k$ and $q \mid P$. Since $P > p_1 \cdot p_2 \cdots p_k$, thus $q \mid (P - p_1 \cdot p_2 \cdots p_k)$. However, $P - p_1 \cdot p_2 \cdots p_k = 1$, therefore $q \mid 1$, which is obviously impossible.
- Kummer (1878).
  Let us suppose that there are finitely many primes. Let $p_1, p_2, \ldots, p_k$ be all of them and let P denote their product: $P = p_1 \cdot p_2 \cdots p_k$. Obviously, $P > 2$. Let us notice that $P - 1$ can be represented as a product of primes. Of course, all factors of this product are taken from the set $\{p_1, p_2, \ldots, p_k\}$. Therefore, there exists at least one prime p_i (for some $i = 1, \ldots, k$) that divides both P and $P - 1$. However, then we get $p_i \mid P - 1$ and $p_i \mid P$, but since $P > P - 1$, we obtain $p_i \mid (P - (P - 1))$, thus $p_i \mid 1$, which is obviously impossible.

- Stieltjes (1890).

  Let us assume that there are finitely many primes. Let $p_1, p_2, \ldots, p_k$ be all of them and let P denote their product: $P = p_1 \cdot p_2 \cdots p_k$. Now, let us represent P as a product of two natural numbers, m and n, greater than or equal 1 (m and n are products of some primes taken from the set $\{p_1, p_2, \ldots, p_k\}$. Thus, none of $p_1, p_2, \ldots, p_k$ divides both m and n. Then, if we consider the sum $m + n$, it turns out that it does not have a prime divisor. But since this sum is greater than 1, it has such a divisor. We obtain a contradiction. $\square$

Below we present more theorems, which imply that there exist infinitely many primes.

Theorem 2.18 *For every natural number $n > 2$ there exists at least one prime greater than n and less than $n!$.*

Proof Let us observe that $N = n! - 1$ is greater than 1 (since $n > 2$). Therefore, N has a prime divisor, which we denote by p. Let us also notice that p cannot be less than or equal to n, as it divides $n! - 1$. Thus, p is greater than n. On the other hand, we know that $p \leq N$, so $p < N - 1$. Finally, we get $n < p < n!$. $\square$

Corollary *It follows from the above theorem that there are infinitely many primes.*

Theorem 2.19 (Chebyshev) *For every natural number $n > 3$ there exists at least one prime greater than n and less than $2n - 2$.*

Theorem 2.20 (Breusch) *For every natural number $n > 7$ there exist at least four primes of the forms $3k + 1$, $3k + 2$, $4k + 1$, $4k + 3$ such that all of them are greater than n and smaller than $2n$.*

It is worth mentioning that despite many efforts no formula for prime numbers has been obtained. Moreover, nobody has proven that such a formula written by means of elementary functions does not exist at all; however, it is assumed that there is no such a formula.

In 1654 Fermat conjectured $2^{2^n} + 1$ to be a formula for primes. However, in 1732 Euler showed that 641 divides $2^{2^5} + 1$. Landry, in 1880, proved that 274177 is another divisor of $2^{2^5} + 1$. Now it is also known that 319489 divides $2^{2^{11}} + 1$ and 114689 divides $2^{2^{12}} + 1$. As an interesting fact let us mention that $2^{2^{38}} + 1$ (which has tens billions of digits) was proven divisible by $3 \cdot 2^{41} + 1$. Furthermore, it was shown that numbers $2^{2^n} + 1$ are composite for $n = 6, 7, 8, 9, 11, 12, 18, 23, 36, 38, 73$.

Another interesting fact concerns the so-called Euler's polynomial $f(x) = x^2 + x + 41$, whose values are prime for all integer arguments taken from the interval $\langle -40, 39 \rangle$.[4]

---

[4]More information about this polynomial can be found in [85].

Table 2.7 Values of Euler's function

$\Phi(n)$	+0	+1	+2	+3	+4	+5	+6	+7	+8	+9
0+		1	1	2	2	4	2	6	4	6
10+	4	10	4	12	6	8	8	16	6	18
20+	8	12	10	22	8	20	12	18	12	28
30+	8	30	16	20	16	24	12	36	18	24
40+	16	40	12	42	20	24	22	46	16	42
50+	20	32	24	52	18	40	24	36	28	58
60+	16	60	30	36	32	48	20	66	32	44
70+	24	70	24	72	36	40	36	60	24	78
80+	32	54	40	82	24	64	42	56	40	88

2.2.3 Euler's Function

Let $\Phi : \mathbf{N} \to \mathbf{N}$ be a function which assigns to each natural number n the number of natural numbers not greater than n and coprime with it. The function Φ is called Euler's function.

Example 2.8 For $n = 4$ there exist only two natural numbers not greater than and coprime with 4. These are 1 and 3, hence $\Phi(4) = 2$.

Similarly, $\Phi(13) = 12$, $\Phi(20) = 8$, $\Phi(143) = 120$.

Euler's function has the following properties.

Theorem 2.21 *If p and q are primes, then*

1. $\Phi(p) = p - 1$,
2. $\Phi(p \cdot q) = (p - 1) \cdot (q - 1)$,
3. $\Phi(p^a) = (p - 1) \cdot p^{a-1}$.

Theorem 2.22 *If a and b are coprime, then $\Phi(ab) = \Phi(a) \cdot \Phi(b)$. If $n = p_1^{\alpha_1} p_2^{\alpha_2} \dots p_k^{\alpha_k}$, then $\Phi(n) = n \cdot (1 - \frac{1}{p_1}) \cdot (1 - \frac{1}{p_2}) \cdots (1 - \frac{1}{p_k})$.*

Table 2.7 provides the values of Euler's function for natural numbers less than 90.

2.2.4 Modular Congruences

Let a, b and n be natural numbers ($a, b, n \in \mathbf{N}, n \neq 0$).

If two integers, a and b, have the same remainder when divided by n, then they are said to be congruent modulo n. We denote this by $a \equiv b \pmod{n}$.

In symbols,

$$a \equiv b \pmod{n} \iff (a \bmod n) = (b \bmod n).$$

Example 2.9 $19 \equiv 7 \pmod{12}$, $42 \equiv 8 \pmod{17}$, $14 \equiv 18 \pmod 4$.

Theorem 2.23 *The congruence relation is an equivalence relation.*

Proof (sketch) Let us notice that for all natural numbers a, b, c, n the congruence relation $\equiv$ has the following properties:

1. reflexivity—$a \equiv a \pmod n$
2. symmetry—$a \equiv b \pmod n \Rightarrow b \equiv a \pmod n$
3. transitivity—$[a \equiv b \pmod n \wedge b \equiv c \pmod n] \Rightarrow a \equiv c \pmod n$

Due to the properties of equivalence relations, each congruence relation (modulo n) determines a partition of the set of natural numbers into disjoint equivalence classes. These classes are formed by natural numbers congruent modulo n. $\qquad \square$

Example 2.10 Let $n = 4$. Then the congruence relation partitions the set of natural numbers into four disjoint classes:

$$[0] = \{0, 4, 8, \ldots\},$$
$$[1] = \{1, 5, 9, \ldots\},$$
$$[2] = \{2, 6, 10, \ldots\},$$
$$[3] = \{3, 7, 11, \ldots\}.$$

Definition 2.21 Let n be a fixed positive natural number.
Then the following implication holds:

$$(a = q \cdot n + r \wedge 0 \leq r < n) \Rightarrow a \equiv r \pmod n.$$

We call r the remainder of a modulo n.

Corollary *For any equivalence class of a there exists some a_0 from the set $\{1, 2, \ldots, n - 1\}$ such that $a \equiv a_0 \pmod n$. Such a_0 is called the canonical representative of the equivalence class of a (the class $[a]$).*
The set $Z_n = \{0, 1, 2, \ldots, n - 1\}$ is called the set of natural numbers modulo n.

Theorem 2.24 *Congruence relations satisfy the following implications:*

1. $[a \equiv b \pmod n \wedge c \equiv d \pmod n] \Rightarrow a \pm b \equiv c \pm d \pmod n$,
2. $[a \equiv b \pmod n \wedge c \equiv d \pmod n] \Rightarrow ac \equiv bd \pmod n$,
3. $[a \equiv b \pmod n \wedge r \mid n] \Rightarrow a \equiv b \pmod r$,
4. $[a \equiv b \pmod n \wedge a \equiv b \pmod m \wedge \gcd(n, m) = 1] \Rightarrow a \equiv b \pmod{n \cdot m}$.

Concerning computational complexity it should be mentioned that the time cost of addition and subtraction modulo n of k-bit integers equals $O(k)$, multiplication and inversion (whenever possible) takes $O(k^2)$, while exponentiation costs $O(k^3)$.[5] These facts are crucial for the complexity of encryption algorithms presented in subsequent chapters.

2.2.5 Simple Modular Equations

Let $d = \gcd(a, n)$.

Theorem 2.25 *The equation $a \cdot x \equiv b \pmod{n}$ has a solution (or solutions) in Z_n if and only if $d \mid b$. Moreover, there exist exactly d solutions and all of them are congruent modulo $\frac{n}{d}$.*

Example 2.11 $3 \equiv 2 \pmod{5}$.
  We have

$$3 \cdot 0 \pmod 5 = 0,$$
$$3 \cdot 1 \pmod 5 = 3,$$
$$3 \cdot 2 \pmod 5 = 1,$$
$$3 \cdot 3 \pmod 5 = 4,$$
$$3 \cdot 4 \pmod 5 = 2.$$

Of course, $d = \gcd(3, 5) = 1$ and $1 \mid 2$ (due to the condition $d \mid b$), hence in fact there is only one solution: $x = 2$.

Example 2.12 $3 \cdot x \equiv 5 \pmod{6}$.
  We get

$$3 \cdot 0 \pmod 6 = 0,$$
$$3 \cdot 1 \pmod 6 = 3,$$
$$3 \cdot 2 \pmod 6 = 0,$$
$$3 \cdot 3 \pmod 6 = 3,$$
$$3 \cdot 4 \pmod 6 = 0,$$
$$3 \cdot 5 \pmod 6 = 3.$$

Obviously, $d = \gcd(3, 6) = 3$ and it is not true that $3 \mid 5$—hence there are no solutions.

---

[5]See Table 2.5 in [68].

Example 2.13 $3 \cdot x \equiv 3 \pmod{6}$.

We get

$$3 \cdot 0 \pmod{6} = 0,$$

$$3 \cdot 1 \pmod{6} = 3,$$

$$3 \cdot 2 \pmod{6} = 0,$$

$$3 \cdot 3 \pmod{6} = 3,$$

$$3 \cdot 4 \pmod{6} = 0,$$

$$3 \cdot 5 \pmod{6} = 3.$$

Obviously, $d = \gcd(3, 6) = 3$ and $3 \mid 3$—therefore there exist 3 solutions.

Theorem 2.26 (Chinese Remainder Theorem) *If natural numbers* $n_1, n_2, \ldots, n_k$ *are pairwise coprime, i.e.,* $\gcd(n_i, n_j) = 1$ *for any distinct* $i, j \in \{1, 2, \ldots, k\}$, *then the system of equations*

$$\begin{cases} x \equiv a_1 \pmod{n_1} \\ x \equiv a_2 \pmod{n_2} \\ \ldots \\ x \equiv a_k \pmod{n_k} \end{cases}$$

has exactly one solution in Z_n, *where* $n = n_1 \cdot n_2 \cdots n_k$.

The system can be solved by applying the technique of the Gaussian elimination:

$$x = \sum_{i-1}^{k} a_i \cdot N_i \cdot M_i \pmod{n},$$

where $N_i = \frac{n}{n_i}$, *a* $M_i = N_i^{-1} \pmod{n}$.

Example 2.14 Let

$$x \equiv 3 \pmod{7}$$

$$x \equiv 7 \pmod{13}$$

We have

$n_1 = 7, \quad n_2 = 13, \quad n = 7 \cdot 13 = 91$

$N_1 = 13, \quad N_2 = 7$

$M_1 = 13^{-1} \pmod{7} = 6^{-1} \pmod{7} = 6$

$M_2 = 7^{-1} \pmod{13} = 2$

$x = 3 \cdot 13 \cdot 6 + 7 \cdot 7 \cdot 2 \pmod{91} = 234 + 98 \pmod{91} = 332 \pmod{91} = 59.$

Corollary (To the CRT) *If* $\gcd(n_1, n_2) = 1$ *and*

$$x \equiv a \pmod{n_1},$$
$$x \equiv a \pmod{n_2},$$

then $x = a \pmod{n_1 \cdot n_2}$ *is the only solution to the above system of equations.*

2.2.6 Euler's Theorem

Theorem 2.27 (Fermat's Little Theorem) *If p is a prime, then for all $a \in Z_p$ such that $a \neq 0$ we have*

$$a^{p-1} \equiv 1 \pmod{p}.$$

Fermat's little theorem can be generalized to the following one.

Theorem 2.28 (Euler's Theorem) *For every positive integer n coprime with a, where $a \in Z_n$ and $a \neq 0$, the following modular equation holds*

$$a^{\Phi(n)} \equiv 1 \pmod{n},$$

where $\Phi(n)$ is Euler's function on n.

2.3 Sieve of Eratosthenes, Euclidean Algorithms

Below we present some of most elementary algorithms in number theory applying notions used in cryptography, along with their applications. We start with the so-called sieve of Eratosthenes, which allows us to select primes from a given initial interval of natural numbers. Next, we describe a few versions of the Euclidean algorithm including the basic one that enables us to compute the greatest common divisor of two natural numbers and the extended version that computes inverse elements in rings Z_n.[6]

2.3.1 Sieve of Eratosthenes

The question of whether there are methods to determine primes in the set of natural numbers was raised already by the ancients. According to current knowledge, the

---

[6]A very intelligible presentation of all these algorithms can be found in [87]. See also [68].

first algorithmic method solving this problem was developed in the second century BC by the ancient Greek mathematician Eratosthenes (276 BC–184 BC).

Its simple idea is to arrange natural numbers in an ascending sequence (or in an array) and eliminate composite numbers by crossing out multiples of, consecutively, two, three, five, and so on.

Let us look at an example that illustrates the search for primes in the set $\{2, 3, \ldots, 60\}$ by means of the sieve of Eratosthenes.

First, we arrange numbers in a sequence (or an array):

2	3	4	5	6	7	8	9	10	11	12	13	14	15	16	17	18	19	20
21	22	23	24	25	26	27	28	29	30	31	32	33	34	35	36	37	38	39	40
41	42	43	44	45	46	47	48	49	50	51	52	53	54	55	56	57	58	59	60

The first number in this sequence is equal to 2 (we do not take 1 into consideration, as according to the definition it is not prime), hence 2 is prime. We cross out all multiples of 2 except itself, which gives the following sequence:

2	3	4	5	~~6~~	7	~~8~~	9	~~10~~	11	~~12~~	13	~~14~~	15	~~16~~	17	~~18~~	19	~~20~~
21	~~22~~	23	~~24~~	25	~~26~~	27	~~28~~	29	~~30~~	31	~~32~~	33	~~34~~	35	~~36~~	37	~~38~~	39	~~40~~
41	~~42~~	43	~~44~~	45	~~46~~	47	~~48~~	49	~~50~~	51	~~52~~	53	~~54~~	55	~~56~~	57	~~58~~	59	~~60~~

The next prime turns out to be 3. We cross out its multiples, as well:

2	3	4	5	~~6~~	7	~~8~~	~~9~~	~~10~~	11	~~12~~	13	~~14~~	~~15~~	~~16~~	17	~~18~~	19	~~20~~
~~21~~	~~22~~	23	~~24~~	25	~~26~~	~~27~~	~~28~~	29	~~30~~	31	~~32~~	~~33~~	~~34~~	35	~~36~~	37	~~38~~	~~39~~	~~40~~
41	~~42~~	43	~~44~~	~~45~~	~~46~~	47	~~48~~	49	~~50~~	~~51~~	~~52~~	53	~~54~~	55	~~56~~	~~57~~	~~58~~	59	~~60~~

Afterwards, we continue this procedure with 5 and 7, respectively:

2	3	4	5	~~6~~	7	~~8~~	~~9~~	~~10~~	11	~~12~~	13	~~14~~	~~15~~	~~16~~	17	~~18~~	19	~~20~~
~~21~~	~~22~~	23	~~24~~	~~25~~	~~26~~	~~27~~	~~28~~	29	~~30~~	31	~~32~~	~~33~~	~~34~~	~~35~~	~~36~~	37	~~38~~	~~39~~	~~40~~
41	~~42~~	43	~~44~~	~~45~~	~~46~~	47	~~48~~	~~49~~	~~50~~	~~51~~	~~52~~	53	~~54~~	~~55~~	~~56~~	~~57~~	~~58~~	59	~~60~~

Let us observe that in order to find all prime numbers in the set $\{1, 2, \ldots, n\}$, it is sufficient to apply the sieve algorithm only for primes not greater than $\sqrt{n}$. This follows from the fact that every composite number greater than $\sqrt{n}$ has to have a prime factor which is less than $\sqrt{n}$. Therefore, it must have already been crossed out by the sieve. For this reason, in the case of the considered set $\{2, 3, \ldots, 60\}$ we can stop the selection procedure on arriving at 7.

We obtain the following primes: $2, 3, 5, 7, 11, 13, 17, 19, 23, 29, 31, 37, 41, 43, 47, 53, 59$.

2.3.2 Euclidean Algorithm

The algorithm presented below is attributed to Euclid (c. 300 BC), who is thought to have been the first chief librarian of the ancient Library of Alexandria and who wrote the famous *Elements*—the first treatise on geometry. The algorithm computes the greatest common divisor of two natural numbers. Its extended version allows us to determine the inverse of a given natural number in Z_n.

The first version of the algorithm, presented in *Elements*, concerned the purely geometric problem of determining whether two line segments are commensurable. Later, it was proven that this problem can be expressed in the language of number theory.

The easiest version of the Euclidean algorithm consists of repeatedly subtracting the smaller number from the greater one until zero is obtained. The last nonzero number achieved in this way is equal to the greatest common divisor of the two input numbers. A faster version applies a function that returns the remainder of the division of two natural numbers. There exist also recursive versions of the algorithm. Below we present them written in pseudocode.

Algorithm 2.1 (Euclid (1))
Input: m, n (positive integers, for the sake of simplicity let m ≤ n)
Output: gcd(m, n)
Auxiliary variables: natural numbers a, b, c

```
1  a := n;
2  b := m;
3  if a=b then gcd(a,b) := a
4         else
5            repeat
6               begin
7                  repeat b := b - a until b < a;
8                     (a,b) := (b,a);
9               end
10           until b=0;
11 gcd(n,m) := a;
```

It is easy to notice that this algorithm can be rewritten in a simpler way using the mod function, which finds the remainder of division:

Algorithm 2.2 (Euclid (2))
Input: m, n (positive integers, let m ≤ n)
Output: gcd(m, n)
Auxiliary variables: natural numbers a, b, c

```
1  a := n;
2  b := m;
3  if a=b then gcd(a,b) := a
4         else
5            repeat
6               begin
7                  b := (b mod a)
8                     (a,b) := (b,a);
```

```
9              end
10             until b=0;
11 gcd(a,b) :=a;
```

The algorithm can also be presented in a recursive version:

Algorithm 2.3 (Euclid (3))
Input: m, n (positive integers, let m ≤ n)
Output: gcd(m, n)
Auxiliary variables: natural numbers a, b

```
1  a := n;
2  b := m;
3  if a=b then gcd(a,b) := a
4        else
5            if a<b then gcd(a,b) := gcd(a, b-a)
6                else
7                    gcd(a,b) := gcd(a-b, b);
```

In order to show the correctness of the Euclidean algorithm, we start by proving the following result.

Theorem 2.29 *For all natural numbers a, b, where $b \neq 0$, the common divisors of a and b are the same as the common divisors of a and $b \bmod a$.*

Proof Let a, b be arbitrary numbers satisfying the assumptions of the theorem. Then, for some q and r,

$$b = a \cdot q + r,$$

where

$$q = (b \operatorname{div} a),$$
$$r = (b \bmod a),$$

thus

$$b = a \cdot (b \operatorname{div} a) + (b \bmod a).$$

Let us assume that the above formula holds also for $a = 1$. We have

$$(b \operatorname{div} a) = (b \operatorname{div} 1) = b, \qquad (b \bmod a) = (b \bmod 1) = 0.$$

Suppose that d is a divisor of both a and b. Then, for some x, y, we get

$$b = d \cdot x \quad \text{and} \quad a = d \cdot y.$$

We have

$$b = a \cdot q + r = d \cdot y \cdot q + r,$$

hence

$$d \cdot x = d \cdot y \cdot q + r, \quad r = d \cdot (x - y \cdot q),$$

therefore

$$(b \bmod a) = d \cdot (x - y \cdot q).$$

It follows that d is also a common divisor of a and $b \bmod a$.
The proof of the other direction is analogous. □

Corollary *If the set of divisors of positive integers a and $b \bmod a$ is equal to the set of divisors of a and b, then the greatest common divisor of both pairs is the same:*

$$\gcd(a, b) = \gcd(a, b \bmod a).$$

Let us take a look at several examples:

Example 2.15 $\gcd(45, 12) = \gcd(45 \bmod 12, 12) = \gcd(9, 12) = \gcd(9, 12 \bmod 9)$
$= \gcd(9, 3) = \gcd(9 \bmod 3, 3) = \gcd(0, 3) = 3.$

Example 2.16 $\gcd(20, 63) = \gcd(63 \bmod 20, 20) = \gcd(3, 20) = \gcd(3, 20 \bmod 3)$
$= \gcd(3, 2) = \gcd(3 \bmod 2, 2) = \gcd(1, 2) = \gcd(1, 2 \bmod 1) = \gcd(1, 1) = 1.$

This shows that 63 and 20 are coprime (indeed, let us notice that $63 = 3^2 \cdot 7$, while $20 = 2^2 \cdot 5$).

Theorem 2.30 *The Euclidean algorithm is correct, i.e., it returns the greatest common divisor of two given positive integers.*

Proof (for the second version of the algorithm) In order to prove the theorem, we need to show two facts. Firstly, it is necessary to justify that the algorithm stops, secondly, that its output is correct.

Let us consider two natural numbers n, m such that $n \leq m$.

1. In the case when $n = m$, then $\gcd(n, m) = n = m$, and hence the algorithm returns the value $\gcd(n, m)$ (3rd line of the algorithm (2)).
2. Let us assume that $n < m$. After executing each loop 6–9, values of the variable b form a strictly decreasing sequence of natural numbers. Obviously, each strictly decreasing sequence of natural numbers is finite and thus the last value of b is equal to 0. Therefore, the algorithm always stops.

As concerns the correctness of the result, let us observe that, due to the last theorem, $\gcd(n, m)$ is constant before and after each loop 6–9. The initial value of $\gcd(n, m)$ is thus equal to the value after the last execution of the loop, where $b = 0$,

Table 2.8 Consecutive values of variables a, b, q and $-q \cdot b$

Loop number	a	b	q	$-q \cdot b$
1	135	40	3	-120
2	40	15	2	-30
3	15	10	1	-10
4	10	5	2	-10
5	5	0		

which gives $\gcd(n, m) = \gcd(a, 0) = a$. The last value of the variable a is the greatest common divisor of n and m.

From the viewpoint of the computational complexity, it should be noticed that the time complexity of the above algorithm applied to k-bit numbers equals $O(k^2)$.[7] $\square$

2.3.3 Extended Euclidean Algorithm

Let us consider one more variant of the Euclidean algorithm which applies the function div instead of mod. This version allows us to present and justify the correctness of the so-called extended Euclidean algorithm.

Algorithm 2.4 (Euclid (4))
Input: m, n (positive integers, let m $\leq$ n)
Output: gcd(m, n)
Auxiliary variables: natural numbers a, b, c

```
1   a := n;
2   b := m;
3   while b <> 0 do
4       begin
5           q := a div b;
6           (a,b) := (b, a - bq)
7       end;
8   gcd(m,n) := a
```

Example 2.17 Let us follow the execution of the above algorithm for $n = 135$ and $m = 40$.

Table 2.8 below provides values of variables a, b, q and $-q \cdot b$ during the algorithm's execution for the numbers n, m set as above.

As can be seen in the presented example, the algorithm generates several sequences of natural numbers $a_0, a_1, a_2, \ldots, a_k, b_0, b_1, b_2, \ldots, b_k, q_1, q_2, \ldots, q_k$ and integers $-q_1 \cdot b_1, -q_2 \cdot b_2, \ldots, -q_k \cdot b_k$ (where $a_0 = m$, while $b_0 = n$).

---

[7]See [68], Fact 2.105.

If a_{i-1} and b_{i-1} are values of variables a and b at the beginning of the loop 4–7, and a_i and b_i are values of these variables after the loop's execution, then, for $i = 1, 2, \ldots, k$, the following properties hold:

1. $a_i = b_{i-1}$,
2. $q_i = a_{i-1} \operatorname{div} a_i$
3. $a_{i+1} = b_i = a_{i-1} - q_i \cdot b_{i-1} = a_{i-1} - q_i \cdot a_i$, hence
4. $a_{i+1} = a_{i-1} - q_i \cdot a_i$

Let us also notice that $a_k = \gcd(n, m)$.

Now, we will construct two useful integer sequences (s_n) and (t_n). Let

$$s_0 = 1, \quad t_0 = 0 \quad \text{and} \quad s_1 = 0, \quad t_1 = 1.$$

Let us observe that for such coefficients s_0, t_0, s_1, t_1 the following relations hold:

$$m = a_0 = s_0 \cdot m + t_0 \cdot n \quad \text{and} \quad n = a_1 = s_1 \cdot m + t_1 \cdot n,$$

as well as $a_{i-1} = s_{i-1} \cdot m + t_{i-1} \cdot n$ and $a_i = s_i \cdot m + t_i \cdot n$.

Now, let us apply formula 4. We get

$$a_{i+1} = a_{i-1} - q_i \cdot a_i = (s_{i-1} \cdot m + t_{i-1} \cdot n) - q_i \cdot (s_i \cdot m + t_i \cdot n)$$

$$= (s_{i-1} - q_i \cdot s_i) \cdot m + (t_{i-1} + t_i \cdot q_i) \cdot n$$

If sequences (s_n) are (t_n) are defined as follows:

$$s_{n+1} = s_{n-1} - q_n \cdot s_n$$

$$t_{n+1} = t_{n-1} - q_n \cdot t_n,$$

then we can see that for all $i = 0, 1, \ldots, k - 1$ the equation $a_{i+1} = s_{i+1} \cdot m + t_{i+1} \cdot n$ is valid.

Therefore, this relation does not depend on the number of executions of the loop 4–7.

Now, let us recall that the last value of a determines $\gcd(n, m)$, which results in the following formula:

$$\gcd(n, m) = a_k = s_k \cdot m + t_k \cdot n.$$

We see that the greatest common divisor of two given numbers can be represented as their linear combination with integer coefficients. This observation turns out to be crucial for determining inverses in rings Z_n.

Finally, we describe the so-called extended Euclidean algorithm, which takes into account our considerations and which determines coefficients s and t mentioned above.

Algorithm 2.5 (Extended Euclidean Algorithm)

Input: m, n (positive integers, let us assume that $m \leq n$)

Output: $\gcd(m, n)$

Auxiliary variables: natural numbers a, a', q, integers s, s', t, t'

```
1    a := m;
2    a' := n;
3    s := 1;
4    t := 0;
5    s' := 0;
6    t' := 1;

{We have: m = a = sm + tn and n = a = s'm + t'n}

7    while a <> 0 do
8      begin
9         q := a div a';
10        (a,a') := (a', a - qa')
11        (s,s') := (s', s - qs')
12        (t,t') := (t', t - qt')
13     end
14  gcd(n,m) := a
```

The extended Euclidean algorithm returns the greatest common divisor of two given numbers, and, moreover, it determines the integer coefficients s and t of a linear combination such that $\gcd(n, m) = s \cdot n + t \cdot m$.

The proof is based on our discussion related to Example 2.17.

The above algorithm allows us, among other things, to find inverses in rings Z_n.

Let us recall that if for a given number $z \in Z_n$ there exists $y \in Z_n$ such that $x \cdot y \equiv 1 \pmod{n}$, then we call x and y mutually inverse. We adopt the following notation: $y = x^{-1}$ and $x = y^{-1}$.

We say that $z \in Z_n$ is invertible if and only if there exists its inverse.

We have the following result.

Theorem 2.31 *A number* $z \in Z_n$ *is invertible in* Z_n *if and only if* $\gcd(z, n) = 1$. *In particular, if p is prime, then every number from the set* $\{1, 2, \ldots, p - 1\}$ *is invertible in* Z_p.

Example 2.18 Let us consider the following problem. We want to compute the inverse, provided it exists, of 10 in the set Z_{37} (37 is a prime, so due to the above theorem 10 is invertible in Z_{37}). Let us denote this inverse by x.

The following modular equation has to be satisfied: $10 \cdot x = 1 \pmod{37}$.

If we apply the extended Euclidean algorithm to 10 and 37, then we obtain $\gcd(10, 37) = 1$, $s = -11$ and $t = 3$. We have

$$1 = -11 \cdot 10 + 3 \cdot 37,$$

and since $(-11 = 26) \bmod 37$, we also get

$$1 = 26 \cdot 10 + 3 \cdot 37 \ (\mathrm{mod}\, 37),$$

therefore

$$1 = 26 \cdot 10 \ (\mathrm{mod}\, 37).$$

Thus, 27 is the inverse of 10 in the set Z_{37}.

It follows from this example that a simple way to determine the inverse of x in Z_n is to apply the extended Euclidean algorithm for numbers x and n.

The time complexity of the described algorithm applied to k-bit numbers is also $O(k^2)$.[8]

2.4   Tests for Primality

This section presents two probabilistic, or randomized, algorithms for testing primality of natural numbers—Fermat's test and the Miller-Rabin test,[9] both often used in practice today. This is followed by pointing out the theoretic role of one of the most important achievements in computer science of the last decade, namely the AKS deterministic test for primality. The section closes with a brief discussion of two computationally hard number theoretic problems—the integer factorization and the discrete logarithm problem. These issues play a fundamental role when it comes to the cryptographic strength of many of today's security systems, considered in the following chapters.

2.4.1   Fermat's Test

Let's recall *Fermat's little theorem*: If p is a prime integer, then for any $a \in Z_p$ and $a \neq 0$,

$$a^{p-1} \equiv 1 \ (\mathrm{mod}\, p).$$

Unfortunately, the primes are not the only numbers that satisfy the above condition. There are also composite numbers, for which the above holds true.

A composite n that satisfies condition $a^{n-1} \equiv 1 \ (\mathrm{mod}\, n)$ for every a coprime to n is called a Carmichael number.

The smallest Carmichael number is 561 $(3 \cdot 11 \cdot 17)$.

---

[8] See [68], Fact 2.108.
[9] See Sect. 4.2. in [68].

A number w satisfying the condition

$$w^{n-1} \equiv 1 \ (\bmod\, n)$$

for the natural number n ($w < n$) is called a witness to the primality of n. Of course, if n is prime, then all natural numbers less than n are witnesses to the primality of n.

It turns out that Fermat's little theorem provides a method for checking primality. The following assertion is true.

Theorem 2.32 *Every number relatively prime to n is a witness to the primality of n or at most half of the numbers relatively prime to n are witnesses to the primality of n.*

Proof Consider a natural n. Let T denote the set of all integers relatively prime to n. Then for each $w \in T$, we have: $\gcd(w, n) = 1$. There are two cases: either all the elements of T are witnesses to the primality of n, that is, for each $w \in T$, we have: $w^{n-1} = 1 \ (\bmod\, n)$, or a number exists in T which is not a witness to the primality of n. In the first case the conclusion is obvious.

Suppose that some $w \in T$ is not a witness to the primality of n, i.e., $w^{n-1} \neq 1$ $(\bmod\, n)$. Then n is composite. Let $T_n = \{w_1, w_2, \ldots, w_t\}$ denote the set of those numbers from T ($T_n \subseteq T$) which are witnesses to the primality of n. We have, for each $k \in \{1, 2, \ldots, t\}$: $w_k^{n-1} = 1 \ (\bmod\, n)$.

Let $u_i = w \cdot w_i$, for each $i \in \{1, 2, \ldots, t\}$. Then any $i, k \in \{1, 2, \ldots, t\}$ satisfy the following relationships:

1. $u_i \neq u_k$, for $i \neq k$.

Because suppose that for some $i \neq j$, we have $u_i = u_k$. Then of course $u_i - u_k = 0$, therefore $w \cdot w_i - w \cdot w_k = 0$, and so $n \mid (w \cdot w_i - w \cdot w_k)$ and finally $n \mid w \cdot (w_i - w_k)$. But $\gcd(w, n) = 1$. Therefore $n \mid (w_i - w_k)$. It is also true that $-n < w_i - w_k < n$. Hence $w_i = w_k$, which contradicts the assumption.

2. $u_i^{n-1} = (w \cdot w_i)^{n-1} = w^{n-1} \cdot w_i^{n-1} = w^{n-1} \neq 1 \ (\bmod\, n)$.

A direct application of these properties is the fact that in the latter case, for t numbers which are witnesses to the primality of n, there exist as many numbers in T which are not witnesses to the primality of n. $\qquad\square$

2.4.2 Fermat's Primality Test

The test consists of k independent trials carried out for a given number n being tested.

The parameter k is chosen by the user, in practice most often k is not less than 20 and not greater than 50.

We choose a random number w such that $w < n$ and

1. we compute $\gcd(w, n)$; if $\gcd(w, n) > 1$, then n is composite;
2. we compute $w^{n-1} \pmod{n}$; if $w^{n-1} \not\equiv 1 \pmod{n}$, then n is composite.

We repeat the test several times. If in k trials we do not get that n is composite, the test concludes: n is prime.

As noted above, there exist composite numbers n satisfying the congruence $w^{n-1} \equiv 1 \pmod{n}$, for each w. The test may therefore mistakenly declare primality. The question arises, how often the test can be mistaken, and when, and whether the probability of a correct result can be determined.

Obviously, the test always gets it wrong, when we test the Carmichael numbers. The probability of a correct result of Fermat's test is provided as a corollary to the theorem proven above:

Theorem 2.33 *If n is not prime and is not a Carmichael number, then, in a single trial a randomly selected number a ($a < n$) is not a witness to the primality of n with probability of at least $\frac{1}{2}$.*

It follows that, if we repeat the test k times and we do not hit on a Carmichael number, the probability of a mistaken result is less than $\frac{1}{2^k}$. For k equal to 20, the result is already satisfactory for our purposes.

Carmichael numbers are believed to be very rare. Their distribution has been studied extensively for over 100 years with no definite answer, so far. Their rarity has been proved for the primes up to 10^{21} (as of August 2012), see [80]. The currently interesting cryptographic prime parameters are much bigger, in the range of size between 160 and 4096 bits, (see [30, 82]). These are still very small from the perspective of asymptotic (i.e., for arbitrarily large n) conjectures currently discussed in number theory research. The probability of randomly hitting a Carmichael number cannot be precisely estimated with present knowledge. It is often believed that they are sufficiently rare among small primes currently used in cryptography to make the risk due to the fallibility of the Fermat test fallibility small enough in practice. However, according to some researchers (e.g., [68]) this uncertainty makes Fermat's test excessively fallible.

It is interesting to note that Fermat's test is now utilized for testing primality of numbers used as keys in the PGP system (discussed thoroughly in the following chapters).

2.4.3 Miller-Rabin Test

This subsection presents the Miller-Rabin test, most often used in practice these days.

Theorem 2.34 *Let n be an odd prime, and let $n - 1 = 2^s \cdot r$ where r is odd. Let a be an integer coprime to n. Then either $a^r \equiv 1 \pmod{n}$ or $a^{2^j \cdot r} \equiv -1 \pmod{n}$ for some $j, 0 \le j \le s - 1$.*

As before, we will examine primality of a natural number n. Since there is only one even prime 2, the other primes are odd, we consider only an odd number n. Of course, the number $n - 1$ is even, so there exist natural numbers r and s such that:

$$n - 1 = 2^s \cdot r \quad \text{where } r \text{ is odd.}$$

As in the previous test, we run k independent trials:

1. we choose a random number $1 < a \le n - 1$ and compute $x = a^r \pmod{n}$;
2. we sequentially compute the powers of x: $x^2, x^4, x^8, x^{16}, \ldots$, until

   (a) the exponent value reaches $2s$, then we check if whether the last computed power is equal to $1 \bmod n$, and if not, then the number a is not a witness to the primality of n, therefore n is composite.
   (b) any of the powers calculated is equal to $1 \bmod n$; if it is 1, then we check whether every previous power is equal to $-1 \bmod n$, if not, the number a is not a witness to the primality of n, therefore n is composite.

The error probability of the Miller–Rabin test is characterized by the following statements.

Theorem 2.35 *If n is prime, the test always gives the correct answer.*

Theorem 2.36 *If n is composite, then the probability that the selected number is a witness to the primality and the test with a single trial declares* prime *is less than $\frac{1}{4}$.*

Thus a single positive Miller–Rabin test trial gives twice the confidence that the result is correct than does Fermat's test. For k trials the confidence rises 2^k-fold.

The seemingly more complicated Miller-Rabin test is in fact computationally no more time-consuming than the Fermat test. The time complexity of each of the two tests for k-bit input numbers is $O(k^3)$.[10]

2.4.4 Algorithm AKS

The tests presented above for primality are probabilistic. This means that the result is correct with a certain large probability but the probability is not equal to 1.

So far, no feasible deterministic algorithm has been developed for checking primality of numbers of size interesting in cryptographic practice these days. Until

---

[10]See Sect. 4.2 in [68].

2002 the only known deterministic algorithms testing primality were of exponential time complexity.

In August 2002, Manindra Agrawal and his two undergraduate students, Neeraj Kayal and Nitin Saxena of the Indian Institute of Technology in Kanpur, published the first polynomial-time algorithm for testing primality.[11] However practical usage of this algorithm for large numbers of current interest is still impossible. The degree of the polynomial is too high. Many research centers are working hard on optimizing this algorithm.

Algorithm AKS (for abbreviation, we omit the names of the coauthors) is based on a generalization of Fermat's little theorem for polynomials.

Theorem 2.37 *A natural number n is prime iff*

$$(x - a)^n \equiv (x^n - a) \ (\mathrm{mod}\, n)$$

for all natural numbers a such that a < n.

Here $x - a$ and $x^n - a$ are polynomials with coefficients in the ring Z_n.

Since the above condition is equivalent to the primality of n, the AKS test is deterministic. If n is prime, the algorithm will always return prime. Conversely, if n is composite, the algorithm will always return composite. There are no liars in this test, and no problem with their probability distribution, unlike in the case of the properties on which the Fermat and Miller-Rabin tests are based. It is much harder to give an intuitive argument for the polynomial run time estimate so we shall not dwell on it here. For a proof of this result and further discussion the interested reader is referred to [4] and [62]. [62] gives a slightly smaller than seventh degree polynomial run time complexity upper bound. It also argues that a fundamentally new idea would be required to obtain a deterministic primality testing algorithm with run time exponent smaller than 6. This leaves the AKS test infeasible for primes in the size range currently used in practical cryptography.

2.5 Computationally Hard Problems in Number Theory

Modern cryptography often employs so-called computationally hard mathematical problems. A computational problem is considered *hard* or *intractable* or *infeasible* if there is no known algorithm solving all the problem instances with a polynomial upper bound on the resources required, in particular polynomial time. Any cryptosystem whose security is based on an intractable problem is considered secure. That is, breaking the cryptosystem would imply the existence of a polynomial-resources (e.g., time) algorithm solving all problem instances, including instances with parameters especially carefully chosen. This section presents two of the most famous such problems: the integer factorization problem, justifying the cryptographic strength

---

[11] See [4].

of the RSA algorithm, and the discrete logarithm problem, employed in the Digital Signature Algorithm.

2.5.1 Factorization

The integer factorization problem is the problem of splitting any given composite positive integer n into (preferably prime) non-trivial factors. The multiplication of integers is instantly executed on any computer. But the inverse operation, i.e., factorization, is computationally hard. This subsection summarizes the current status of the integer factorization problem to the extent of its interest for cryptology.

In general running times of the factoring algorithms are functions of the size of n only. In some special cases, these times may depend also on some specific properties of n, e.g., on the size of the prime factors of n. It is advisable to try the algorithms for finding small prime factors first. The hardest case is when n is the product of two primes of roughly the same size.

In 1991, a global contest was started, the *RSA Factoring Challenge*,[12] organized by *RSA Security* in order to stimulate the scientific community to study efficient algorithms for factoring large integers. A list of numbers was published, which were known to be the products of two primes. These numbers are called *RSA numbers*.

A cash prize was offered for factorization of some of them. The first one, a 100-digit RSA-100 number was factored out within a few days, but most of them still remain unbroken. The contest lasted for sixteen years and was officially closed in May 2007. Some of the smaller prizes had been awarded at the time. The remaining prizes were retracted. Many numbers were factored during the challenge. Even today, these results still determine the bounds of feasible factorization.

Here are some of the challenge details. In August 1999, the cryptological community was electrified to learn that a 512-bit number (155 decimal digits) was factored out into prime factors.

10941738641570527421809707322040357612003732945449205990913842131 47634998428893478471799725789126733249762575289978183379707653724 402714674353159335433897.

It turned out to be the product of the following two 78-decimal-digit primes:

10263959282974110577205419657399167590071656780803806680334193352 1790711307779

×

10660348838016845482092722036001287867920795857598929152227060823 7193062808643.

Finding these factors took four months. Multiple computers were involved in the calculations.

In March 2002, nCipher Inc. announced that it had developed software that allowed it to break the 512-bit RSA key within six weeks, using tens of computers. A little later, the computing time was shortened to one day.

These are obviously very good results, but it should be noted and emphasized that increasing the number of bits by one doubles the search space.

In December 2003, factorization of the next RSA Challenge number was announced. This time it was RSA-576, a 576-bit (174-decimal-digit) integer. This number is:

18819881292060796383869723946165043980716356337941738270076335642
29888597152346654853190606065047430453173880113033967161996923212
05734031879550656996221305168759307650257059.

It is the product of the following primes:

39807508642406493739712550055038649119906436234252670840638518957
5946388957261768583317

×

47277214610743530253622307197304822463291469530209711645985217113
0520711256363590397527.

The team that managed to factorize RSA-576 received the $10,000 prize, as promised by the RSA Challenge.

As of August 2012, the largest RSA Challenge cryptographically hard integer (i.e., one that was chosen specifically to resist all known factoring attacks, and is a product of two roughly equal primes) that has been factored is RSA-768, a 768-bit (232-decimal-digit) integer:

12301866845301177551304949583849627207728535695953347921973224521
51726400507263657518745202199786469389956474942774063845925192557
32630345373154826850791702612214291346167042921431160222124047927
473779408066535141959745985690214341

=

33478071698956898786044169848212690817704794983713768568912431388
982883793878002287614711652531743087737814467999489

×

36746043666799590428244633799627952632279158164343087642676032283
815739666511279233373417143396810270092798736308917

This was the result of a large collaboration across the globe stretching over more than two years and using the general-purpose factoring algorithm called the general number field sieve. The overall effort required more than 10^{20} operations, on the

Table 2.9 RSA numbers

RSA Number	Digits	Bits	Awards	Decomposed	Solving team
RSA-100	100	330		April 1991	A.K. Lenstra
RSA-110	110	364		April 1992	A.K. Lenstra and M. Manasse
RSA-120	120	397		June 1993	T. Denny and others
RSA-129	129	426	US $00	April 1994	A.K. Lenstra and others
RSA-130	130	430		April 10, 1996	A.K. Lenstra and others
RSA-140	140	463		February 2, 1999	H.J. te Riele and others
RSA-150	150	496		April 16, 2004	K. Aoki and others
RSA-155	155	512		August 22, 1999	H.J. te Riele and others
RSA-160	160	530		April 1, 2003	J. Franke and others
RSA-576	174	576	US $10000	3 December 2003	J. Franke and others
RSA-640	193	640	US $20000	2 November 2005	J. Franke and others
RSA-200	200	663		9 May 2005	J. Franke and others
RSA-704	212	704	US $30000	prize withdrawn	
RSA-768	232	768	US $50000	prize withdrawn	
RSA-896	270	896	US $75000	prize withdrawn	
RSA-1024	309	1024	US $100000	prize withdrawn	
RSA-1536	463	1536	US $150000	prize withdrawn	
RSA-2048	617	2048	US $200000	prize withdrawn	

order of 2^{67} instructions. This is sufficiently low that even for short-term protection of data of little value, 768-bit RSA moduli can no longer be recommended [58].

More RSA numbers are waiting in the queue (Table 2.9). For a person who manages to decompose RSA-704, a US $30000 award was offered, and for the longest presented number, the RSA-2048, a US $200000. Table 2.9 shows more on the RSA Challenge.[13]

The longest number presented to the contest was the RSA-2048:

2519590847565789349402718324004839857142928212620403202777713783604366202070759555626401852588078440691829064124951508218929855914917618450280848912007284499268739280728777673597141834727026189637501497182469116507761337985909570009733045974880842840179742910064245869181719511874612151517265463228221686998754918242243363725908514186546204357679842338718477444792073993423658482382428119816381501067481045166037730605620161967625613384414360383390441495263443219011465754445417842402092461651572335077870774981712577246796292638635637328991215483143816789988504044536402352738195137863656439121201039712282212072035 7.

─────────────────────
[13] See also [88].

Comparing this number to RSA-576, one can easily forecast that even using modern technology the factorization will remain an open problem for a very long time. The best algorithms currently used for factorization of k-bit integers have the time complexity $O(e^{k \cdot lg(k)})$[14] (see [68]). The work on them, and on new algorithms, does not give much hope for easy and fast factorization of large numbers. A very nice survey of integer factorization methods and their complexities is given by [68], Chap. 3 and [75].

2.5.2 Discrete Logarithm Problem

Another computationally hard problem is the calculation of discrete logarithm. This section gives a brief account of its current status. This is similar to that of factorization, in a way, due to its computational hardness, uncertain future, and its role in modern cryptography.

Let's recall that the logarithm of a number $a > 0$ to the base $0 < b \neq 1$ is the number c such that $b^c = a$, i.e., $\log_b a = c \Leftrightarrow b^c = a$. In other words, the search for the logarithm of a number is the search for a suitable exponent by which the base has to be raised to give that number. It is the inverse function to exponentiation.

Discrete logarithm is a direct analog in a finite group of the usual log in the field of reals. In general, in a finite multiplicative group G the discrete logarithm of $a \in G$ to the base $b \in G$ is defined to be $c \in G$ such that $b^c = a$ in G, provided that such a c exists. In cryptography, only logs in cyclic groups are considered and the base b is assumed to be a generator of G. The exponent can only be a positive integer, say n, and both $a, b \neq 0$. The logarithm is well defined for every $a \in G$ (i.e., there exists such an exponent c), under these assumptions. Most often, G is the multiplicative group of a finite field and the order of b in G is known. (This is the case of ElGamal and the Digital Signature Algorithm, for example.)

The discrete logarithm problem (DLP) is the following: given a prime p, a generator g of Z_p, and an element $x \in Z_p^*$ find the integer y, $0 \leq y \leq p - 2$, such that $g^y = x \pmod{p}$.

Let us recall that Z_p^* denotes the multiplicative group of Z_p, and for a prime p, $Z_p^* = \{a \mid 1 \leq a \leq p - 1\}$ with multiplication modulo p. In particular, if p is a prime, then Z_p has a generator; i.e., an element $g \in Z_p$ such that for each $y \in Z_p$ there is an integer i with $y = g^i \bmod p$. In other words, every finite field of size prime; has at least one generator (also called primitive element) g; i.e., all nonzero elements of the field are expressible as powers of g.

It is easy and fast to calculate the powers in Z_n, even for large n. But computing the inverse function to exponentiation, or searching for the discrete logarithm, is computationally hard, similar to integer factorization. To date, nobody knows of a time-efficient algorithm for the discrete logarithm of large enough numbers.

---

[14]The lg function is the logarithm to base 2.

The most obvious algorithm for DLP is exhaustive search: successively compute g^0, g^1, g^2 until y is obtained. It takes $O(p)$ multiplications. This is exponential in the bit-length of p, and is therefore infeasible if n is large, i.e., in cases of current cryptographic interest.

In some important applications, in particular in the Digital Signature Algorithm (DSA), operations are performed in a field Z_p with a prime p which nowadays is recommended to be of at least 2048 bits. This prime p is selected so that $p - 1$ is divisible by a much smaller prime q specified in the standard *FIPS 186-3* to be of 160-, 224-, or 256-bit length.

The currently best method known for computing discrete logs in finite fields Z_p is called the number field sieve, with a subexponential expected running time, roughly equal to $\exp((\log(m))^{\frac{1}{3}})$, where m is the order of the group. The currently best general algorithms for computing discrete logs (including probabilistic or parallelized ones) in cyclic groups run in (expected) exponential time $O(m^{\frac{1}{2}})$, and with low memory requirements.

The so-far largest discrete log case for a prime field Z_p (with p chosen with all the recommended precautions to resist the known simple attacks) that has been solved, up to August 2012, is for a 530-bit (160 decimal digit) prime p, [57]. The largest finite group discrete log problem with hard parameters that has been solved is that of discrete logs over an elliptic curve modulo a 112-bit prime, i.e., in a group of about 2^{112} elements [21].

The Diffie-Hellman problem (DHP) is the following: given a prime p, a generator g of Z_p^* and elements $g^a \bmod p$ and $g^b \bmod p$, compute $g^{ab} \bmod p$. From the complexity theory standpoint, DHP is at most as hard as DLP; i.e., it is polytime reducible to DLP. Whether these problems are computationally equivalent remains unknown.

The hardness of the discrete logarithm problem is the basis for the security justification of the Digital Signature Algorithm, presented in the next section, and for the Diffie-Hellman key exchange protocol. The discrete log problem in elliptic curve groups is not explicitly considered in this book. We mention in passing that, elliptic curve cryptosystems currently use much smaller key sizes than would be required by DSA and RSA with comparable security.

It appears that computing like discrete logs in prime fields or in elliptic curve groups is harder than factoring integers of the same size. However, one of the reasons for this impression might be that much less attention and effort has been given to discrete logs than to integer factorization, while many leading algorithms are similar.

More on the discrete logarithm problem can be found in Sect. 3.6 of [68] and a beautiful survey [74]. For recent advances see [75], and the references therein.

Chapter 3
Foundations of Symmetric Cryptography

This chapter presents theoretical foundations of symmetric-key cryptography, or secret-key cryptography. The currently most widely used symmetric algorithms are given. It starts with the concept of a Feistel network which constitutes an important design principle underlying many advanced symmetric encryption schemes. Among the most well-known symmetric-key ciphers are DES (Data Encryption Standard) and its official successor AES (Advanced Encryption Standard), followed by several others also well known and also often used in practice such as IDEA (International Data Encryption Algorithm) or the RC (Rivest Cipher) family of algorithms.

3.1 Idea of Symmetric Cryptography

As indicated in Chap. 1, symmetric-key cryptography uses the same key for encryption and decryption, or the decryption key can easily be computed from the encryption key, and the other way round. Usually, symmetric-key ciphers are very fast. Their main disadvantage is that a secret key must be agreed or transferred securely between two parties before they can start communicating with such a cipher. It always requires an earlier-established secure method of key exchange. In the traditional framework this used to be arranged via special couriers. In the computerized world, however, there is always a serious threat that the secret key could be intercepted by an unauthorized party. (In this book for simplicity such an unauthorized party is called an intruder, or adversary.) Since every symmetric cipher's security is based on the security of its keys, the keys must be kept secret. Compromising a key in such ciphers enables anyone who has the key to decrypt all the communication cryptograms. Also in future, as long as communication is required to remain secret, the key must be kept secret. Figure 3.1 illustrates the idea of symmetric cryptography.

C. Kościelny et al., *Modern Cryptography Primer*,
DOI 10.1007/978-3-642-41386-5_3, © Springer-Verlag Berlin Heidelberg 2013

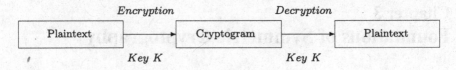

Fig. 3.1 Encryption and decryption with the same key

3.1.1 The Feistel Network

Many of the currently used symmetric algorithms apply some modifications of the so-called Feistel network, i.e., an encryption algorithm introduced by Horst Feistel and published by IBM at the beginning of the 1970s.[1]

The Feistel network is a block algorithm which takes as an input blocks of an arbitrary even length. A given block is divided into halves, left and right, denoted by L and R respectively. During the encryption process a function f_S, dependent on the key S is applied. It returns a pair of transformed halves, L' and R', as a result.

Proper encryption consists of two substitutions:

1. $L' := R$.
2. $R' := L \ XOR \ f_S(R)$.

In the first substitution we replace the left half with the value of the right half, while in the second substitution first we apply the function f_S to the right half and then the obtained value along with the left half are processed by the *XOR* operation. The course of the Feistel algorithm is depicted in Fig. 3.2.

Let us recall two basic properties of the *XOR* function:

1. $x \ XOR \ x = 0$,
2. $x \ XOR \ 0 = x$.

It is easy to notice that the ciphertext obtained by means of the Feistel network can be effortlessly decrypted by applying the function f_S, which is used also for encryption. We have

$$L = L \ XOR \ f_S(R) \ XOR \ f_S(R) = R' \ XOR \ f_S(R).$$

Let us recall that $R = L'$. Hence, it is possible to recover the plaintext.

Leaving half of the plaintext unmodified might raise some doubts. However, the security of the algorithm can be increased by repeating the whole procedure any number of times. Symmetric algorithms used in practice usually apply several rounds similar to the round of the Feistel cipher. Often, each of them uses a different key S.

It is worth emphasizing that the function f_S is an arbitrary function that maps bit sequences into sequences of the same length. This means that we can design f_S arbitrarily.

---

[1] See also Sect. 7.4 in [68].

Fig. 3.2 Principle of the
Feistel network

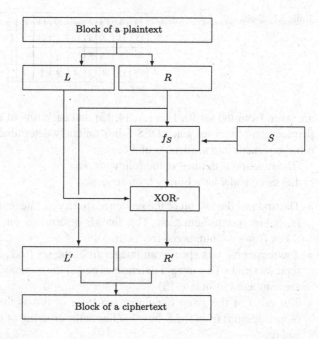

3.2 The DES Algorithm

The Data Encryption Standard (DES)[2] was commissioned by the US National Bureau of Standards. In 1973 NBS solicited proposals for a uniform and reliable encryption algorithm that could be applied, among other places, in commercial communication systems. For over a year all of the submitted algorithms were rejected since they did not meet the rigorous design criteria. In 1974 the DES algorithm developed at IBM by Horst Feistel and Dan Coppersmith was thoroughly examined and finally accepted by NBS, introduced and specified in [41], superseded by [42, 43], and [44]. It was withdrawn as a US NIST standard in 2005. Its 56-bit key size is now considered to be small and insecure. Although many years have passed, DES is still used for symmetric encryption in numerous cryptographic systems or packages. Due to the rapid increase of computational power, so-called 3DES (Triple DES), see [70], i.e., an algorithm that uses three DES executions for encryption, is often applied.

DES applies transformations with the help of so-called S-boxes, presented in the following subsection.

3.2.1 S-Boxes

The algorithm for transforming data by means of S-boxes (S stands for substitution) is a block algorithm. A DES S-box is represented as a 4×16 matrix whose entries

---

[2]See Sect. 7.4 in [68].

Table 3.1 S-box

14	4	13	1	2	15	11	8	3	10	6	12	5	9	0	7
0	15	7	4	14	2	13	1	10	6	12	11	9	5	3	8
4	1	14	8	13	6	2	11	15	12	9	7	3	10	5	0
15	12	8	2	4	9	1	7	5	11	3	14	10	0	6	13

are taken from the set $\{0, 1, 2, \ldots, 14, 15\}$ and each row of the matrix forms some permutation of this set. Each DES S-box uniquely determines a function that maps 6-bit sequences into sequences of 4 bits.

The function is defined in the following way.

Let us consider an arbitrary 6-bit sequence.

- The first and the last bit of the sequence specify an integer from the set $\{0, 1, 2, 3\}$ in its binary representation. This integer determines one of the rows from the S-box (rows are numbered from 0 to 3).
- The remaining bits specify an integer from the set $\{0, 1, 2, \ldots, 15\}$ in its binary representation. This integer determines one of the columns of the S-box (columns are numbered from 0 to 15).
- The value of the given 6-element sequence of bits is the integer (in its binary representation) from the S-box that lies at the crossing of the appropriate column and row.

Let us consider the following S-box (Table 3.1) and the bit sequence 110010.

The first and the last bit indicate the row number of the S-box, in our case this is the row numbered 2 (10). The remaining bits form the integer 9 (1001), thus the value of the ciphertext is the integer that lies at the crossing of the third row (numbered 2) and the column numbered 9. This gives us 12, which in binary representation is equal to 1100.

Let us notice that a transformation executed by means of such S-boxes is not invertible, i.e., it is not possible to uniquely recover the input on the basis of the output. Therefore, such a transformation cannot be called encryption. However, the construction of the DES algorithm that uses S-boxes allows us to apply them in order to encrypt and decrypt data.

Information about constructing S-boxes can be found, e.g., in [79].

3.2.2 Description of the DES Algorithm

Below we list some characteristic features of the DES cryptosystem.

- DES is a block algorithm—it transforms 64-bit blocks of a plaintext into 64-bit blocks of a ciphertext.
- It applies 16 rounds of some modification of the Feistel network.
- It uses a 56-bit key, but this is often placed within a 64-bit block where one bit in eight is used as a parity bit.

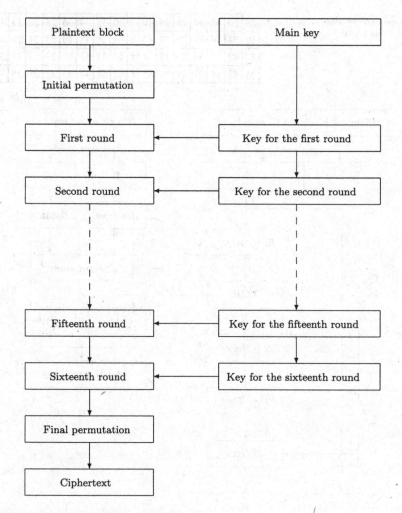

Fig. 3.3 Scheme of the DES algorithm

- An appropriate modification of the main key is used for encryption in each of 16 rounds.
- Special permutations of block bits are used before the first and after the last round.

The algorithm is presented as follows: first, we show its simplified scheme and then we describe in detail how each component of the algorithm works. The simplified scheme is depicted in Fig. 3.3.

As can be seen in Fig. 3.3, the plaintext (given as a 64-bit block) is first transformed by the initial permutation P. Next, we perform 16 rounds of the modified Feistel network. Each round has its own round key obtained from the master key. At the end of the algorithm, we transform the block by the final permutation.

Table 3.2 Consecutive
values of the initial
permutation P

58	50	42	34	26	18	10	2	60	52	44	36	28	20	12	4
62	54	46	38	30	22	14	6	64	56	48	40	32	24	16	8
57	49	41	33	25	17	9	1	59	51	43	35	27	19	11	3
61	53	45	37	29	21	13	5	63	55	47	39	31	23	15	7

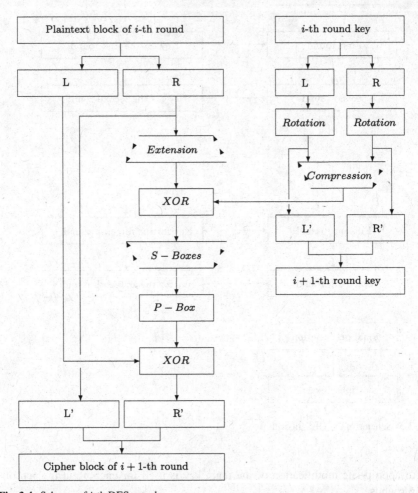

Fig. 3.4 Scheme of i-th DES round

The initial permutation P is the first operation performed by DES. Its values
are presented in Table 3.2 (a bit at the n-th position in the plaintext is shifted to the
position $P(n)$). The purpose of this permutation is to disperse bits in the transformed
block. The obtained rearrangement is quite regular. This can be seen by drawing the
diagram of the permutation as a directed graph.

Next, the algorithm consecutively performs sixteen rounds of the modified Feistel network (Fig. 3.4).

Table 3.3 Initial permutation *PC*1 of the key

57	49	41	33	25	17	9	1	58	50	42	34	26	18
10	2	59	51	43	35	27	19	11	3	60	52	44	36
63	55	47	39	31	23	15	7	62	54	46	38	30	22
14	6	61	53	45	37	29	21	13	5	28	20	12	4

Table 3.4 Rotation of key bits in consecutive rounds

Round	1	2	3	4	5	6	7	8
Rotation	1	1	2	2	2	2	2	2
Round	9	10	11	12	13	14	15	16
Rotation	1	2	2	2	2	2	2	1

Table 3.5 Function *PC*2

14	17	11	24	1	5	3	28	15	6	21	10
23	19	12	4	26	8	16	7	27	20	13	2
41	52	31	37	47	55	30	40	51	45	33	48
44	49	39	56	34	53	46	42	50	36	29	32

Table 3.6 Extension of the right half

32	1	2	3	4	5	4	5	6	7	8	9
8	9	10	11	12	13	12	13	14	15	16	17
16	17	18	19	20	21	20	21	22	23	24	25
24	25	26	27	28	29	28	29	30	31	32	1

Before each round, 56 out of the 64 bits of the key are chosen and permuted by the function *PC*1 (denoted so according to the standard). This function is presented in Table 3.3.

Thereafter, the 56-bit key is divided into halves. Bits from both halves are then shifted to the left by one or two places, depending on the round number (the first bit(s) of both halves are shifted to the end). The value of each shift is given in Table 3.4.

After this operation, we merge the halves into a modified 56-bit key. Then we choose, in a suitable way, and permute 48 bits. The choice is determined by the function *PC*2, whose values are shown in Table 3.5. Due to all these procedures, in each round we use a different key for encryption; moreover, different bits of the main key are applied in each round.

Just as in each execution of the Feistel network, a 64-bit block of the plaintext is then divided into halves L and R. The right half is appropriately extended to 48 bits. Consecutive values of the function that maps 32 bits of the right half into a new 48-bit block are given in Table 3.6.

Next, the *XOR* operation is applied to the obtained block and the modified round key. The result is divided into eight groups of six bits each. Every group is transformed by means of S-boxes. The outcome consists of eight groups, each with four bits. Therefore, as the result of all these operations, we again get 32 bits in the right half. Next, this bit sequence is permuted by the *P*-box (see Table 3.7) and *XOR*ed

Table 3.7 Permutation
P-box

16	7	20	21	29	12	28	17	1	15	23	26	5	18	31	10
2	8	24	14	32	27	3	9	19	13	30	6	22	11	4	25

with the left half according to the Feistel network. The obtained sequence constitutes the right half ready for the next round of DES.

The following relations hold:

1. $L' = R$,
2. $R' = L \; XOR \; f(R, K_i)$,

where $f(R, K_i)$ denotes the value of the block with the P-box omitted in the i-th round.

After 16 rounds described above, the ciphertext is permuted by the inverse of the function P.

Now, let us see how to decrypt DES ciphertexts. It seems that the simplest way is to repeat the whole encryption process in the reversed order. But, of course, this is not feasible, since S-box transformations are not invertible.

It turns out that an attempt to reverse the process is not necessary. Let us consider the second equality that characterizes an algorithm round:

$$R' = L \; XOR \; f(R, K_i).$$

Of course, we get

$$R' \; XOR \; f(R, K_i) = L \; XOR \; f(R, K_i) \; XOR \; f(R, K_i).$$

Applying one of the properties of the XOR function, we obtain

$$R' \; XOR \; f(R, K_i) = L.$$

Finally, after a suitable substitution,

$$L = R' \; XOR \; f(L', K_i).$$

Thus, the following equations are valid

1. $R = L'$,
2. $L = R' \; XOR \; f(L', K_i)$.

It can be seen that in order to recover the contents of the text encrypted in a given round, it is sufficient to know the cryptogram and an appropriate part of the modified key (i.e., the part that corresponds to the given round). Therefore, decryption consists of applying the same algorithm as for encryption using modified keys in the reversed order.

At the first glance, the DES algorithm may appear to be complicated, hard to implement and, most importantly, computationally laborious. However, if we look at it more closely, we notice that all performed operations are simply bit shifts, permutations, XOR operations or substitutions. All these procedures are easy for hardware implementation and can be executed very quickly.

3.2.3 Breaking DES

For many years the DES algorithm was thoroughly analysed. The only publicly known, and most importantly practically executable way to break the algorithm is, until today, the brute force method which is the search of the entire space of all cryptographic keys. The number of keys is 2^{56}. In decimal format this is about 72000000000000000, or approximately 72 quadrillion. This many decryptions are required to check every possible key-candidate to decipher a given cryptogram. At the beginning of the use of DES as a symmetric encryption standard, which was in the late 1970s and throughout the 1980s, the number was too big for contemporary computers.

However, often what cannot be calculated by commonly available computers may be calculated by systems specially dedicated to specific calculations. Already in 1977, Hellman and Diffie estimated that for about \$20 million, a specially dedicated computing machine could be designed and constructed that would be able to find the encryption key by the brute force method in just one day. In 1981, Diffie revised his estimates and said it would be possible to identify the key within two days, providing that the attacker had equipment worth \$50 million. In 1993 Michael Weiner suggested a construction which would break DES in a few hours. The cost of building such a device was to estimated be about one million dollars. However, publicly no organization or individual has claimed responsibility for building such a device [92]. (For more details about the cryptographic power of DES code and attempts to break it, the reader is referred to Sect. 7.4.3 in [68].)

Over the years, the computing power of computers and their number has increased. The first practical breaking of DES was achieved and publicly demonstrated at the end of the 1990s. It all started in 1997 when RSA Security offered \$10000 for practical breaking of the code. The winners were the members of the DESCHALL project founded by Rocke Verser, Matt Curtin, and Justin Dolske. They made the first well-known, publicly announced, and successful attempt to break DES in 1997. It took them 96 days. To break the code they used thousands of computers scattered all over the internet [51]. The next edition of the contest—in 1998—was won by the *distributed.net* project, which got the key within 41 days. In the same year the Electronic Frontier Foundation demonstrated the DES Cracker device, which cost \$250000 and deciphered the code within 56 hours [36]. A year later, in 1999, distributed.net and RSA Labs broke the code in less than 24 hours [36].

Another well-known project dealing with breaking the DES code was the CO-PACOBANA project run by the German Universities of Bochum and Kiel [59]. A machine developed in 2006 within the framework of this project consisted of 120 reconfigurable computing FPGA cards of XILINX Spartan3-1000 type running in parallel. The cost of the device was very low, about \$10000. Fully breaking DES was possible within a week. In 2008 the successor to the COPACOBANA project, the COPACOBANA RIVYERA machine broke DES in less than one day [25]. It used 128 FPGA Spartan-3 5000 cards. Nowadays some specialised systems based on FPGA architectures cope with DES within several hours.

There are also other methods of attack, which in theory are more effective than brute force. One of these is the attack using differential cryptanalysis, specially developed for this purpose by Eli Biham and Adi Shamir [17, 18]. This method involves comparing pairs of ciphertexts provided as a result of encryption using the same key of explicit texts that differ in a certain prescribed way. Carrying out the attack, however, requires preparation of a large number of data and, therefore, it is infeasible [17, 92]. Another theoretical method is linear analysis, developed by Mitsuru Matsui [67]. Research in this area continues. More methods are being developed, including hybrid methods. Also version of DES limited or modified in different ways are being broken.

Currently, one solution to the insecurity of DES is to use repeated encryption with the algorithm. Even double encryption reduces the risk of being broken 72 quadrillion times, while only doubling the encryption time. In practice, Triple DES (3DES) encryption is used. 3DES applies triple encryption with DES. Today breaking this algorithm is infeasible. However, it is three times slower than DES which is why it sometimes loses out to other symmetric algorithms.

3.3 Extensions of the DES Algorithm

Many users of the DES cryptosystem are not satisfied with a 56-bit key, therefore some modifications of this algorithm have been developed.

3.3.1 Triple DES

This method applies two keys: K_1 and K_2, and the encryption algorithm operates according to the formula

$$C = DES_{K_1}\left(DES_{K_2}^{-1}\left(DES_{K_1}(M)\right)\right). \tag{3.1}$$

Thus, first a message M is encrypted by means of the key K_1, then the result of this encryption is decrypted with the use of the key K_2 and, finally, the outcome of decryption is again encrypted with the key K_1. Hence, the decryption algorithm corresponds to the equation

$$M = DES_{K_1}^{-1}\left(DES_{K_2}\left(DES_{K_1}^{-1}(C)\right)\right). \tag{3.2}$$

Of course, $DES_K(T)$ stands in the above equations for the algorithm encrypting a 64-bit block T with a key K, while $DES_K^{-1}(T)$ denotes the inverse operation, i.e., the procedure of decrypting the block T with the key K. Therefore, the length of the encryption key is doubled.

3.3.2 DESX

When applying this method for encrypting a 64-bit data block M, three keys: K_{out}, K_{in}, K_{DES}, the *DES* algorithm, and the *XOR* operation are used. The first two keys are 64 bits long. A cryptogram is generated according to the formula

$$C = K_{out} \; XOR \; DES_{K_{DES}}(M \; XOR \; K_{in}), \qquad (3.3)$$

while correct decryption corresponds to the equation

$$M = K_{in} \; XOR \; DES^{-1}_{K_{DES}}(C \; XOR \; K_{out}). \qquad (3.4)$$

This version of the *DES* algorithm, even when the recently invented so-called differential cryptanalysis is applied, requires checking $2^{120} = 10^{36}$ keys in order to break the cipher.

3.4 Modes of Operation of the DES Algorithm

It hardly happens that a plaintext contains only 64 bits, which correspond to 8 ASCII symbols. Thus, a plaintext is usually divided into 64-bit blocks and the DES algorithm with the same key is applied several times.

3.4.1 Electronic Codebook Mode of Operation

A scheme of this mode of operation is depicted in Fig. 3.5, where each 64-bit block M_i of a plaintext is encrypted with the same key K. Within this system cryptograms corresponding to plaintext blocks are all distinct. Let us then imagine that $2^{64} = 1.844674407 \cdot 10^{19}$ possible plaintexts are included in a book in which a cryptogram is assigned to every plaintext block. This justifies the name of the mode.

When using this mode it may happen that an encrypted message contains the same ciphertext blocks corresponding to the same plaintext blocks, which provides cryptanalysts with data that facilitates breaking the cipher. The electronic codebook mode is thus unusable for encrypting long messages.

3.4.2 Cipher Block-Chaining Mode of Operation

A technique that guarantees to generate different ciphertext blocks for identical blocks of plaintext is called the cipher block-chaining mode of operation and its scheme is illustrated in Fig. 3.6. Here the input for the *DES* algorithm is here formed by the result of the *XOR* operation applied to a plaintext block and the previous ciphertext block. In order to create the first block of the cryptogram, a 64-bit sequence *IV*, called the Initialization Vector, has to be generated at random. It can

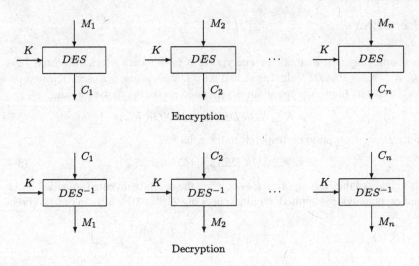

Fig. 3.5 Application of the *DES* algorithm in the electronic codebook mode

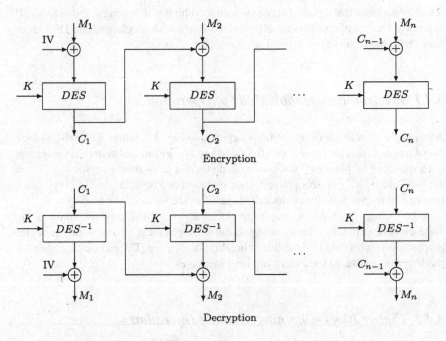

Fig. 3.6 Application of the *DES* algorithm in cipher-block chaining mode

safely be sent through an open access channel to a receiver so that the latter is able to decrypt the message correctly.

The decryption procedure is very similar: now the sequence *IV* along with the outcome of the *DES*-algorithm applied to the first ciphertext block are *XOR*ed,

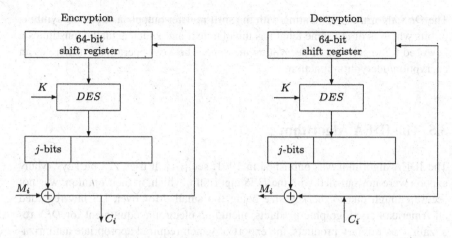

Fig. 3.7 Application of the *DES* algorithm in the cipher feedback mode

which results in the first block of the plaintext. In a similar way the other plaintext blocks of the received message are obtained.

3.4.3 Cipher Feedback Mode of Operation

This method is used to encrypt long texts and the principle of its operation is presented in Fig. 3.7.

Unlike previous modes, in this case not whole blocks are encrypted, but their j-bit fragments. In practice, $j = 1$ or $j = 8$. When $j = 1$, then bits are encrypted one by one, while in case $j = 8$ single ASCII symbols are encrypted consecutively. Such a mode of operation can be applied in order to transmit data generated by means of a keyboard to a server. In this case each generated symbol has to be sent immediately, without waiting for the block to be completed with eight symbols. Now let us look more closely at the process of encrypting symbol by symbol. In the beginning the shift register contains a random sequence IV of zeroes and ones which is encrypted with a key K. First, the eight leftmost bits of the created cryptogram are *XOR*ed with the first typed symbol M_1, which results in the first symbol C_1 of the ciphertext. After sending the symbol C_1 to the receiver, it is placed in the register, and at the same time the eight leftmost bits are deleted. Next, the second symbol M_2 is typed and all the operations executed for generating the symbol C_1 are repeated in order to generate the second symbol C_2 of the ciphertext. This process is repeated as many times as there are symbols contained in the message undergoing the encryption process. The decryption procedure is analogous, but it is performed according to a slightly different scheme.

It is worth noticing that in this mode of operation the input of the algorithm is in the form of a stream of plaintext or ciphertext symbols or bits and a 56-bit key K.

The *DES* algorithm cooperating with the shift register outputs a stream of symbols or bits which is of the same length as the plaintext and which actually constitutes a key used for encrypting or decrypting message. The *XOR* operation acts here as an encryption/decryption function.

3.5 The IDEA Algorithm

The IDEA algorithm was published in 1991, see [61]. It uses 128-bit keys. Many experts were not satisfied with the *DES* algorithm, which, in their opinion, was not secure enough due to the key size being too small. Moreover, US law regarded all American cryptographic products, including electronic equipment for *DES* realization, as military products, the export of which required appropriate authorization. This situation has caused conflicts when transmitting data to the US with the (US) National Security Agency. For these reasons Xuejia Lai and James L. Massey from ETH Zurich designed the *International Data Encryption Algorithm* (*IDEA* for short).

Like the *DES* cryptosystem, the *IDEA* algorithm generates 64-bit blocks of a cryptogram from 64-bit blocks of a plaintext; however, it uses a key of size 128 bits. *IDEA*, instead of the explicit use of permutations, applies only the three following operations, which are easy to realize in both software and hardware:

- bitwise addition modulo 2, denoted by $\oplus$,
- addition modulo 2^{16} (neglecting overflows), denoted by $\boxplus$,
- multiplication modulo $2^{16} + 1$ (neglecting overflows), denoted by $\odot$.

The above operations are executed on 16-bit blocks, therefore the algorithm can be performed on 16-bit processors very efficiently.

The scheme of the algorithm is depicted in Fig. 3.8.

As the input of the algorithm we take four 16-bit subblocks of a block of the plaintext: X_1, X_2, X_3 and X_4. These four subblocks, which—as can be seen in the figure—constitute the input for the first transformation round (there are eight such rounds), are processed by 14 operations with six blocks of subkeys. After swapping two inner subblocks obtained after the first round, we get the input block for the second round. After the eighth round the final transformation is executed and then inner blocks are not swapped any more.

According to the scheme, the algorithm uses 52 subblocks of the key: six of them after each round and four subblocks in the final transformation. The principle of generating 16-bit subkey blocks is quite simple. First, 128 bits of the key are divided into eight subkeys: six of them are used to begin the first iteration round, leaving the other two subkeys for the second iteration. Next, the key cycles by shifting 25 bits to the left, then it is again divided into eight 16-bit subkeys, yielding four more subkeys for the second round and four subkeys for the third one. This procedure is repeated until all the required keys are obtained.

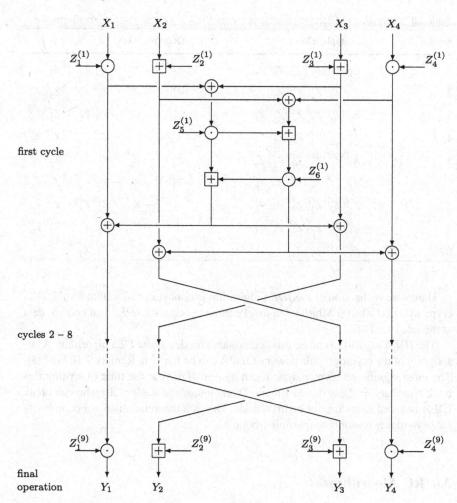

Fig. 3.8 The IDEA algorithm

Exactly the same algorithm is used for decryption; however, in this case other blocks of subkeys are used (see Table 3.8). In order to compute subkeys for the decryption process, multiplicative or additive inverses of encryption subkeys have to be applied. For example, the multiplicative inverse of the encryption subkey $Z_1^{(1)}$ is denoted by $Z_1^{(1)-1}$, while $-Z_1^{(1)}$ stands for the additive inverse (we assume that $0^{-1} = 0$). Hence,

$$Z_1^{(1)} \cdot Z_1^{(1)-1} \equiv 1 \pmod{2^{16}+1},$$

$$Z_1^{(1)} + \left(-Z_1^{(1)}\right) \equiv 0 \pmod{2^{16}}.$$

Table 3.8 Encryption and decryption subkeys for the *IDEA* algorithm (ft—final transformation)

Round	Encryption key	Decryption key
1	$Z_1^{(1)} Z_2^{(1)} Z_3^{(1)} Z_4^{(1)} Z_5^{(1)} Z_6^{(1)}$	$Z_1^{(9)-1} - Z_2^{(9)} - Z_3^{(9)} Z_4^{(9)-1} Z_5^{(8)} Z_6^{(8)}$
2	$Z_1^{(2)} Z_2^{(2)} Z_3^{(2)} Z_4^{(2)} Z_5^{(2)} Z_6^{(2)}$	$Z_1^{(8)-1} - Z_3^{(8)} - Z_2^{(8)} Z_4^{(8)-1} Z_5^{(7)} Z_6^{(7)}$
3	$Z_1^{(3)} Z_2^{(3)} Z_3^{(3)} Z_4^{(3)} Z_5^{(3)} Z_6^{(3)}$	$Z_1^{(7)-1} - Z_3^{(7)} - Z_2^{(7)} Z_4^{(7)-1} Z_5^{(6)} Z_6^{(6)}$
4	$Z_1^{(4)} Z_2^{(4)} Z_3^{(4)} Z_4^{(4)} Z_5^{(4)} Z_6^{(4)}$	$Z_1^{(6)-1} - Z_3^{(6)} - Z_2^{(6)} Z_4^{(6)-1} Z_5^{(5)} Z_6^{(5)}$
5	$Z_1^{(5)} Z_2^{(5)} Z_3^{(5)} Z_4^{(5)} Z_5^{(5)} Z_6^{(5)}$	$Z_1^{(5)-1} - Z_3^{(5)} - Z_2^{(5)} Z_4^{(5)-1} Z_5^{(4)} Z_6^{(4)}$
6	$Z_1^{(6)} Z_2^{(6)} Z_3^{(6)} Z_4^{(6)} Z_5^{(6)} Z_6^{(6)}$	$Z_1^{(4)-1} - Z_3^{(4)} - Z_2^{(4)} Z_4^{(4)-1} Z_5^{(3)} Z_6^{(3)}$
7	$Z_1^{(7)} Z_2^{(7)} Z_3^{(7)} Z_4^{(7)} Z_5^{(7)} Z_6^{(7)}$	$Z_1^{(3)-1} - Z_3^{(3)} - Z_2^{(3)} Z_4^{(3)-1} Z_5^{(2)} Z_6^{(2)}$
8	$Z_1^{(8)} Z_2^{(8)} Z_3^{(8)} Z_4^{(8)} Z_5^{(8)} Z_6^{(8)}$	$Z_1^{(2)-1} - Z_2^{(2)} - Z_2^{(2)} Z_3^{(2)-1} Z_5^{(1)} Z_6^{(1)}$
ft	$Z_1^{(9)} Z_2^{(9)} Z_3^{(9)} Z_4^{(9)}$	$Z_1^{(1)-1} - Z_2^{(1)} - Z_3^{(1)} Z_4^{(1)-1}$

Hardware realization of the *IDEA* algorithm is almost as fast as that for the *DES* cryptosystem (50–200 Mbit/s). On fast Pentium processors, *IDEA* can encrypt data at the rate of 40 MB/s.

The *IDEA* algorithm can be used in the same modes as the *DES* algorithm. A description of the cryptographic power of IDEA can be found in Remark 7.107 in [68]. The most significant cryptanalytic result against IDEA, at the time of writing this book (August, 2012), is due to Biham, Dunkelman, and Keller [20] who can break IDEA reduced to six (out of eight) rounds. This is a theoretic attack, of complexity far beyond any reasonable feasibility bounds.

3.6 RC Algorithms

Now we are going to describe a few algorithms developed mainly by Ronald Rivest. These algorithms are briefly denoted by RC (Ron's Cipher or Rivest's cipher). The first one, widely applied in practice, is the RC4 algorithm.

3.6.1 RC4 Algorithm

The RC4 algorithm [47], sometimes called ARC4 or ARCFOUR, is the first RC algorithm applied commercially in systems used in practice. Nowadays, it is also applied in security protocols in computer networks such as SSL or WEP. Although RC4 is resistant to linear and differential cryptanalysis, due to its short key and other imperfections it is currently not considered a safe cryptosystem. At present, RC4 is not recommended for use in new systems.

As already mentioned, RC4 was designed by Ron Rivest of RSA Security in 1987 and it was initially a trade secret. At the end of 1994, a *C* implementation of the cipher leaked to the Internet via the *sci.crypt* newsgroup. Since then the algorithm is no longer a secret, though its name, RC4, is still a registered trademark. In view of international law, unofficial cipher implementations are legal, but they carry the other names mentioned before: ARC4 or ARCFOUR.

The algorithm applies a basic key containing from 40 to 128 bits. Let us denote it by *key* and its length by d. The algorithm can be briefly described by the following scheme.

1. First, we generate a pseudorandom bit sequence based on the basic key.
2. Then, we determine an auxiliary pseudorandom permutation S of 256 bits.
3. By means of permutation S we generate a bit sequence whose length corresponds to the length of a plaintext. This sequence is called a *keystream* and we denote it by K.
4. The keystream acts as an encryption key in the Vernam cipher, which was described in the first chapter, i.e., the encryption process consists of performing the *XOR* operation on the stream (key) and the plaintext.
5. According to the XOR encryption principle, the decryption process consists of applying the XOR function once more to the cryptogram and the key (a recipient of a potential message holds the same basic key, thus they are able to generate the same pseudorandom sequence of bits—the encryption key).

In order to generate a keystream, the cipher makes use of a secret *initial state*, which consists of two parameters:

1. a permutation S of all 256 possible states,
2. two 8-bit pointers, i and j.

The process to create the keystream works as follows. First, the table S is initialized to the identity permutation. Then, S is processed in 256 iterations according to the algorithm for pseudorandom generation presented below, but at the same time it is interleaved with consecutive bytes of the key. In detail, the process is carried out as follows:

We generate the 256-element identity permutation S:

Algorithm 3.1
```
for i from 0 to 255
S[i] := i
```

Now, we create a new alternative pseudorandom permutation that depends on the basic key.

Algorithm 3.2
```
j: = 0
for i from 0 to 255
j := (j + S[i] + key[i mod d]) mod 256
swap(S[i],S[j])
```

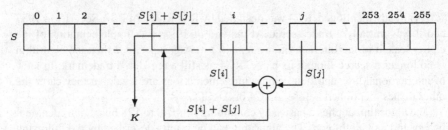

Fig. 3.9 General scheme of RC4

As can be seen, we compute the sum modulo 256 of the pointer j and the i-th element of the permutation S and the i-th bit of the basic key *key* (if i is greater than d, then we take the $(i \bmod d)$-th bit of the key. The so-obtained pointer j specifies some value of the permutation $S[j]$. This value is switched in S with the value $S[i]$. We get a new permutation S, which depends on the basic key *key*.

Now, an intermediate stage of the RC4 algorithm takes place. The value of the keystream K results from applying S on $S[i] + S[j]$ (mod 256), where i and j are pointers modified during the algorithm execution.

Algorithm 3.3
```
i := 0
j := 0
while CreatingCipherStream:
    i := (i + 1) mod 256
    j := (j + S[i]) mod 256
    swap(S[i],S[j])
    out S[(S[i] + S[j]) mod 256]
```

As can be noticed, the pseudorandom generation algorithm repeatedly modifies the permutation S by replacing its values. As long as it is needed, we generate consecutive bytes of the key, which will later be used for encryption of subsequent plaintext bytes. At each step the algorithm increments the variable i by 1, takes the index j and the i-th element of the permutation S, adds these numbers modulo 256, and finally applies S to the so-obtained value. The result is switched in S with the value $S[i]$. As output we take the element of S with the index $(S[i] + S[j]) \bmod 256$. This operation is continued as long as bytes of the stream are needed to encrypt successive bytes of the plaintext. Let us notice that every value of the permutation S is replaced at least once every 256 iterations.

The general scheme of RC4 consisting of all the described operations is illustrated in Fig. 3.9.

3.6.2 RC5 Algorithm

Another RC algorithm is RC5, announced in 1994. When designing the algorithm, Ron Rivest set himself the following objectives [104].

- The algorithm should be easy to implement with regard to both software and hardware.
- The algorithm should be fast (therefore RC5 applies only operations on blocks which correspond to words in terms of hardware, e.g., when run on 32-bit processors, the algorithm executes operations on 32-bit blocks).
- The algorithm should be flexible as concerns encryption parameters used (sizes of a block and a key, as well as the number of rounds should be modifiable). The user should be able to set cipher parameters in order to have control over the relation between the algorithm's efficiency and its security level.
- The algorithm should be as simple as possible, so that the cryptographic strength of RC5 can be rapidly determined.
- The algorithm should have low memory requirements, so that it may easily be implemented, e.g., on smart cards.
- The algorithm should provide a suitably high security level.

The algorithm uses three operations: addition modulo n, addition modulo 2^{32}, and permutations (cyclic shifts, to be precise). It is also possible to apply plaintext blocks of variable length, but in the example described below we make use of 64-bit data blocks. The number of algorithm cycles can also vary; we denote it by r. As in the previous case, also here the algorithm uses a basic key, on which 32-bit auxiliary keys used for plaintext processing are based. There are $2r + 2$ such keys; we denote them by $S(0), S(1), S(2), \ldots, S(2r + 1)$.

In the encryption process the plaintext block is first divided into 32-bit words: A and B. Then, by means of keys $S(i)(i = 1, \ldots, 2r + 1)$, the following operations are performed:

Algorithm 3.4
```
A = A + S(0)
B = B + S(1)
For i = 1 to r
    A = ((A XOR B) <<< B) + S(2i)
    B = ((B XOR A) <<< A) + S(2i+1)
```

The cryptogram results from concatenating blocks A and B.

In the notation above, the symbol >>> stands for a cyclic bit-shift to the right (analogously, >>> denotes a cyclic bit-shift to the left). All addition operations are performed modulo 2^{32}.

The decryption process is equally easy. The ciphertext block is divided into two words, A and B, and then the following operations are executed:

Algorithm 3.5
```
For  i = r downto 1
    B = ((B -- S(2i+1)) >>> A) XOR A
    A = ((A -- S(2i)) >>> B) XOR B
    B = B -- S(1)
    A = A -- S(0)
```

Once again, the symbol >>> denotes a bit-shift and all subtraction operations are performed modulo 2^{32}.

Creating the vector $S(i)$ of keys is just a bit more complicated. First, bytes of the key are copied to a vector L with 32-bit words (if needed, any unfilled byte positions of the last word are zeroed). Next, the vector S, which applies a linear generator modulo 2^{32}, is initialized.

Algorithm 3.6
```
S(0) = P
For i = 1 to 2(r+1)
S(i) = (S(i-1) + Q)
```

Constants $P = 0xb7e15163$ and $Q = 0x9e3779b9$ are counterparts of the values e and ϕ in the hexadecimal representation. Once again, addition is performed modulo 2^{32}.

Finally, we apply S to L:

Algorithm 3.7
```
i = j = 0
A = B = 0
For i = 1 to 3n (n is the greater of two values 2(r+1) and c)
A = S(i) = (S(i) + A + B) <<< 3
B = L(j) = (L(j) + A + B) <<< (A+B)
i = (i + 1) mod 2(r+1)
j = (j + 1) mod c
```

Actually, RC5 constitutes a family of algorithms. In the example presented above, we considered 32-bit words and a 64-bit block. It is possible, however, to process 64-bit words and a 128-bit block. For $w = 64$, the values of constants P and Q are equal to 0x7e151628aed2a6b and 0x9e3779b97f4c15, respectively. Rivest denoted different algorithm implementations by RC5-$w/r/b$, where w is the size of a word, r is the number of cycles, and b is the size of the key given in bytes.

RSA Laboratories spent a lot of time on the cryptanalysis of the 64-bit block version. After five cycles the statistics are very good. After eight cycles each bit of a plaintext is the subject of at least one shift. An attack by means of differential cryptanalysis in the case of five cycles of the RC5 algorithm requires 2^{34} plaintexts, 10 cycles require 2^{45}, 12 cycles require 2^{53}, and 15 cycles require 2^{68} plaintexts. Studies with the use of linear cryptanalysis showed that the algorithm provides an appropriate level of security for more than six cycles. Ron Rivest recommended the use of 12 or even 16 cycles, however, this number may grow with increases in computational power.

3.6.3 RC5-Breaking Project

In 1997 RSA Security Inc. proposed a challenge to break several algorithms, including RC5. The company offered a $10000 prize for breaking any of them. In the

Table 3.9 Project RC5-56
statistics (completed)

Total blocks to search:	268435456
Total blocks tested:	98068754
Overall rate:	6 blocks/s
Total keys to search:	72057594037927940
Total keys tested:	26325130699341825
Overall rate:	1578699548 keys/s
Percent complete:	36.533
Time working:	193 days

Table 3.10 Project RC5-64
statistics (completed)

Total blocks to search:	68719476736
Total blocks tested:	56878907073
Overall rate:	381 blocks/s
Total keys to search:	18446744073709552000
Total keys tested:	15268315356922380000
Overall rate:	102385059633 keys/s
Percent complete:	82.770
Time working:	1726 days

same year, an organization called distributed.net was founded, aimed at the brute-force breaking of the RC5-32/12/7 cipher (with a 56-bit key). It was one of the first distributed processing projects ever. The idea of distributed.net was to make use of thousands of PCs in order to create a system of enormous computational power. Users (from all over the world) of the system install a small application, which analyzes downloaded data blocks whenever a computer is idle. By now, cryptograms encrypted with 56- and 64-bit keys have been already broken, see Tables 3.9 and 3.10. Currently the project aims at breaking RC5 with a 72-bit key [36].

On a particular day in mid-February 2012, data about the searched keyspace were as follows. On that day 2444 users took part in the project (in 2009 there were daily 3500 users on average). 4060996 key blocks were searched, which amounts to 0.002176 % of the space of blocks at the rate of 83 blocks per second (in June 2005 the rate reached only 32 blocks). This gave altogether 1005004909696777824 keys (1163200126964 keys per second). Up to that day, there were 90811 users participating in the projects. They also try to break the algorithm by working in groups.

Tables describing attacks on RC-72 are worth some attention. They demonstrate the progress of brute-force breaking that was achieved in just a few years of the project (June 2005–December 2012).

Some statistics of the project, illustrating the computational power of cipher breaking and obtained results, are presented in Table 3.11.

Table 3.11 Project RC5-72
statistics

Time	Total blocks to search:	1099511627776
	Total keys to search:	4722366482869646000000
June 2005	Total blocks tested:	2485337292
	Total keys tested:	10674442388669202000
	Overall rate:	136969830273 keys/s
	Percent complete:	0.226
	Time working:	902 days
June 2007	Total blocks tested:	4402572198
	Total keys tested:	18908903608688840000
	Overall rate:	139042599127 keys/s
	Percent complete:	0.40
	Time working:	1574 days
September 2008	Total blocks tested:	5702917070
	Total keys tested:	24493842307450145000
	Overall rate:	134229898307 keys/s
	Percent complete:	0.519
	Time working:	2112 days
May 2009	Total blocks tested:	6711832495
	Total keys tested:	28827101062255085000
	Overall rate:	141435779159 keys/s
	Percent complete:	0.61
	Time working:	2359 days
September 2011	Total blocks tested:	20262298665
	Total keys tested:	87025910107959459840
	Overall rate:	314665520135 keys/s
	Percent complete:	1.843
	Time working:	3201 days
February 2012	Total blocks tested:	23986713948
	Total keys tested:	103022151945167044608
	Overall rate:	354665680513 keys/s
	Percent complete:	2.182
	Time working:	3362 days
September 2012	Total blocks tested:	27946339728
	Total keys tested:	120028615174665535488
	Overall rate:	388158726751 keys/s
	Percent complete:	2.542
	Time working:	3579 days
December 2012	Total blocks tested:	29380323401
	Total keys tested:	126187571102871253696
	Overall rate:	396552890354 keys/s
	Percent complete:	2.672
	Time working:	3679 days
September 2013	Total blocks tested:	32515503820
	Total keys tested:	139653025519863070720
	Overall rate:	410138153270 keys/s
	Percent complete:	2.957
	Time working:	3941 days

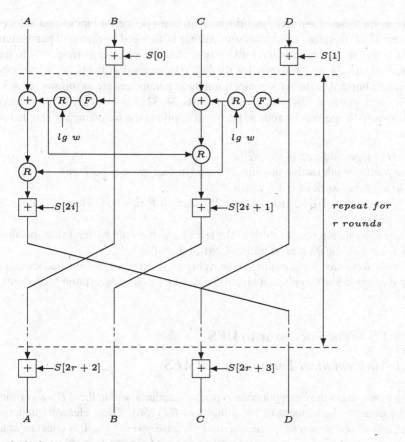

Fig. 3.10 General scheme of RC6 encryption algorithm

3.6.4 RC6 Algorithm

The RC6 algorithm [86] was designed in RSA Laboratories and submitted to the AES competition in 1998. It was created by Ronald Rivest, Matthew Robshaw, Ray Sidney and Yiqun Yin. The algorithm is based on the RC5 cipher presented above. The authors introduced some modifications to meet the requirements of the AES competition. Block and key sizes changed and due to some other improvements security and efficiency of the algorithm increased.

According to the AES requirements, the algorithm supports 128-, 192- and 258-bit encryption keys, while the size of a processed data block equals 128 bits. In the algorithm a plaintext block is divided into four 32-bit fragments in order to apply the 32-bit architecture of most currently used processors. The RC6 cipher, similarly to RC5, makes use of only those operations that can be efficiently implemented on modern processors. In the encryption process integer multiplication is applied for interleaving bits.

The general scheme of one round of the RC6 algorithm is depicted in Fig. 3.10.

As in the case of the RC5 algorithm, RC6 can operate on blocks and keys of different sizes, therefore its various versions can be denoted by means of parameters by RC6-$w/r/b$, where w is the bit size of a plaintext block, r corresponds to the number of rounds, and b stands for the key size counted in bytes. In the version that was submitted to the AES competition these parameters are as follows: $w = 32$ (32 bits $\times$ 4 words = 128 bits), $r = 20$, $b = 16, 24, 32$ ($b \times 8 = 128, 192, 256$ bits).

RC6-$w/r/b$ operates on four w-bit words applying the following six simple operations:

- $a \boxplus b$ integer addition modulo 2^w,
- $a - b$ integer subtraction modulo 2^w (used in decryption procedure),
- $a \oplus b$ bitwise XOR of w-bit words,
- $a \otimes b$ integer multiplication modulo 2^w (used in F function, where $F(x) = x \otimes (2x \boxplus 1)$),
- $a <<< b$ rotation (cyclic shift) to the left of a w-bit word by the value specified by the $\log_2 w$ ($\lg w$) least significant bits of the word b,
- $a >>> b$ rotation (cyclic shift) to the right of a w-bit word by the value specified by the $\log_2 w$ least significant bits of the word b (used in decryption procedure).

3.7 AES—The Successor to DES

3.7.1 Mathematical Foundations of AES

Every byte used in the encryption/decryption procedures within the AES algorithm is considered as an element of the finite field $GF(256)$. These elements undergo operations of addition, multiplication, multiplicative inverse, etc. It is convenient to represent bytes as polynomials of degree seven over $GF(2)$. In such a representation consecutive bits correspond to the coefficients of an appropriate polynomial. Addition of two elements from $GF(256)$ represented as polynomials corresponds to ordinary polynomial addition, which is obtained by adding appropriate coefficients modulo 2. For example, if we want to add two bytes—elements of $GF(256)$ represented by the following polynomials $\mathbf{a}(x)$ and $\mathbf{b}(x)$:

$$\mathbf{a}(x) = a_7 x^7 + a_6 x^6 + a_5 x^5 + a_4 x^4 + a_3 x^3 + a_2 x^2 + a_1 x + a_0$$

and

$$\mathbf{b}(x) = b_7 x^7 + b_6 x^6 + b_5 x^5 + b_4 x^4 + b_3 x^3 + b_2 x^2 + b_1 x + b_0,$$

then their sum is given by

$$\mathbf{c}(x) = \mathbf{a}(x) + \mathbf{b}(x) = c_7 x^7 + c_6 x^6 + c_5 x^5 + c_4 x^4 + c_3 x^3 + c_2 x^2 + c_1 x + c_0,$$

where $c_i = a_i \oplus b_i$, $0 \leq i \leq 7$, and $\oplus$ stands for addition modulo 2. For instance, let

$$\mathbf{a}(x) = x^7 + x + 1, \qquad \mathbf{b}(x) = x^5 + x^2 + x.$$

Then

$$\mathbf{a}(x) + \mathbf{b}(x) = x^7 + x^5 + x^2 + 1.$$

When executing the procedures of the algorithm, each byte is represented as a sequence of 8 bits or 2 hexadecimal digits:

$$\mathbf{a} = \{a_7 \, a_6 \, a_5 \, a_4 \, a_3 \, a_2 \, a_1 \, a_0\} = \{A_1 \, A_0\},$$
$$\mathbf{b} = \{b_7 \, b_6 \, b_5 \, b_4 \, b_3 \, b_2 \, b_1 \, b_0\} = \{B_1 \, B_0\},$$
$$\mathbf{a} + \mathbf{b} = \mathbf{c} = \{c_7 \, c_6 \, c_5 \, c_4 \, c_3 \, c_2 \, c_1 \, c_0\} = \{C_1 \, C_0\}.$$

Similarly to the case of polynomials $c_i = a_i \oplus b_i$, $0 \le i \le 7$, and given a_i, b_i and c_i it is easy to compute A_i, B_i and C_i.

Let $\mathbf{a} = (10101110) = \{\mathtt{ae}\}$, $\mathbf{b} = \{01111111\} = \{\mathtt{7f}\}$. Then $\mathbf{a} + \mathbf{b} = \{11010001\} = \{\mathtt{d1}\}$.

Multiplication in the field $GF(256)$, denoted by $\bullet$, is much harder and corresponds to multiplying in $GF(2)$ polynomials representing elements of $GF(256)$ modulo some irreducible polynomial of degree eight over $GF(2)$.

Irreducible polynomials of degree 8 over $GF(2)$

$$x^8 + x^7 + x^5 + x + 1, \quad x^8 + x^7 + x^6 + x^3 + x^2 + x + 1,$$
$$x^8 + x^7 + x^6 + x^4 + x^3 + x^2 + 1, \quad x^8 + x^7 + x^5 + x^4 + 1,$$
$$x^8 + x^6 + x^4 + x^3 + x^2 + x + 1, \quad x^8 + x^5 + x^3 + x^2 + 1,$$
$$x^8 + x^7 + x^6 + x^4 + x^2 + x + 1, \quad x^8 + x^6 + x^5 + x^2 + 1,$$
$$x^8 + x^7 + x^3 + x^2 + 1, \quad x^8 + x^6 + x^5 + x^4 + x^3 + x + 1,$$
$$x^8 + x^6 + x^5 + x^3 + 1, \quad x^8 + x^7 + x^4 + x^3 + x^2 + x + 1,$$
$$x^8 + x^5 + x^3 + x + 1, \quad \underline{x^8 + x^4 + x^3 + x + 1},$$
$$x^8 + x^6 + x^5 + x + 1, \quad x^8 + x^7 + x^5 + x^4 + x^3 + x^2 + 1,$$
$$x^8 + x^6 + x^3 + x^2 + 1, \quad x^8 + x^7 + x^2 + x + 1,$$
$$x^8 + x^5 + x^4 + x^3 + x^2 + x + 1, \quad x^8 + x^7 + x^6 + x^5 + x^4 + x^3 + 1,$$
$$x^8 + x^7 + x^6 + x^5 + x^4 + x + 1, \quad x^8 + x^7 + x^6 + x^5 + x^4 + x^2 + 1,$$
$$x^8 + x^6 + x^5 + x^4 + x^2 + x + 1, \quad x^8 + x^7 + x^5 + x^3 + 1,$$
$$x^8 + x^7 + x^6 + x + 1, \quad x^8 + x^7 + x^3 + x + 1,$$
$$x^8 + x^5 + x^4 + x^3 + 1, \quad x^8 + x^4 + x^3 + x^2 + 1,$$
$$x^8 + x^6 + x^5 + x^4 + 1, \quad x^8 + x^7 + x^6 + x^5 + x^2 + x + 1.$$

There exist 30 such polynomials. For the *AES* cryptosystem the following irreducible polynomial

$$m(x) = x^8 + x^4 + x^3 + x + 1$$

was chosen.

Multiplication of elements from $GF(256)$ in the form of polynomials

$$\mathbf{a}(x) = a_7 x^7 + a_6 x^6 + a_5 x^5 + a_4 x^4 + a_3 x^3 + a_2 x^2 + a_1 x + a_0,$$
$$\mathbf{b}(x) = b_7 x^7 + b_6 x^6 + b_5 x^5 + b_4 x^4 + b_3 x^3 + b_2 x^2 + b_1 x + b_0,$$

modulo the chosen polynomial $m(x)$ is performed as follows:

$$\mathbf{a}(x) \bullet \mathbf{b}(x) \quad (\mathrm{mod}\ m(x))$$
$$\equiv \mathbf{c}(x) = c_7 x^7 + c_6 x^6 + c_5 x^5 + c_4 x^4 + c_3 x^3 + c_2 x^2 + c_1 x + c_0,$$

where

$$
\begin{aligned}
c_0 =\ & a_5 b_3 + a_5 b_7 + a_6 b_2 + a_6 b_7 + a_6 b_6 + a_7 b_1 + a_7 b_6 + a_7 b_5 + a_0 b_0 + a_4 b_4 \\
& + a_2 b_6 + a_3 b_5 + a_1 b_7 \quad (\mathrm{mod}\ 2), \\
c_1 =\ & a_1 b_0 + a_1 b_7 + a_2 b_7 + a_2 b_6 + a_3 b_6 + a_3 b_5 + a_4 b_5 + a_4 b_4 + a_5 b_4 + a_5 b_3 \\
& + a_5 b_7 + a_6 b_3 + a_6 b_2 + a_6 b_6 + a_7 b_2 + a_7 b_7 + a_7 b_1 + a_7 b_5 \\
& + a_0 b_1 \quad (\mathrm{mod}\ 2), \\
c_2 =\ & a_2 b_0 + a_2 b_7 + a_3 b_7 + a_3 b_6 + a_4 b_6 + a_4 b_5 + a_5 b_5 + a_5 b_4 + a_6 b_4 + a_6 b_3 \\
& + a_6 b_7 + a_7 b_3 + a_7 b_2 + a_7 b_6 + a_0 b_2 + a_1 b_1 \quad (\mathrm{mod}\ 2), \\
c_3 =\ & a_4 b_4 + a_2 b_6 + a_3 b_5 + a_1 b_7 + a_5 b_7 + a_5 b_3 + a_7 b_5 + a_7 b_6 + a_7 b_1 + a_6 b_6 \\
& + a_6 b_7 + a_6 b_2 + a_7 b_7 + a_3 b_7 + a_4 b_6 + a_5 b_5 + a_6 b_4 + a_7 b_3 + a_0 b_3 + a_1 b_2 \\
& + a_2 b_1 + a_3 b_0 + a_4 b_7 + a_5 b_6 + a_6 b_5 + a_7 b_4 \quad (\mathrm{mod}\ 2), \\
c_4 =\ & a_1 b_3 + a_1 b_7 + a_2 b_2 + a_2 b_7 + a_2 b_6 + a_3 b_1 + a_3 b_6 + a_3 b_5 + a_4 b_0 + a_4 b_7 \\
& + a_4 b_5 + a_4 b_4 + a_5 b_6 + a_5 b_4 + a_5 b_3 + a_6 b_2 + a_6 b_3 + a_6 b_5 + a_7 b_1 + a_7 b_2 \\
& + a_7 b_4 + a_7 b_7 + a_0 b_4 \quad (\mathrm{mod}\ 2), \\
c_5 =\ & a_2 b_3 + a_2 b_7 + a_3 b_2 + a_3 b_7 + a_3 b_6 + a_4 b_1 + a_4 b_6 + a_4 b_5 + a_5 b_0 + a_5 b_7 \\
& + a_5 b_5 + a_5 b_4 + a_6 b_6 + a_6 b_4 + a_6 b_3 + a_7 b_2 + a_7 b_3 + a_7 b_5 + a_0 b_5 \\
& + a_1 b_4 \quad (\mathrm{mod}\ 2), \\
c_6 =\ & a_3 b_3 + a_3 b_7 + a_4 b_2 + a_4 b_7 + a_4 b_6 + a_5 b_1 + a_5 b_6 + a_5 b_5 + a_6 b_0 + a_6 b_7 \\
& + a_6 b_5 + a_6 b_4 + a_7 b_6 + a_7 b_4 + a_7 b_3 + a_0 b_6 + a_1 b_5 + a_2 b_4 \quad (\mathrm{mod}\ 2), \\
c_7 =\ & a_4 b_3 + a_4 b_7 + a_5 b_2 + a_5 b_7 + a_5 b_6 + a_6 b_1 + a_6 b_6 + a_6 b_5 + a_7 b_0 + a_7 b_7 \\
& + a_7 b_5 + a_7 b_4 + a_3 b_4 + a_2 b_5 + a_0 b_7 + a_1 b_6 \quad (\mathrm{mod}\ 2).
\end{aligned}
$$

For instance, if $\mathbf{a}(x) = x^7 + x + 1$ and $\mathbf{b}(x) = x^5 + x^2 + x$, then $\mathbf{a}(x) \bullet \mathbf{b}(x) = x^7 + x^6 + x^5 + x^3 + x^2$. Rewriting this operation with field elements in their binary and hexadecimal representations gives

$$\mathbf{a} = \{10000011\} = \{83\}, \qquad \mathbf{b} = \{00100110\} = \{26\},$$
$$\{10000011\} \bullet \{00100110\} = \{11101100\}, \qquad \{83\} \bullet \{26\} = \{ec\}.$$

The *AES* specification takes into account the case of multiplying an arbitrary element of $GF(256)$ in its polynomial representation $\mathbf{a}(x) = a_7 x^7 + a_6 x^6 + a_5 x^5 + a_4 x^4 + a_3 x^3 + a_2 x^2 + a_1 x + a_0$ by the element x:

$$x \bullet \mathbf{a}(x) = x \mathbf{a}(x)$$
$$\equiv a_7 x^8 + a_6 x^7 + a_5 x^6 + a_4 x^5 + a_3 x^4 + a_2 x^3 + a_1 x^2 + a_0 x \quad (\mathrm{mod}\ m(x)).$$

When $a_7 = 0$, then

$$x \bullet \mathbf{a}(x) = a_6 x^7 + a_5 x^6 + a_4 x^5 + a_3 x^4 + a_2 x^3 + a_1 x^2 + a_0 x,$$

otherwise

$$x \bullet \mathbf{a}(x) = a_6 x^7 + a_5 x^6 + a_4 x^5 + (1 \oplus a_3) x^4 + (1 \oplus a_2) x^3 + a_1 x^2 + (1 \oplus a_0) x + 1.$$

Hence, multiplication of $\mathbf{a}(x)$ by x corresponds at the byte level to multiplication by $\{00000010\}$, while in the hexadecimal representation to multiplication by $\{02\}$, and in fact it consists of shifting bits of the byte

$$\mathbf{a} = \{a_7 \, a_6 \, a_5 \, a_4 \, a_3 \, a_2 \, a_1 \, a_0\}$$

by one to the left if $a_7 = 0$, and if $a_7 = 1$, then to the so-shifted bits we have to add modulo 2 the byte $\{00011011\}$. Therefore,

$$\{00000010\} \bullet \{a_7 \, a_6 \, a_5 \, a_4 \, a_3 \, a_2 \, a_1 \, a_0\}$$
$$= \begin{cases} \{a_6 \, a_5 \, a_4 \, a_3 \, a_2 \, a_1 \, a_0 \, 0\} & \text{if } a_7 = 0, \\ \{a_6 \, a_5 \, a_4 \, a_3 \, a_2 \, a_1 \, a_0 \, 0\} \oplus \{00011011\} & \text{if } a_7 = 1. \end{cases}$$

An efficient hardware implementation of the above is important for of multiplication in the field $GF(256)$—it is then possible to perform multiplication by x several times. For instance,

$$\{10000011\} \bullet \{00100110\}$$
$$= \{10000011\} \bullet \left(\{00000010\} \oplus \{00000100\} \oplus \{00100000\}\right) = \{11101100\},$$

since

$$\{10000011\} \bullet \{00000010\} = \{00011101\},$$
$$\{10000011\} \bullet \{00000100\} = \{00111010\},$$
$$\{10000011\} \bullet \{00001000\} = \{01110100\},$$
$$\{10000011\} \bullet \{00010000\} = \{11101000\},$$
$$\{10000011\} \bullet \{00100000\} = \{11001011\},$$

thus

$$\{10000011\} \bullet \{00100110\} = \{11001011\} \oplus \{00111010\} \oplus \{00011101\}$$
$$= \{11101100\}.$$

In the encryption and decryption processes multiplicative inverses are computed. For this purpose the extended Euclidean algorithm for polynomials is used. Given a polynomial $m(x)$ and an element $\mathbf{a}(x) \in GF(256)$, the algorithm outputs the element $\mathbf{b}(x) = \mathbf{a}^{-1}(x)$ and the polynomial $c(x)$ which satisfy the formula

$$\mathbf{a}(x)\mathbf{b}(x) + m(x)c(x) = 1,$$

from which it follows that $\mathbf{a}(x)\mathbf{b}(x) \equiv 1 \pmod{m(x)}$. Here we present one version of this algorithm:

input $a(x)$, $m(x)$, $s_2(x) \leftarrow 1$, $s_1(x) \leftarrow 0$, $t_2(x) \leftarrow 0$, $t_1(x) \leftarrow 1$,
while $m(x) \neq 0$ **do**
begin
   $q(x) \leftarrow a(x) \textbf{ div } m(x)$, $r(x) \leftarrow a(x) \textbf{ mod } m(x)$,
   $s(x) \leftarrow s_2(x) - q(x)s_1(x)$, $t(x) \leftarrow t_2(x) - q(x)t_1(x)$,
   $a(x) \leftarrow m(x)$, $m(x) \leftarrow r(x)$,
   $s_2(x) \leftarrow s_1(x)$, $s_1(x) \leftarrow s(x)$, $t_2(x) \leftarrow t_1(x)$, $t_1(x) \leftarrow t(x)$,
   $b(x) \leftarrow s_2(x)$
   $c(x) \leftarrow t_2(x)$
end
output $b(x), c(x)$.

Every byte may be represented by some number taken from the interval $[0, 255]$. Similarly, it is possible to represent each element from the field $GF(256)$ as a number from the same interval. To this end, the following isomorphism should be applied:

$$\sigma : W \rightarrow \{0, 1, \ldots, 255\}.$$

W stands here for the set of polynomials of degree at most 7 over $GF(2)$, i.e., for the underlying set of the field $GF(256)$:

$$W = \left\{ w_i(x) = v_{i,7}x^7 + v_{i,6}x^6 + \cdots + v_{i,2}x^2 + v_{i,1}x + v_{i,0}, i = 0, 1, \ldots, 255 \right\}$$

The function σ, given by

$$\sigma\big(w_i(x)\big) = w_i(2),$$

is an isomorphism, hence there exists the inverse function σ^{-1} which can be represented by a simple algorithm that transforms a polynomial $w_i(x)$ into a number from the interval $[0, 255]$.

All operations over $GF(256)$ required during the *AES* encryption and decryption procedures can be efficiently performed in any programming language.

During realization of the *AES* procedures it may be necessary to compute the multiplicative inverse of $\{00000000\}$, therefore it was additionally assumed that this element is self-inverse, which is in contradiction to the general rules of algebra, yet it makes the algorithm work. The fastest way to compute the multiplicative inverses in $GF(256)$ is to determine and store all of them as shown below. Notice that in fact, it is a one-dimensional array which takes 256 bytes, even though it looks like two-dimensional.

Table of multiplicative inverses in $GF(256)$

x	00	01	02	03	04	05	06	07	08	09	0a	0b	0c	0d	0e	0f
inv(x)	00	01	8d	f6	cb	52	7b	d1	e8	4f	29	c0	b0	e1	e5	c7
x	10	11	12	13	14	15	16	17	18	19	1a	1b	1c	1d	1e	1f
inv(x)	74	b4	aa	4b	99	2b	60	5f	58	3f	fd	cc	ff	40	ee	b2
x	20	21	22	23	24	25	26	27	28	29	2a	2b	2c	2d	2e	2f
inv(x)	3a	6e	5a	f1	55	4d	a8	c9	c1	0a	98	15	30	44	a2	c2

x	30	31	32	33	34	35	36	37	38	39	3a	3b	3c	3d	3e	3f
inv(x)	2c	45	92	6c	f3	39	66	42	f2	35	20	6f	77	bb	59	19
x	40	41	42	43	44	45	46	47	48	49	4a	4b	4c	4d	4e	4f
inv(x)	1d	fe	37	67	2d	31	f5	69	a7	64	ab	13	54	25	e9	09
x	50	51	52	53	54	55	56	57	58	59	5a	5b	5c	5d	5e	5f
inv(x)	ed	5c	05	ca	4c	24	87	bf	18	3e	22	f0	51	ec	61	17
x	60	61	62	63	64	65	66	67	68	69	6a	6b	6c	6d	6e	6f
inv(x)	16	5e	af	d3	49	a6	36	43	f4	47	91	df	33	93	21	3b
x	70	71	72	73	74	75	76	77	78	79	7a	7b	7c	7d	7e	7f
inv(x)	79	b7	97	85	10	b5	ba	3c	b6	70	d0	06	a1	fa	81	82
x	80	81	82	83	84	85	86	87	88	89	8a	8b	8c	8d	8e	8f
inv(x)	83	7e	7f	80	96	73	be	56	9b	9e	95	d9	f7	02	b9	a4
x	90	91	92	93	94	95	96	97	98	99	9a	9b	9c	9d	9e	9f
inv(x)	de	6a	32	6d	d8	8a	84	72	2a	14	9f	88	f9	dc	89	9a
x	a0	a1	a2	a3	a4	a5	a6	a7	a8	a9	aa	ab	ac	ad	ae	af
inv(x)	fb	7c	2e	c3	8f	b8	65	48	26	c8	12	4a	ce	e7	d2	62
x	b0	b1	b2	b3	b4	b5	b6	b7	b8	b9	ba	bb	bc	bd	be	bf
inv(x)	0c	e0	1f	ef	11	75	78	71	a5	8e	76	3d	bd	bc	86	57
x	c0	c1	c2	c3	c4	c5	c6	c7	c8	c9	ca	cb	cc	cd	ce	cf
inv(x)	0b	28	2f	a3	da	d4	e4	0f	a9	27	53	04	1b	fc	ac	e6
x	d0	d1	d2	d3	d4	d5	d6	d7	d8	d9	da	db	dc	dd	de	df
inv(x)	7a	07	ae	63	c5	db	e2	ea	94	8b	c4	d5	9d	f8	90	6b
x	e0	e1	e2	e3	e4	e5	e6	e7	e8	e9	ea	eb	ec	ed	ee	ef
inv(x)	b1	0d	d6	eb	c6	0e	cf	ad	08	4e	d7	e3	5d	50	1e	b3
x	f0	f1	f2	f3	f4	f5	f6	f7	f8	f9	fa	fb	fc	fd	fe	ff
inv(x)	5b	23	38	34	68	46	03	8c	dd	9c	7d	a0	cd	1a	41	1c

In a similar way multiplication and addition over $GF(256)$ may be expressed by means of tables, to which one can refer and which are larger than the table of multiplicative inverses as they take 65536 bytes each.

Other mathematical operations, used in the AES algorithm, are performed on polynomials of degree at most three with coefficients taken from the field $GF(256)$. The algorithm uses two such polynomials:

$$a(x) = a_3 x^3 + a_2 x^2 + a_1 x + a_0,$$
$$b(x) = b_3 x^3 + b_2 x^2 + b_1 x + b_0, \quad a_i, b_i \in GF(256),$$

which are considered as 4-byte words

$$\mathbf{a} = [a_3, a_2, a_1, a_0], \qquad \mathbf{b} = [b_3, b_2, b_1, b_0].$$

They are added in the following way:

$$a(x) + b(x) = (a_3 \oplus b_3)x^3 + (a_2 \oplus b_2)x^2 + (a_1 \oplus b_1)x + (a_0 \oplus b_0)$$
$$\mathbf{a} + \mathbf{b} = \big[(a_3 \oplus b_3), (a_2 \oplus b_2), (a_1 \oplus b_1), (a_0 \oplus b_0)\big].$$

Multiplication of the polynomials is executed in two phases. First, we expand the product

$$a(x) \bullet b(x) = c(x) = c_6 x^6 + c_5 x^5 + c_4 x^4 + c_3 x^3 + c_x^2 + c_1 x + c_0,$$

where

$$c_0 = a_0 \bullet b_0,$$
$$c_1 = a_1 \bullet b_0 \oplus a_0 \bullet b_1,$$
$$c_2 = a_2 \bullet b_0 \oplus a_1 \bullet b_1 \oplus a_0 \bullet b_2,$$
$$c_3 = a_3 \bullet b_0 \oplus a_2 \bullet b_1 \oplus a_1 \bullet b_2 \oplus a_0 \bullet b_3,$$
$$c_4 = a_3 \bullet b_1 \oplus a_2 \bullet b_2 \oplus a_1 \bullet b_3,$$
$$c_5 = a_3 \bullet b_2 \oplus a_2 \bullet b_3,$$
$$c_6 = a_3 \bullet b_3.$$

The polynomial $c(x)$ does not represent a 4-byte word, thus in the second phase of multiplication it is reduced modulo $x^4 + 1$, i.e., we apply the following substitution: $x^4 = 1, x^5 = x, x^6 = x^2$. Therefore,

$$a(x) \otimes b(x) = d(x) = d_3 x^3 + d_2 x^2 + d_1 x + d_0,$$

with

$$d_0 = (a_0 \bullet b_0) \oplus (a_3 \bullet b_1) \oplus (a_2 \bullet b_2) \oplus (a_1 \bullet b_3),$$
$$d_1 = (a_1 \bullet b_0) \oplus (a_0 \bullet b_1) \oplus (a_3 \bullet b_2) \oplus (a_2 \bullet b_3),$$
$$d_2 = (a_2 \bullet b_0) \oplus (a_1 \bullet b_1) \oplus (a_0 \bullet b_2) \oplus (a_3 \bullet b_3),$$
$$d_3 = (a_3 \bullet b_0) \oplus (a_2 \bullet b_1) \oplus (a_1 \bullet b_2) \oplus (a_0 \bullet b_3).$$

If $a(x)$ is a fixed polynomial of degree ≤ 3 over $GF(256)$ and $b(x)$ is an arbitrary polynomial of the same type, then multiplication of these two polynomials over $GF(256)$ modulo $x^4 + 1$, i.e., the operation $d(x) = a(x) \otimes b(x)$, can be rephrased by the following matrix equation:

$$\begin{bmatrix} d_0 \\ d_1 \\ d_2 \\ d_3 \end{bmatrix} = \begin{bmatrix} a_0 & a_3 & a_2 & a_1 \\ a_1 & a_0 & a_3 & a_2 \\ a_2 & a_1 & a_0 & a_3 \\ a_3 & a_2 & a_1 & a_0 \end{bmatrix} \begin{bmatrix} b_0 \\ b_1 \\ b_2 \\ b_3 \end{bmatrix}.$$

The polynomial $x^4 + 1$ is reducible over $GF(256)$ into the product

$$(x+1)(x+1)(x+1)(x+1),$$

hence the operation $\otimes$ is not always invertible. However, the *AES* algorithm applies the following pair of polynomials, one of which is the inverse of the second:

$$a(x) = \{03\}x^3 + \{01\}x^2 + \{01\}x + \{02\},$$
$$a(x)^{-1} = \{0b\}x^3 + \{0d\}x^2 + \{09\}x + \{0e\},$$

since

$$a(x) \otimes a(x)^{-1} = \begin{bmatrix} \{02\} & \{03\} & \{01\} & \{01\} \\ \{01\} & \{02\} & \{03\} & \{01\} \\ \{01\} & \{01\} & \{02\} & \{03\} \\ \{03\} & \{01\} & \{01\} & \{02\} \end{bmatrix} \begin{bmatrix} \{0e\} \\ \{09\} \\ \{0d\} \\ \{0b\} \end{bmatrix} = \{01\}.$$

Another polynomial over $GF(256)$, applied in AES, is the following: $a(x) = \{01\}x^3 + \{00\}x^2 + \{00\}x + \{00\} = x^3$. Multiplying an arbitrary polynomial $b(x) = b_3 x^3 + b_2 x^2 + b_1 x + b_0$ by $a(x)$ can be described by the matrix equation

$$a(x) \otimes b(x) = \begin{bmatrix} \{00\} & \{01\} & \{00\} & \{00\} \\ \{00\} & \{00\} & \{01\} & \{00\} \\ \{00\} & \{00\} & \{00\} & \{01\} \\ \{01\} & \{00\} & \{00\} & \{00\} \end{bmatrix} \begin{bmatrix} b_0 \\ b_1 \\ b_2 \\ b_3 \end{bmatrix} = \begin{bmatrix} b_1 \\ b_2 \\ b_3 \\ b_0 \end{bmatrix},$$

which corresponds to a cyclic byte shift of an input word by one to the left.

Beside the above-mentioned operations, the AES algorithm also uses the following affine transformation over $GF(2)$:

$$\begin{bmatrix} b'_0 \\ b'_1 \\ b'_2 \\ b'_3 \\ b'_4 \\ b'_5 \\ b'_6 \\ b'_7 \end{bmatrix} = \begin{bmatrix} 1 & 0 & 0 & 0 & 1 & 1 & 1 & 1 \\ 1 & 1 & 0 & 0 & 0 & 1 & 1 & 1 \\ 1 & 1 & 1 & 0 & 0 & 0 & 1 & 1 \\ 1 & 1 & 1 & 1 & 0 & 0 & 0 & 1 \\ 1 & 1 & 1 & 1 & 1 & 0 & 0 & 0 \\ 0 & 1 & 1 & 1 & 1 & 1 & 0 & 0 \\ 0 & 0 & 1 & 1 & 1 & 1 & 1 & 0 \\ 0 & 0 & 0 & 1 & 1 & 1 & 1 & 1 \end{bmatrix} \begin{bmatrix} b_0 \\ b_1 \\ b_2 \\ b_3 \\ b_4 \\ b_5 \\ b_6 \\ b_7 \end{bmatrix} + \begin{bmatrix} 1 \\ 1 \\ 0 \\ 0 \\ 0 \\ 1 \\ 1 \\ 0 \end{bmatrix}$$

which can be described by the formula

$$b'_i = b_i \oplus b_{(i+4) \,(\mathrm{mod}\,8)} \oplus b_{(i+5) \,(\mathrm{mod}\,8)} \oplus b_{(i+6) \,(\mathrm{mod}\,8)} \oplus b_{(i+7) \,(\mathrm{mod}\,8)} \oplus c_i,$$

where c_i is the i-th bit of the byte $\{63\} = \{01100011\}$. Therefore, the affine transformation consists of determining the byte $\mathbf{b'} = \{b'_7 \, b'_6 \, b'_5 \, b'_4 \, b'_3 \, b'_2 \, b'_1 \, b'_0\}$, whose components are computed by means of equations over $GF(2)$:

$$b'_0 = b_0 + b_4 + b_5 + b_6 + b_7 + 1,$$
$$b'_1 = b_1 + b_5 + b_6 + b_7 + b_0 + 1,$$
$$b'_2 = b_2 + b_6 + b_7 + b_0 + b_1,$$
$$b'_3 = b_3 + b_7 + b_0 + b_1 + b_2,$$
$$b'_4 = b_4 + b_0 + b_1 + b_2 + b_3,$$
$$b'_5 = b_5 + b_1 + b_2 + b_3 + b_4 + 1,$$
$$b'_6 = b_6 + b_2 + b_3 + b_4 + b_5 + 1,$$
$$b'_7 = b_7 + b_3 + b_4 + b_5 + b_6.$$

Of course, there exists the inverse function to the above affine transformation given by

$$
\begin{bmatrix} b_0' \\ b_1' \\ b_2' \\ b_3' \\ b_4' \\ b_5' \\ b_6' \\ b_7' \end{bmatrix} = \begin{bmatrix} 0 & 0 & 1 & 0 & 0 & 1 & 0 & 1 \\ 1 & 0 & 0 & 1 & 0 & 0 & 1 & 0 \\ 0 & 1 & 0 & 0 & 1 & 0 & 0 & 1 \\ 1 & 0 & 1 & 0 & 0 & 1 & 0 & 0 \\ 0 & 1 & 0 & 1 & 0 & 0 & 1 & 0 \\ 0 & 0 & 1 & 0 & 1 & 0 & 0 & 1 \\ 1 & 0 & 0 & 1 & 0 & 1 & 0 & 0 \\ 0 & 1 & 0 & 0 & 1 & 0 & 1 & 0 \end{bmatrix} \left(\begin{bmatrix} b_0 \\ b_1 \\ b_2 \\ b_3 \\ b_4 \\ b_5 \\ b_6 \\ b_7 \end{bmatrix} + \begin{bmatrix} 1 \\ 1 \\ 0 \\ 0 \\ 0 \\ 1 \\ 1 \\ 0 \end{bmatrix} \right)
$$

$$
= \begin{bmatrix} 0 & 0 & 1 & 0 & 0 & 1 & 0 & 1 \\ 1 & 0 & 0 & 1 & 0 & 0 & 1 & 0 \\ 0 & 1 & 0 & 0 & 1 & 0 & 0 & 1 \\ 1 & 0 & 1 & 0 & 0 & 1 & 0 & 0 \\ 0 & 1 & 0 & 1 & 0 & 0 & 1 & 0 \\ 0 & 0 & 1 & 0 & 1 & 0 & 0 & 1 \\ 1 & 0 & 0 & 1 & 0 & 1 & 0 & 0 \\ 0 & 1 & 0 & 0 & 1 & 0 & 1 & 0 \end{bmatrix} \begin{bmatrix} b_0+1 \\ b_1+1 \\ b_2 \\ b_3 \\ b_4 \\ b_5+1 \\ b_6+1 \\ b_7 \end{bmatrix} = \begin{bmatrix} b_2+b_5+b_7+1 \\ b_0+b_3+b_6 \\ b_1+b_4+b_7+1 \\ b_0+b_2+b_5 \\ b_1+b_3+b_6 \\ b_2+b_4+b_7 \\ b_0+b_3+b_5 \\ b_1+b_3+b_6 \end{bmatrix}
$$

hence

$$
b_0' = b_2 + b_5 + b_7 + 1,
$$
$$
b_1' = b_0 + b_3 + b_6,
$$
$$
b_2' = b_1 + b_4 + b_7 + 1,
$$
$$
b_3' = b_0 + b_2 + b_5,
$$
$$
b_4' = b_1 + b_3 + b_6,
$$
$$
b_5' = b_2 + b_4 + b_7,
$$
$$
b_6' = b_0 + b_3 + b_5,
$$
$$
b_7' = b_1 + b_3 + b_6.
$$

3.7.2 Description of the Algorithm

The encryption standard AES [46] is a block cipher which is a variant of the larger collection of ciphers called Rijndael. The AES standard supports a symmetric-key cipher transforming a 128-bit block of a plaintext into a ciphertext block of the same size. In the encryption process the key length varies between 128, 192 and 256 bits (16, 24 and 32 bytes). Rijndael can use also other key lengths and plaintext block sizes but AES does not allow such cases.

The input and output of the AES algorithm are 128-bit sequences, called blocks of size 128 (the size of a block is the number of bits occurring in this block). A cipher key for the algorithm is a 128-, 192- or 256-bit sequence. Bits in these sequences are enumerated starting with 0 up to the number smaller by one than the sequence length. Bit numbers in a sequence are called indices of the bits.

The basic unit of encryption in the process of the AES algorithm is a byte, a sequence of eight bits. Input, output and key sequences are divided into groups consisting of eight consecutive bits, forming tables of bytes. Therefore, if each of an input, an output and a cipher key is considered as a table of bytes, denoted by $\mathbf{a}$, then it is possible to access elements of this table by their indices. So an element from a table $\mathbf{a}$ is given by some $\mathbf{a}_n$ (or $\mathbf{a}[n]$), where $0 \leq n \leq 15$ for the input and output blocks and $0 \leq n \leq 15$, $0 \leq n \leq 23$ and $0 \leq n \leq 31$ for the block of the cipher key of size 128, 192 and 256, respectively.

The value of each byte, denoted by $\{b_7\,b_6\,b_5\,b_4\,b_3\,b_2\,b_1\,b_0\}$, is determined by bits forming a given byte. The following notation is considered as the polynomial representation of elements from the Galois field $GF(256)$

$$b_7x^7 + b_6x^6 + b_5x^5 + b_4x^4 + b_3x^3 + b_2x^2 + b_1x + b_0 = \sum_{k=1}^{8} b_{8-k}x^{8-k}.$$

For example, the byte with the value $\{10000011\}$ corresponds to the polynomial $x^7 + x + 1$ over $GF(2)$.

In practice, to denote the value of a byte it is easier to use the hexadecimal representation, where eight bits of one byte are replaced by two hexadecimal digits, according to the following table:

Hexadecimal representation of 4-bit sequences

0000	0	0100	4	1000	8	1100	c
0001	1	0101	5	1001	9	1101	d
0010	2	0110	6	1010	a	1110	e
0011	3	0111	7	1011	b	1111	f

For example, the hexadecimal entry $\{ab\}$ corresponds to $\{10101011\}$ written in the binary representation.

A table $\mathbf{a}$ of bytes is represented by its elements $\mathbf{a}_0, \mathbf{a}_1, \ldots, \mathbf{a}_{15}$. Bytes are created from a 128-bit sequence

$$input_0,\ input_1,\ \ldots,\ input_{127}$$

in the following way:

$$a_0 = \{input_0, input_1, \ldots, input_7\},$$
$$a_1 = \{input_8, input_9, \ldots, input_{15}\},$$
$$\vdots$$
$$a_{15} = \{input_{120}, input_{121}, \ldots, input_{127}\},$$

where indices of bytes are related to the order of bit occurrences according to the table:

Indices of bits and bytes

input sequence of bits	0 1 2 3 4 5 6 7	8 9 10 11 12 13 14 15	...
byte number	0	1	...
bit numbers in the byte	7 6 5 4 3 2 1 0	7 6 5 4 3 2 1 0	...

This method of creating a table of bytes is also applicable to 192- and 256-bit key sequences.

Table of input bytes, table of the state, table of output bytes

in_0	in_4	in_8	in_{12}
in_1	in_5	in_9	in_{13}
in_2	in_6	in_{10}	in_{14}
in_3	in_7	in_{11}	in_{15}

$s_{0,0}$	$s_{0,1}$	$s_{0,2}$	$s_{0,3}$
$s_{1,0}$	$s_{1,1}$	$s_{1,2}$	$s_{1,3}$
$s_{2,0}$	$s_{2,1}$	$s_{2,2}$	$s_{2,3}$
$s_{3,0}$	$s_{3,1}$	$s_{3,2}$	$s_{3,3}$

out_0	out_4	out_8	out_{12}
out_1	out_5	out_9	out_{13}
out_2	out_6	out_{10}	out_{14}
out_3	out_7	out_{11}	out_{15}

Internal operations executed by the *AES* algorithm during encryption and decryption processes are performed on a two-dimensional table of bytes, called the state. The state is a table consisting of 4 rows, each with **Nb** bytes, where **Nb** is the length of a plaintext block divided by 32. Elements of the state are denoted by $s_{r,c}$ or $s[r, c]$, where r stands for a row number of the state, c is a column number and

$$0 \leq r \leq 3, \quad 0 \leq c \leq \mathbf{Nb} - 1.$$

At the beginning of the encryption/decryption procedure, the input table **in** is copied to the state table according to the equation

$$\mathbf{s}[r, c] = \mathbf{in}[r + 4c], \quad 0 \leq r \leq 3, \ 0 \leq c \leq \mathbf{Nb} - 1,$$

and after that the state table is copied to the output table **out**, according to the equation

$$\mathbf{out}[r + 4c] = \mathbf{s}[r, c], \quad 0 \leq r \leq 3, \ 0 \leq c \leq \mathbf{Nb} - 1.$$

Four bytes of each column from the state table form a 32-bit word and a row number r is an index of four bytes of each word. Therefore, we can look at the state as a one-dimensional table **w** of 32-bit words, consisting of 4 elements: $\mathbf{w}_0, \mathbf{w}_1, \mathbf{w}_2, \mathbf{w}_3$ ($\mathbf{w}[0], \mathbf{w}[1], \mathbf{w}[2], \mathbf{w}[3]$), where

$$\mathbf{w}_0 = s_{0,0} \, s_{1,0} \, s_{2,0} \, s_{3,0},$$
$$\mathbf{w}_1 = s_{0,1} \, s_{1,1} \, s_{2,1} \, s_{3,1},$$
$$\mathbf{w}_2 = s_{0,2} \, s_{1,2} \, s_{2,2} \, s_{3,2},$$
$$\mathbf{w}_3 = s_{0,3} \, s_{1,3} \, s_{2,3} \, s_{3,3}.$$

According to the standard, the *AES* algorithm transforms input and output blocks and the state table of length 128, which means that **Nb** = 4. A cipher key **K** can be of length 128, 192 or 256 bits, so **Nk** = 4, 6 or 8. The number of rounds is strictly related with the key length, according to the following table:

	key length (**Nk** words)	block size (**Nb** words)	number of rounds (**Nr**)
AES-128	4	4	10
AES-192	6	4	12
AES-256	8	4	14

Under the standard, these are the only possible combinations of the parameters.

During encryption and decryption procedures in the *AES* algorithm, some number of rounds is performed and each of them consists of four different transformations executed on bytes from the state table.

3.7.3 Key Expansion

Before the encryption/decryption procedures it is necessary to generate $Nb * (Nr+1)$ 4-byte auxiliary keys and to store them in a table w. For this purpose the procedure KeyExpansion(), whose pseudocode is given below, is applied.

```
KeyExpansion(byte key[4*Nk], word w[Nb*(Nr+1)], Nk) begin
    word temp
    i = 0
    while (i < Nk)
       w[i] = word(key[4*i], key[4*i+1], key[4*i+2], key[4*i+3])
       i = i+1
    end while
    i = Nk
    while (i < Nb * (Nr+1))
       temp = w[i-1]
       if (i mod Nk = 0)
          temp = SubWord(RotWord(temp)) xor Rcon[i/Nk]
       else if (Nk > 6 and i mod Nk = 4)
          temp = SubWord(temp)
       end if
       w[i] = w[i-Nk] xor temp
       i = i + 1
    end while
end
```

The formal parameters of this procedure are: the table key, which represents the encryption key, the table w, and the parameter Nk. The function SubWord() takes a 4-byte word as an input, applies to each byte the substitution S-box, i.e., it computes the multiplicative inverse of a given byte in $GF(256)$, and finally executes the afore mentioned affine transformation on the so-computed inverse. In the encryption algorithm, the procedure SubBytes(), operating on bytes instead of words, is the counterpart of the SubWord() function.

Values of the function SubBytes (S-box substitution)

```
x            00 01 02 03 04 05 06 07 08 09 0a 0b 0c 0d 0e 0f
SubBytes(x)  63 7c 77 7b f2 6b 6f c5 30 01 67 2b fe d7 ab 76
x            10 11 12 13 14 15 16 17 18 19 1a 1b 1c 1d 1e 1f
SubBytes(x)  ca 82 c9 7d fa 59 47 f0 ad d4 a2 af 9c a4 72 c0
x            20 21 22 23 24 25 26 27 28 29 2a 2b 2c 2d 2e 2f
SubBytes(x)  b7 fd 93 26 36 3f f7 cc 34 a5 e5 f1 71 d8 31 15
x            30 31 32 33 34 35 36 37 38 39 3a 3b 3c 3d 3e 3f
SubBytes(x)  04 c7 23 c3 18 96 05 9a 07 12 80 e2 eb 27 b2 75
x            40 41 42 43 44 45 46 47 48 49 4a 4b 4c 4d 4e 4f
SubBytes(x)  09 83 2c 1a 1b 6e 5a a0 52 3b d6 b3 29 e3 2f 84
x            50 51 52 53 54 55 56 57 58 59 5a 5b 5c 5d 5e 5f
SubBytes(x)  53 d1 00 ed 20 fc b1 5b 6a cb be 39 4a 4c 58 cf
x            60 61 62 63 64 65 66 67 68 69 6a 6b 6c 6d 6e 6f
SubBytes(x)  d0 ef aa fb 43 4d 33 85 45 f9 02 7f 50 3c 9f a8
x            70 71 72 73 74 75 76 77 78 79 7a 7b 7c 7d 7e 7f
SubBytes(x)  51 a3 40 8f 92 9d 38 f5 bc b6 da 21 10 ff f3 d2
x            80 81 82 83 84 85 86 87 88 89 8a 8b 8c 8d 8e 8f
SubBytes(x)  cd 0c 13 ec 5f 97 44 17 c4 a7 7e 3d 64 5d 19 73
x            90 91 92 93 94 95 96 97 98 99 9a 9b 9c 9d 9e 9f
SubBytes(x)  60 81 4f dc 22 2a 90 88 46 ee b8 14 de 5e 0b db
x            a0 a1 a2 a3 a4 a5 a6 a7 a8 a9 aa ab ac ad ae af
SubBytes(x)  e0 32 3a 0a 49 06 24 5c c2 d3 ac 62 91 95 e4 79
x            b0 b1 b2 b3 b4 b5 b6 b7 b8 b9 ba bb bc bd be bf
SubBytes(x)  e7 c8 37 6d 8d d5 4e a9 6c 56 f4 ea 65 7a ae 08
x            c0 c1 c2 c3 c4 c5 c6 c7 c8 c9 ca cb cc cd ce cf
SubBytes(x)  ba 78 25 2e 1c a6 b4 c6 e8 dd 74 1f 4b bd 8b 8a
x            d0 d1 d2 d3 d4 d5 d6 d7 d8 d9 da db dc dd de df
SubBytes(x)  70 3e b5 66 48 03 f6 0e 61 35 57 b9 86 c1 1d 9e
x            e0 e1 e2 e3 e4 e5 e6 e7 e8 e9 ea eb ec ed ee ef
SubBytes(x)  e1 f8 98 11 69 d9 8e 94 9b 1e 87 e9 ce 55 28 df
x            f0 f1 f2 f3 f4 f5 f6 f7 f8 f9 fa fb fc fd fe ff
SubBytes(x)  8c a1 89 0d bf e6 42 68 41 99 2d 0f b0 54 bb 16
```

On the other hand, the function RotWord() permutes an input word $[a_0, a_1, a_2, a_3]$ cyclically and outputs $[a_1, a_2, a_3, a_0]$. The so-called round constant Rcon[i] is a table containing words

$$\text{Rcon}[i] = \big[\{02\}^{i-1}, \{00\}, \{00\}, \{00\}\big], \quad i = 1, 2, \ldots$$

whose first byte is given by the i-th power of the element $\{02\}$ in the field $GF(256)$. Therefore,

i	1	2	3	4	5	6	7	8	9	10
$\{02\}^{i-1}$	{01}	{02}	{04}	{08}	{10}	{20}	{40}	{80}	{1b}	{36}

It follows from the algorithm that the first Nk words of the extended key w[0], w[1], ..., w[Nk − 1] constitute the encryption key key. Every subsequent word w[i] is equal to the sum modulo two of the previous word (w[i − 1]) and the word occurring Nk positions before (w[i − Nk]). In case of words whose indices are multiples of Nk, first, the word w[i-1] is transformed by functions RotWord()

and `SubWord()`, then the round constant `Rcon[i/Nk]` is added modulo two to the result, and, finally, the word `w[i-Nk]` is added modulo two to the outcome. It should be noticed that if the length of the encryption key equals 256 bits, i.e., $Nk = 8$, and $i - 4$ is a multiple of Nk, then before determining `w[i]` the function `SubWord()` must be applied to the word `w[i-1]`. It is also worth mentioning that the *XOR* operation corresponds to addition in the field $GF(256)$.

3.7.4 Encryption Algorithm

The encryption algorithm can be precisely described by means of the following pseudocode:

```
Cipher(byte in[4*Nb], byte out[4*Nb], word w[Nb*(Nr+1)]) begin
    byte state[4,Nb]
    state = in
    AddRoundKey(state, w[0, Nb-1])
    for round = 1 step 1 to Nr--1
        SubBytes(state)
        ShiftRows(state)
        MixColumns(state)
        AddRoundKey(state, w[round*Nb, (round+1)*Nb-1])
    end for
    SubBytes(state)
    ShiftRows(state)
    AddRoundKey(state, w[Nr*Nb, (Nr+1)*Nb-1])
    out = state
end
```

The formal parameters of the program are two 16-byte tables: `in` and `out`, as well as a table `w` storing $4*(Nr+1)$ 4-byte words, which are the auxiliary keys for each round (Table 3.12). The `state`, a 16-byte table on which some cryptographic transformations are performed, is an important local variable of the program.

At the beginning, an input block `in` is copied to the `state` in the way presented before. Then the procedure `AddRoundKey()` is applied. Its operation consists of adding modulo two a round key to columns of the `state`, which is described mathematically as follows:

$$\left[s'_{0,c}, s'_{1,c}, s'_{2,c}, s'_{3,c}\right] = \left[s_{0,c}, s_{1,c}, s_{2,c}, s_{3,c}\right] \oplus w_{\text{round}*Nb} + c,$$

$$0 \le c < Nb, \ 0 \le \text{round} < Nr.$$

The function `SubBytes()` operates similarly to the function `SubWord` used in the expansion key algorithm, but the substitution `S-box` is here applied to every byte of the `state`.

Table 3.12 Table of input
state bytes and table of output
state bytes

$s_{0,0}$	$s_{0,1}$	$s_{0,2}$	$s_{0,3}$
$s_{1,0}$	$s_{1,1}$	$s_{1,2}$	$s_{1,3}$
$s_{2,0}$	$s_{2,1}$	$s_{2,2}$	$s_{2,3}$
$s_{3,0}$	$s_{3,1}$	$s_{3,2}$	$s_{3,3}$

$\Rightarrow$

$s'_{0,0}$	$s'_{0,1}$	$s'_{0,2}$	$s'_{0,3}$
$s'_{1,0}$	$s'_{1,1}$	$s'_{1,2}$	$s'_{1,3}$
$s'_{2,0}$	$s'_{2,1}$	$s'_{2,2}$	$s'_{2,3}$
$s'_{3,0}$	$s'_{3,1}$	$s'_{3,2}$	$s'_{3,3}$

Next, the transformation ShiftRows() shifts the last three rows of the state cyclically by one, two and three to the left, i.e., it modifies the state according to the equation

$$s_{r,c} = s'_{r,(c+r) \ (\mathrm{mod}\,4)}, \quad 0 \le r \le 3,\ 0 \le c \le 3.$$

Finally, the procedure MixColumns() works on columns of the state, regarding them as polynomials of degree at most 3 over $GF(256)$ which are to be multiplied modulo $x^4 + 1$ by the polynomial $\{03\}x^3 + \{01\}x^2 + \{01\}x + \{02\}$. This operation, denoted by the symbol $\otimes$, has already been described.

Hence, the procedure MixColumns() performs the following operations:

$$s'_{0,c} = (\{02\} \bullet s_{0,c}) \oplus (\{03\} \bullet s_{1,c}) \oplus s_{2,c} \oplus s_{3,c},$$
$$s'_{1,c} = s_{0,c} \oplus (\{02\} \bullet s_{1,c}) \oplus (\{03\} \bullet s_{2,c}) \oplus s_{3,c},$$
$$s'_{2,c} = s_{0,c} \oplus s_{1,c} \oplus (\{02\} \bullet s_{2,c}) \oplus (\{03\} \bullet s_{3,c}),$$
$$s'_{3,c} = (\{03\} \bullet s_{0,c}) \oplus s_{1,c} \oplus s_{2,c} \oplus (\{02\} \bullet s_{3,c}).$$

where $0 \le c \le 3$.

All rounds are identical but the last one, in which the function MixColumns() is not executed. The encryption algorithm finishes with copying the state to the table out.

3.7.5 Decryption Algorithm

The decryption algorithm consists of transformations inverse to those used in the encryption algorithm, however, in the reverse order. The algorithm may be briefly presented by the following pseudocode:

```
InvCipher(byte in[4*Nb], byte out[4*Nb], word w[Nb*(Nr+1)]) begin
    byte state[4,Nb]
    state = in
    AddRoundKey(state, w[Nr*Nb, (Nr+1)*Nb-1])
    for round = Nr-1 step -1 downto 1
        InvShiftRows(state)
        InvSubBytes(state)
        AddRoundKey(state, w[round*Nb, (round+1)*Nb-1])
        InvMixColumns(state)
    end for
    InvShiftRows(state)
    InvSubBytes(state)
```

```
    AddRoundKey(state, w[0, Nb-1])
    out = state
end
```

The function `AddRoundKey()`, which is self-inverse, is the first transformation. The second one, `InvShiftRows()`, is an inverse to the function `ShiftRows()`, and as such it modifies the state according to the equation

$$s'_{r,(c+r)\ (\mathrm{mod}\,4)} = s_{r,c}, \quad 0 \le r \le 3,\ 0 \le c \le 3.$$

The easiest way to present how the next function, `InvSubBytes`, operates is to use the table below.

Values of the function `InvSubBytes`

```
x              00 01 02 03 04 05 06 07 08 09 0a 0b 0c 0d 0e 0f
InvSubBytes(x) 52 09 6a d5 30 36 a5 38 bf 40 a3 9e 81 f3 d7 fb
x              10 11 12 13 14 15 16 17 18 19 1a 1b 1c 1d 1e 1f
InvSubBytes(x) 7c e3 39 82 9b 2f ff 87 34 8e 43 44 c4 de e9 cb
x              20 21 22 23 24 25 26 27 28 29 2a 2b 2c 2d 2e 2f
InvSubBytes(x) 54 7b 94 32 a6 c2 23 3d ee 4c 95 0b 42 fa c3 4e
x              30 31 32 33 34 35 36 37 38 39 3a 3b 3c 3d 3e 3f
InvSubBytes(x) 08 2e a1 66 28 d9 24 b2 76 5b a2 49 6d 8b d1 25
x              40 41 42 43 44 45 46 47 48 49 4a 4b 4c 4d 4e 4f
InvSubBytes(x) 72 f8 f6 64 86 68 98 16 d4 a4 5c cc 5d 65 b6 92
x              50 51 52 53 54 55 56 57 58 59 5a 5b 5c 5d 5e 5f
InvSubBytes(x) 6c 70 48 50 fd ed b9 da 5e 15 46 57 a7 8d 9d 84
x              60 61 62 63 64 65 66 67 68 69 6a 6b 6c 6d 6e 6f
InvSubBytes(x) 90 d8 ab 00 8c bc d3 0a f7 e4 58 05 b8 b3 45 06
x              70 71 72 73 74 75 76 77 78 79 7a 7b 7c 7d 7e 7f
InvSubBytes(x) d0 2c 1e 8f ca 3f 0f 02 c1 af bd 03 01 13 8a 6b
x              80 81 82 83 84 85 86 87 88 89 8a 8b 8c 8d 8e 8f
InvSubBytes(x) 3a 91 11 41 4f 67 dc ea 97 f2 cf ce f0 b4 e6 73
x              90 91 92 93 94 95 96 97 98 99 9a 9b 9c 9d 9e 9f
InvSubBytes(x) 96 ac 74 22 e7 ad 35 85 e2 f9 37 e8 1c 75 df 6e
x              a0 a1 a2 a3 a4 a5 a6 a7 a8 a9 aa ab ac ad ae af
InvSubBytes(x) 47 f1 1a 71 1d 29 c5 89 6f b7 62 0e aa 18 be 1b
x              b0 b1 b2 b3 b4 b5 b6 b7 b8 b9 ba bb bc bd be bf
InvSubBytes(x) fc 56 3e 4b c6 d2 79 20 9a db c0 fe 78 cd 5a f4
x              c0 c1 c2 c3 c4 c5 c6 c7 c8 c9 ca cb cc cd ce cf
InvSubBytes(x) 1f dd a8 33 88 07 c7 31 b1 12 10 59 27 80 ec 5f
x              d0 d1 d2 d3 d4 d5 d6 d7 d8 d9 da db dc dd de df
InvSubBytes(x) 60 51 7f a9 19 b5 4a 0d 2d e5 7a 9f 93 c9 9c ef
x              e0 e1 e2 e3 e4 e5 e6 e7 e8 e9 ea eb ec ed ee ef
InvSubBytes(x) a0 e0 3b 4d ae 2a f5 b0 c8 eb bb 3c 83 53 99 61
x              f0 f1 f2 f3 f4 f5 f6 f7 f8 f9 fa fb fc fd fe ff
InvSubBytes(x) 17 2b 04 7e ba 77 d6 26 e1 69 14 63 55 21 0c 7d
```

The function `InvMixColumns()`, as the inverse transformation to `MixColumns()`, operates on columns of the state regarding them as polynomials of degree at most 3 over $GF(256)$, which are to be multiplied by

$$(\{03\}x^3 + \{01\}x^2 + \{01\}x + \{02\})^{-1} = \{0b\}x^3 + \{0d\}x^2 + \{09\}x + \{0e\} \text{ modulo}$$

the polynomial $x^4 + 1$. Hence, the function `InvMixColumns()` has to satisfy the following relations:

$$s'_{0,c} = \left(\{0e\} \bullet s_{0,c}\right) \oplus \left(\{0b\} \bullet s_{1,c}\right) \oplus \left(\{0d\} \bullet s_{2,c}\right) \oplus \left(\{09\} \bullet s_{3,c}\right),$$
$$s'_{1,c} = \left(\{09\} \bullet s_{0,c}\right) \oplus \left(\{0e\} \bullet s_{1,c}\right) \oplus \left(\{0b\} \bullet s_{2,c}\right) \oplus \left(\{0d\} \bullet s_{3,c}\right),$$
$$s'_{2,c} = \left(\{0d\} \bullet s_{0,c}\right) \oplus \left(\{09\} \bullet s_{1,c}\right) \oplus \left(\{0e\} \bullet s_{2,c}\right) \oplus \left(\{0b\} \bullet s_{3,c}\right),$$
$$s'_{3,3c} = \left(\{0b\} \bullet s_{0,c}\right) \oplus \left(\{0d\} \bullet s_{1,c}\right) \oplus \left(\{09\} \bullet s_{2,c}\right) \oplus \left(\{0e\} \bullet s_{3,c}\right),$$

for $0 \le c \le 3$.

The decryption procedure finishes with rewriting the table `state` to the table `out`.

The *AES* standard documentation also includes the pseudocode of an equivalent decryption algorithm.

```
EqInvCipher(byte in[4*Nb], byte out[4*Nb], word dw[Nb*(Nr+1)])
begin
    byte state[4,Nb]
    state = in
    AddRoundKey(state, dw[Nr*Nb, (Nr+1)*Nb-1])
    for round = Nr-1 step -1 downto 1
        InvSubBytes(state)
        InvShiftRows(state)
        InvMixColumns(state)
        AddRoundKey(state, dw[round*Nb, (round+1)*Nb-1])
    end for
    InvSubBytes(state)
    InvShiftRows(state)
    AddRoundKey(state, dw[0, Nb-1])
    out = state
end
```

In this version another set of round keys is used, thus applying this algorithm for decryption requires to be modified the procedure `KeyExpansion` by appending two loop instructions at the end of the code:

```
for i = 0 step 1 to (Nr+1)*Nb-1
    dw[i] = w[i]
end for
for round = 1 step 1 to Nr-1
    InvMixColumns(dw[round*Nb, (round+1)*Nb-1])
end for
```

The description of the encryption/decryption procedures of the *AES* cryptosystem is precise. Therefore, it is easy to implement them in any programming language.

The *AES* algorithm is under constant surveillance. Three international conferences dedicated to this standard have already been organized. Finally, it is worth mentioning that the *AES* cipher can operate in the same modes as DES.

3.8 Generalizations and Refinements of DES, IDEA and AES

DES, IDEA and AES belong to the class of iterated block ciphers whose encryption procedure repeats cryptographic procedures sequentially in consecutive rounds and applies a special encryption subkey for each round. Hence, an encryption process for such ciphers can be described by the formula

$$C = E\big(ks(K), M\big), \tag{3.5}$$

where E stands for the encryption function, K is a secret key chosen by a user, M denotes a message that is to be encrypted, and C its cryptogram. The secret key K is not directly applied in encryption, but it is used as an input for the function ks that generates subkeys for each round. Many cryptographers suspect that the function ks, which should maximize diffusion and confusion processes, is meant to, 'stuff' the cryptogram C with some additional information about bits of the secret key K that need to be either eliminated during the decryption process or computed directly from the cryptogram on the basis of some hard to get properties of the function ks. It is believed that this additional information may sometimes allow, with appropriate powerful computers, to decrypt the cryptogram C without knowing the key K. In order to verify this suspicion, it is necessary to find and analyze the function F that satisfies the formula

$$C = F(K, M), \tag{3.6}$$

and which, given the encryption procedure, the way round subkeys are generated, the secret key K, and the message M, allows us to represent symbolically and compute the cryptogram in one step. However, in the case of iterated block ciphers this task is practically infeasible. Therefore, if we do not apply the function ks for generating subkeys and instead we determine the whole set of subkeys for all rounds regarding this set as a secret key, then the cipher strength will increase considerably.

3.8.1 Algorithms DES-768, IDEA-832, AES-1408, AES-1664, and AES-1920

In order to replace currently recommended iterated block ciphers by even stronger ones without changing the hardware or software implementation modules of encryption/decryption algorithms, it is sufficient to eliminate the algorithm generating subkeys, generate, preferably randomly, a set K_s of subkeys for all iterations treating this set as a modified secret key, and, finally, determine a cryptogram according to the formula

$$C = E(K_s, M). \tag{3.7}$$

In such a situation we are certain that all bits of the secret key K_s are involved in the encryption process. Given the DES algorithm, requiring sixteen 48-bit subkeys, in this way we are able to encrypt a 64-bit block of a plaintext with the use of a 768-bit key. In the case of the IDEA algorithm fifty-two 16-bit subkeys, used as an 832-bit secret key, will protect 64 bits of the message. On the other hand, algorithms AES-128, AES-192 and AES-256 apply eleven, thirteen, and fifteen 128-bit subkeys, respectively, thus using these sets of subkeys as secret keys we are able to encrypt a 128-bit data block using keys of size 1408, 1664, and 1920 bits, respectively.

3.8.2 Generalized DES and AES Ciphers

By introducing slight changes in the standard cryptographic algorithms DES and AES, we can significantly increase their resistance to breaking. In case of the DES cryptosystem, we may regard an initial permutation IP, functions $S_1 - S_8$, a permutation P, and a choice function E as variables and hence enlarge the key space. It is known that there are

- $x = 64!$ permutations IP,
- $y = (4 \cdot 16!)^8$ sets of eight S-boxes,
- $z = 32!$ permutations P,
- $u = 2^{40}$ choice functions E,

thus considering these parameters as elements of the key we get the following growth of the key size:

$$\Delta_{DES} = \left\lfloor \frac{\ln(x \cdot y \cdot z \cdot u)}{\ln(2)} \right\rfloor, \tag{3.8}$$

which gives additional 1591 bits. Taking into account considerations from the previous section, we see that the generalized DES algorithm allows us to encrypt 64-bit data blocks with a key of maximum length equal to 2359 bits.

Applying an approach similar to the AES one, we can choose one out of 30 irreducible polynomials of degree eight over $GF(2)$ to perform operations in the field $GF(256)$, the transformation SubBytes() can be replaced by any permutation of 256 elements, functions ShiftRows() and InvShiftRows() can be replaced by a random pair of mutually inverse permutations operating on the state, and transformations MixColumns() and InvMixColumns() by a random pair of mutually inverse nonsingular matrices of size 4×4 over $GF(256)$. Such a generalization of the AES cryptosystem allows us to encrypt a 128-bit data block with a secret key of maximum length of 3736 bits.

Chapter 4
Foundations of Asymmetric Cryptography

This chapter presents asymmetric key cryptography, also known as public-key cryptography. It introduces the first asymmetric algorithm, invented by Diffie and Hellman, as well as the ElGamal algorithm. Moreover, we describe in detail a very well-known example of an asymmetric cryptosystem called RSA.

4.1 Idea of Asymmetric Cryptography

Asymmetric algorithms differ from the symmetric ones significantly. In the case of symmetric cryptography, in general the same key is used for encryption and decryption, or the decryption key can be determined from the encryption key. Hence, it can be said that only one key is used to encrypt and decrypt messages. In the case of asymmetric algorithms, a pair of two different keys is used, with computationally infeasible mutual reconstruction.

Customarily, the key used for encryption is called public and the one for decryption is called private. The essence of the idea of this kind of cryptography is that a ciphertext encrypted with a given public key can be decrypted only with the corresponding private key.

A public key, as its name suggests, can be publicized and widely available. Everyone may know this key and everyone can encrypt data with it. The point, as already mentioned, is that the same key cannot be applied for data decryption. This can be done only with the private key corresponding to the one used for encryption. The private key is known only to its owner and therefore only the owner is able to decrypt the data.

It is also possible to encrypt data in asymmetric algorithms (e.g., RSA) using a private key. This is an example of a digital signature. In such a case a ciphertext can be decrypted only with the corresponding public key, as in the procedure of signature verification. For details see the next chapter.

Distribution of the public keys does not need any secure channel, contrary to the case of symmetric keys. However, public-key cryptography requires a lot of infrastructure taking care of matching the appropriate private and public keys. Also, public

C. Kościelny et al., *Modern Cryptography Primer*,
DOI 10.1007/978-3-642-41386-5_4, © Springer-Verlag Berlin Heidelberg 2013

key computations are substantially more time consuming than those in symmetric cryptography.

4.2 The Diffie-Hellman Algorithm

This algorithm was published in 1976 by Whitfield Diffie and Martin Hellman [31]. Its cryptographic power is based on the problem of computing the discrete logarithm in Z_n (discussed in Chap. 2).[1] The original version of the algorithm can be used only for distribution or exchange of (usually symmetric) session keys and cannot be used for encryption. However, we present it here due to its historical value and also as an introduction to the ElGamal algorithm. The latter is a well-known cipher. Diffie-Hellman key exchange is also widely used in Web security with SSL (Socket Layer Security) and TLS (Transport Layer Security) protocols, and in the IPSec protocol key exchange framework.

Let us suppose that two entities (denoted by A and B) want to communicate with each other by means of some symmetric algorithm that requires a secret key k which is a natural number.

Algorithm 4.1 (The D-H Algorithm)

1. Users A and B agree upon two numbers: n and g (where $g \in Z_n$). These two numbers are not necessarily kept secret and A and B may establish them in an arbitrary way.
2. A chooses a large integer x randomly and computes $X = g^x \bmod n$.
3. A sends the value X to B.
4. B chooses a large integer y and computes $Y = g^y \bmod n$.
5. B sends the value Y to A.
6. A computes $k = Y^x \bmod n$.
7. B computes $k' = X^y \bmod n$.

Let us notice that

$$k = Y^x \bmod n = (g^y)^x \bmod n = g^{yx} \bmod n$$

and

$$k' = X^y \bmod n = (g^x)^y \bmod n = g^{xy} \bmod n.$$

Therefore, $k = k'$.

The integer k is thus known to both users and can be applied as a symmetric key for further communication with any symmetric cipher.

Let us recall that in this scheme only numbers n, g, X and Y are transmitted in an unencrypted way, i.e., they can be eavesdropped by a potential intruder. No one

---

[1] See also [68, 76].

except A and B respectively knows the integers x and y necessary for determining k. It would be possible to compute the value of k if one could extract x from the equation $X = g^x \bmod n$ or y from $Y = g^y \bmod n$. However, as we already pointed in Chap. 2, this is infeasible now for appropriately chosen sufficiently large integers. There is no proof to date that either the Diffie-Hellman Problem (DHP) or the Discrete Logarithm Problem (DLP) is a hard problem. The DHP is conjectured (but not proven) to be equivalent to the DLP.[2]

The Diffie-Hellman algorithm was patented in the US but its patent expired in 1997. Therefore, the algorithm can be used without any restrictions.

The time complexity of this algorithm depends on modular exponentiation and equals $O(l^3)$, where l is the bit length of the parameters used.

4.3 The ElGamal Algorithm

The algorithm was published in 1985 by Tahir ElGamal.[3] It can be considered a modification of the Diffie-Hellman algorithm. In this algorithm, as usual in asymmetric cryptosystems, we have two keys: a public and a private one.

Algorithm 4.2 (ElGamal Key-Generation Algorithm)

1. Choose a prime p and two arbitrary integers g and x $(g, x < p)$.
2. Compute $y = g^x \bmod p$.

Integers g and p may be commonly known and together with the number y they form the public key. The private key is given by x (of course, we still have to know the numbers g and p).

Let us suppose that we want to encrypt a message M $(M < p)$ with the public key (g, p, y).

Algorithm 4.3 (ElGamal Encryption Algorithm)

1. Choose randomly an integer k such that $GCD(k, p - 1) = 1$ (k and $p - 1$ are co-prime).
2. Compute $a = g^k \bmod p$.
3. Compute $b = y^k \cdot M \bmod p$.

The pair (a, b) forms the ciphertext of the given message M.

In order to decrypt it, the data decryption algorithm presented below has to be used:

---

[2]See [19, 22, 68, 74].

[3]See also [68, 104].

Algorithm 4.4 (ElGamal Decryption Algorithm)

1. Compute the inverse of $a^x \bmod p$ ($(a^x)^{-1} \bmod p$); let us notice that due to the primality of p, such an inverse always exists.
2. Compute $b \cdot (a^x)^{-1} \bmod p$.
3. This value is equal to the plaintext M ($M = b \cdot (a^x)^{-1} \bmod p$).

Let us notice that after suitable substitutions we get:

$$b \cdot (a^x)^{-1} \bmod p = y^k \cdot M \cdot (a^x)^{-1} \bmod p$$

$$= (g^x)^k \cdot M \cdot ((g^k)^x)^{-1} \bmod p = g^{xk} \cdot M \cdot (g^{kx})^{-1} \bmod p.$$

Finally, due to the commutativity of multiplication,

$$g^{xk} \cdot M \cdot (g^{kx})^{-1} \bmod p = g^{xk} \cdot (g^{xk})^{-1} \cdot M \bmod p = M.$$

Example 4.1 Let $p = 37$, $g = 7$ and $x = 6$. Then $y = g^x \bmod p = 4$. The public key is thus given by the triple $(g, p, y) = (7, 37, 4)$, and the private key by $(g, p, x) = (7, 37, 6)$. Let us take $k = 7$. (It is prime, therefore $GCD(k, p - 1) = 1$.) Let $M = 26$ be a plaintext. We compute $a = g^k \bmod p = 28$ and $b = y^k \cdot M \bmod p = 13$. The ciphertext is given by the pair $(28, 13)$. In order to decrypt the ciphertext, we have to compute $(a^x)^{-1} \bmod p = 2$. Now, we compute $b \cdot (a^x)^{-1} \bmod p = 26$. Finally, $b \cdot (a^x)^{-1} \bmod p = M$.

The cryptographic power of the algorithm is based, like D-H above, upon the Discrete Logarithm Problem. The problem of breaking the ElGamal encryption scheme, i.e., recovering M given g, p, y, a, and b, is equivalent to solving the Diffie-Hellman problem. The security of the ElGamal scheme is said to be based on the Discrete Logarithm Problem, however, their equivalence has not been proven. It is not known if there exists an efficient algorithm able to recover the message M, given its ciphertext and the public key.

The ElGamal algorithm has never been patented, since from its beginning it was covered by the patent protection of the Diffie-Hellman algorithm. Since the patent for the latter expired in 1997, the ElGamal algorithm was for some time the only asymmetric cryptosystem not protected by any patent.

Similarly to the case of the Diffie-Hellman algorithm, the time complexity of the ElGamal encryption algorithm requires two modular exponentiation and it is $O(l^3)$, where l is the bit length of the parameters used. Decryption requires only one exponentiation. The ElGamal encryption algorithm is probabilistic, meaning that each plaintext can be encrypted to many possible ciphertexts. One consequence of this is that an ElGamal ciphertext is twice as long in bit length as its plaintext.

4.4 The RSA Algorithm

The RSA algorithm[4] is well known, deeply examined by researchers, and currently widely used. It was developed in 1977 by three professors from the Massachusetts Institute of Technology (MIT): Ron Rivest, Adi Shamir and Leonard Adleman. The name of the algorithm comes from the initials of their surnames. The RSA cryptosystem was patented in 1983 by MIT. However, its patent expired in 2000 and now it can be used with no restrictions.

The algorithm enables encryption and decryption with the use of a pair of keys: a public and a private one, according to the idea of asymmetric cryptography. RSA is a cryptosystem that also allows encryption of messages with a private key and, in such a case, to decrypt them with a public key (used for digital signatures).

4.4.1 Key Generation

Below, we present methods to generate keys for encrypting and decrypting messages.

Algorithm 4.5 (RSA Key Generation Algorithm)
1. Choose two large random primes p and q.
2. Choose a random integer e such that $1 < e < (p - 1) \cdot (q - 1)$ and $GCD((p - 1) \cdot (q - 1), e) = 1$.
3. Find an integer d that is the inverse of e modulo $(p - 1) \cdot (q - 1)$ (if such an inverse does not exist, then choose another e), i.e., such that $e \cdot d = 1 \bmod (p - 1) \cdot (q - 1)$.
4. Compute $n = p \cdot q$ (at this moment it is recommended to delete p and q in order to prevent them from being obtained by an eavesdropper).
5. Your public key is (e, n) and the private key is (d, n).

The cryptographic power of the RSA cryptosystem is based upon the factorization problem. If someone could factorize the number n, being a part of the corresponding public key, then they would be able to obtain d, being a part of a private key. Thus the integers p and q need to be carefully chosen. One of the choice criteria is to take numbers that are not too close to each other. (Otherwise, it would be easy to find them by looking for primes close to the square root of n.) Also, when choosing the integer e, one can follow some recommendations that increase the speed of the algorithm. In general, it is advised to take a prime in the form $2^{2^m} + 1$. (In binary representation such numbers have only two bits equal to 1, while the other bits are equal to 0, therefore the arithmetic operations performed on such integers are optimally fast.)

---

[4]See also Sect. 8.2 in [68].

4.4.2 Encryption and Decryption

Let a pair (e, n) be a public key and a pair (d, n) a private one.

Let us suppose that we want to encrypt a message given by an integer M ($M < n$). The corresponding ciphertext is equal to $S = M^e \bmod n$. In order to decrypt it, we compute $S^d \bmod n$.

The following transformations prove the correctness of the algorithm, i.e., that $M = S^d \bmod n$.

Let us recall that $e \cdot d = 1 \bmod (p - 1) \cdot (q - 1)$, which means that for some integer k the following equation holds:

$$e \cdot d = 1 + k \cdot (p - 1) \cdot (q - 1).$$

Let us also recall that if p and q are primes, then

$$\Phi(p \cdot q) = (p - 1) \cdot (q - 1),$$

where $\Phi(p \cdot q)$ is the value of the Euler function applied to the product $p \cdot q$.

We obtain

$$e \cdot d = 1 + k \cdot (p - 1) \cdot (q - 1) = 1 + k \cdot \Phi(p \cdot q).$$

Now, let us recall Euler's theorem discussed in Chap. 2. It states that for any two co prime natural numbers n and a, the following equation is valid:

$$a^{\Phi(n)} = 1 \bmod n.$$

If $n = p \cdot q$, then we get:

$$a^{\Phi(p \cdot q)} = 1 \bmod p \cdot q,$$

hence

$$a^{(p-1) \cdot (q-1)} = 1 \bmod p \cdot q.$$

Now, taking into account all these preparations and after a suitable substitution we get:

$$
\begin{aligned}
S^d \bmod n = \left(M^e\right)^d \bmod n &= M^{e \cdot d} \bmod n \\
&= M^{1 + k \cdot \Phi(p \cdot q)} \bmod n = M \cdot M^{k \cdot \Phi(p \cdot q)} \bmod n \\
&= M \cdot M^{k \cdot \Phi(n)} \bmod n = M \cdot \left(M^{\Phi(n)}\right)^k \bmod n \\
&= M \cdot 1^k \bmod n = M \bmod n = M.
\end{aligned}
$$

These equations hold when $GCD(M, n) = 1$ (the assumption in Euler's Theorem). Otherwise, it would be easy to find the common divisor of M and n, by the Euclidean Algorithm. This would have to be either p or q. The number n would get factorized and the algorithm with the given key would get broken. However, it has been proven that also for M and n with a common divisor, the equality guaranteeing the algorithms correctness holds. Also, it has been proven that the probability of generating a message not coprime with n is close to 0.

Let us notice that we have assumed $M < n$. In the case when a plaintext is longer than n, we can break it into blocks and encrypt it blockwise.

Example 4.2 Let us consider the following example of execution of the RSA algorithm.

Let $p = 37$ and $q = 71$ (both integers are prime).

Then, we get their product $n = p \cdot q = 2627$. According to the afore mentioned recommendations, we take e in the form $2^{2^m} + 1$ for $m = 2$, hence $e = 17$.

The integer d satisfying the equation $d \cdot e = 1 \bmod (p - 1) \cdot (q - 1)$, so the inverse of e modulo $(p - 1) \cdot (q - 1)$, is equal to 593.

Therefore, a public key is given by the pair $(e, n) = (17, 2627)$, and a private key by $(d, n) = (593, 2627)$.

Let us take a plaintext $M = 258566522$. Of course, this number is greater than 2627.

Thus, we divide it into 3-digit blocks $M = m_1 m_2 m_3$, where:

$$m_1 = 258,$$
$$m_2 = 566,$$
$$m_3 = 522.$$

Following the algorithm, we raise these blocks to the power e modulo n. We get

$$s_1 = m_1^e \bmod n = 258^e \bmod n = 813,$$
$$s_2 = m_2^e \bmod n = 566^e \bmod n = 1840,$$
$$s_3 = m_3^e \bmod n = 522^e \bmod n = 1619.$$

The ciphertext S is thus the following: 813–1840–1619 (it is necessary to separate encryption values for each block in order to prevent ambiguity, e.g., the cryptogram of the plaintext 121222444 encrypted as stated above: 1691592925 could be read as 1691–592–925 or 169–1592–925. Of course, the decrypted messages are then different, they are equal to 121222444 and 228889444, respectively).

If we decrypt consecutive blocks of the ciphertext with the key (d, n), then we obtain consecutive blocks of the plaintext M:

$$s_1^d \bmod n = 813^d \bmod n = 258 = m_1,$$
$$s_2^d \bmod n = 1840^d \bmod n = 566 = m_2,$$
$$s_3^d \bmod n = 1619^d \bmod n = 522 = m_3.$$

To sum up, the RSA algorithm is the most popular and widely known asymmetric cryptosystem. Its cryptographic power has been thoroughly examined.[5] Basic RSA security relies on the intractability of the integer factorization problem. The problem of computing the RSA decryption exponent d from the public key (e, n), and the problem of factoring n, are computationally equivalent.[6]

Numbers p and q used for generating the public and private keys can be chosen in such a way that there is no feasible algorithm known for breaking RSA. Due to

---

[5]More information can be found in Sect. 8.2.2 in [68].

[6]See [68], Fact 8.6.

recent progress in the study of factorization, it is recommended to use sufficiently large numbers p and q, so that the integer n has 2048 bits in its binary representation. (Let us recall that numbers with hundreds of digits only are already now factorizable.) It is believed that such long keys will stay unbroken for at least two decades. Currently, keys of this size are used for encryption by large companies that develop cryptographic software and hardware. On the other hand, one can think of breaking RSA by finding the e-th root modulo a composite integer n, i.e., recovering the plaintext message M from its ciphertext $M^e \bmod n$ without actually knowing d. This problem is believed to be computationally equivalent to the integer factorization problem, although no proof of this is known.

Due to the complexity of operations performed during the algorithm execution, the speed of the RSA cryptosystem is not impressive. In the case of 1024-bit parameters, even when special integrated circuits dedicated particularly to the needs of RSA encryption are applied, the algorithm still remains slower than DES by a factor of 100 to even 1000. Modular exponentiation, i.e., integer exponentiation modulo n, is the most expensive operation since for a k-bit base and a k-bit exponent $O(k)$ multiplication, and squaring have to be executed. Let us assume that each of them requires k^2 elementary operations for k-bit numbers. Now, let p and q be t-bit primes and $n = p \cdot q$. Finally, let d be a $2t$-bit private key. Then the encryption process with this key (or the corresponding public key) or generating/verifying the signature, which consists of computing $x^d \bmod n$, for some $x < n$, require $O(t^3)$ elementary operations. The constants occurring in the O notation are smaller than 15 (see [68], Remark 14.78.). Due to its time complexity the RSA algorithm is rarely used for data encryption but it can be applied to encrypt and transport a session key to be used for encrypting data by means of some symmetric algorithm, for instance AES or 3DES.

For the same reason the RSA cryptosystem has limited applications in chip cards since most microprocessors cannot perform computations with keys longer than 1024 bits. In practice, small public keys are usually applied. Decryption and verification of signatures is much faster in such cases.

Security of the RSA cryptosystem is based on the hardness of the factorization problem, which, for k-digit numbers, can be performed in time $O(e^{k \cdot \lg(k)})$ by means of the best currently known algorithms (see [28, 68]). Due to technological progress in expanding the computational power of computers, the necessity of increasing the length of keys should also be taken into account.

Chapter 5
An Electronic Signature and Hash Functions

This chapter presents one of the most important uses of cryptography today—electronic signature algorithms.[1] This is a relatively new alternative to traditional handwritten signatures on paper documents. The electronic signature, analogous to the handwritten signature, is used for signing electronic documents. It can be used online for authentication.

Section 5.2 presents cryptographic hash functions, as used nowadays by the signature schemes. In the last decade these have got a lot of attention in both academia and industry, due to their widespread vital applications and the research challenges associated with them.

5.1 Digital Signature Algorithms

An electronic signature can be realized in many ways. European Union legislation [35] defines an electronic signature as *data in electronic form which are attached to or logically associated with an electronic document and which serve as a method of authentication*. Furthermore, it defines an advanced electronic signature as meeting the following requirements: *it is uniquely linked to the signatory; it is capable of identifying the signatory; it is created using means that the signatory can maintain under their sole control; it is linked to the document to which it relates in such a manner that any subsequent change in the document is feasibly detectable*. Most often suitable cryptographic algorithms are used to generate and verify the e-signature. Some asymmetric algorithms are ideally suited. These techniques will be discussed in detail in the following sections of this chapter.

---

[1] The interested reader can find more on electronic signature in [68, 79, 92]. Legal aspects of an e-signature and its usage in administration across the globe can be read about in [5, 65, 66].

C. Kościelny et al., *Modern Cryptography Primer*,
DOI 10.1007/978-3-642-41386-5_5, © Springer-Verlag Berlin Heidelberg 2013

Besides the methods of asymmetric cryptography, methods using biometric identification of a human are in use. Such methods have been used for a long time to check or confirm the identity of a person. These are the characteristics of each person: handwriting, fingerprints, iris patterns, hand or facial geometry (setting of the eyes, width of the mouth, etc.), and the characteristics of DNA. Unfortunately, no method is yet known for combining biometric identification of a human with a document, which could be signed in that way. Biometric identification methods are used for personal identification nowadays. It is expected that in the near future some new methods of combining some biometric characteristics of a human with a document will be discovered. Some regulations concerning stock exchange transactions by phone can be perceived as an important confirmation of trends of the future. A recorded stock exchange order can be evidence in criminal or administrative proceedings according to the law. In such a case the order (its content) is the document and the characteristics of the voice uniquely identify the person who placed the order. The original recording clearly binds the document and the person. However, the legal and technological problem is that it is easy to make subsequent changes to a digital voice recording.

In practice there are four main indispensable features of any electronic signature scheme:

1. *verifiability*—a practical possibility to check unambiguously the authenticity of a signature,
2. *unforgeability*—forging a signature must be at least as difficult as it is in the hand-written case,
3. *non-repudiation*—the signer cannot successfully repudiate their signature,
4. *integrity of the signed document*—a practical possibility to detect any changes in a document made after it has been signed.

The above features (requirements) make today's communication by electronic devices analogous to a face-to-face communication. Such features enable us, due to the cryptographic power of the algorithms, to check whether a person really is who he/she claims to be.

5.1.1 A Digital Signature

An electronic signature is realized on computers by the algorithms of asymmetric cryptography. As a characteristic of a signing person we take a sequence of digits (a number). That is why it is called a digital signature. The idea of generating and verifying digital signatures is depicted below. Due to the computational hardness of the problem of breaking the most important electronic signature schemes, it is practically impossible to forge an e-signature and thanks to that it can be considered even more reliable than a traditional handwritten signature.

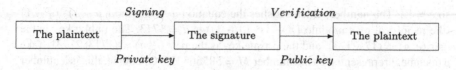

Fig. 5.1   The idea of a digital signature realized with an asymmetric algorithm

In asymmetric cryptography two keys are used. A private key, known only to the owner, serves in general to decrypt the data encrypted by a public key. The private and public keys are essentially a matching pair, which means that the data encrypted by a certain public key can be decrypted only by the corresponding private key.

In the last chapter it was mentioned that some asymmetric algorithms have the property that the data can be encrypted by a private key, then using the corresponding public key the data can be decrypted. Let us have a closer look at the scheme of operation (Fig. 5.1).

In general signing a document means transforming it using the signatory's private key. Everyone knowing the corresponding public key can verify the signature (using a suitable transformation). So, in practice everyone can do it. The point is not to keep secret the signed data. If we can verify the signature with the public key of a certain person it means that only the owner of the corresponding private key was able to encrypt the data properly. This subsection presents in detail three digital signature algorithms using asymmetric cryptography: RSA, ElGamal and DSA.

5.1.2   The RSA Signature

Let the pair of numbers (e, n) be the public key according to the RSA algorithm (see Sect. 4.4), and the pair of numbers (d, n) be the private key. For some prime numbers p and q, the following hold:

1. $GCD((p-1) \cdot (q-1), e) = 1$,
2. $d \cdot e = 1 \bmod (p-1) \cdot (q-1)$,
3. $n = p \cdot q$.

Let us recall that RSA is a cryptosystem with the property that you can also encrypt data with your private key. Suppose we want to digitally sign a message represented as a number M $(M < n)$.

The signature is the number $S = M^d \bmod n$. To verify the signature you can compute $S^e \bmod n$ and check whether the result is equal to M.

The cryptographic power of the RSA digital signature algorithm, as in the case of RSA encryption, is based on the hardness of factorization of large natural numbers (see Sect. 2.5.1).

Example 5.1 Let us consider another example of using the RSA algorithm to generate an electronic signature. Take $p = 53$ and $q = 41$ (both numbers are prime numbers). Then the product $n = p \cdot q = 2173$. As e take the number $2^{2^n} + 1$ for $n = 2$, so $e = 17$. The number which satisfies the equation $d \cdot e = 1 \bmod (p - 1) \cdot (q - 1)$ (the reciprocal of e modulo $(p - 1) \cdot (q - 1)$) is $d = 1713$. The public key is the pair $(e, n) = (17, 2173)$, and the private key is the pair $(d, n) = (1713, 2173)$. Take a document represented as the number $M = 585665223$. Of course, this is a number bigger than 2173. Split it into three-digit blocks $M = m_1 m_2 m_3$, where $m_1 = 585$, $m_2 = 665$, $m_3 = 223$.

The blocks according to the signature algorithm are raised to the power d modulo n. We obtain

$$p_1 = m_1^d \bmod n = 585^d \bmod n = 1381,$$
$$p_2 = m_2^d \bmod n = 665^d \bmod n = 2018,$$
$$p_3 = m_3^d \bmod n = 223^d \bmod n = 912.$$

The signature S has the form $1381, 2018, 912$. If the successive blocks of the signature are decrypted using the key (e, n), we obtain the original blocks of document M:

$$p_1^e \bmod n = 1381^e \bmod n = 585 = m_1,$$
$$p_2^e \bmod n = 2018^e \bmod n = 665 = m_2,$$
$$p_3^e \bmod n = 912^e \bmod n = 223 = m_3.$$

This proves the correctness of the generated signature.

5.1.3 The ElGamal Signature

The ElGamal public key encryption algorithm was presented in the previous chapter. Let us introduce its modification used in digital signatures. Let us recall the key generation algorithm:

Algorithm 5.1 (The ElGamal Key Generation Algorithm)

1. Choose a large prime number p and any two numbers g and x ($g, x < p$).
2. Compute $y = g^x \bmod p$.

The numbers g and p can be made publicly available and together with number y they form the public key (g, p, y). The private key is the number x (as we know g and p anyway, the private key can be the triple (g, p, x)). Suppose we want to sign a document M ($M < p$) using the private key (g, p, x).

Algorithm 5.2 (The ElGamal Signature Algorithm)

1. Choose a random number k such that $GCD(k, p - 1) = 1$ (k and $p - 1$ are relatively prime).
2. Compute $a = g^k \bmod p$.

3. Using the extended Euclidean algorithm, find the number b such that: $M = (a \cdot x + k \cdot b) \bmod (p - 1)$.
4. The signature is (as in the encryption algorithm) the pair of numbers: (a, b).

Algorithm 5.3 (The ElGamal Signature Verification Algorithm)

- To verify the signature (a, b) on a message M, take the signatory's public key (g, p, y) and check whether $y^a \cdot a^b = g^M \bmod p$. If yes, the signature is accepted.

Notice that the random number k should be different in every run of the signing algorithm.

Example 5.2 Let us take the private key $(g, p, x) = (2, 11, 8)$. It is easy to compute the public key $(g, p, y) = (2, 11, 3)$. We will sign the message $M = 5$. For the random number k take 9 (of course $\gcd(10, 9) = 1$).

Compute $a = g^k \bmod p = 2^9 \bmod 11 = 6$.

Determine b using the expanded Euclidean algorithm from the following equation:

$$M = (a \cdot x + k \cdot b) \bmod (p - 1) :$$
$$5 = (6 \cdot 8 + 9 \cdot b) \bmod 10$$
$$b = 3.$$

The signature is the pair $(a, b) = (6, 3)$.

To verify the signature we check the following equation for the numbers just calculated:

$$y^a \cdot a^b = g^M \bmod p :$$
$$3^6 \cdot 6^3 = 2^5 \bmod 11.$$

5.1.4 DSA Signature

The Digital Signature Algorithm was published by the US National Institute of Standards and Technology (NIST) in 1991 as the Digital Signature Standard (DSS), approved as specified in [32] and expanded as [33] in 2009. It is available free of charge. It is a variant of the ElGamal signature algorithm. Here we present in brief the main idea of DSA.

It starts off with specially selected random large integers p, q and g. The NIST standard specifies the (p, q) bit-lengths as $(1024, 160)$, $(2048, 224)$, $(2048, 256)$, or $(3072, 256)$. g is usually set to $2^{\frac{p-1}{q}} \bmod p$.

Every user receives (or chooses randomly) its own individual secret key x (from the interval between 0 and q) and computes $y = g^x \bmod p$. This is the user's public key, as in the ElGamal algorithm. The digital signature on a document M, using an auxiliary (secret) randomized every time number k (of the same size as q), is a pair integers (r, s) satisfying:

$$r = \left(g^k \bmod p\right) \bmod q,$$

$$s = \frac{M + x \cdot r}{k} \bmod q.$$

To verify the signature one checks whether

$$r = \left(g^{\left(\frac{M}{s} \bmod q\right)} \cdot y^{\left(\frac{r}{s} \bmod q\right)} \bmod p\right) \bmod q.$$

Note that the computations are more complicated than in the ElGamal encryption algorithm. As private keys in this system big enough numbers should be used in order to prevent forgery of the signature by trying one by one every possible candidate as a key (the brute force attack).

If the key was a 2-digit number it would not be difficult to try out every candidate from 0 to 99. If the key has, for example, 60 decimal digits the best networked computers nowadays are not able to try out each candidate one by one. It would require more than a couple of years of work. The public key should be a number for which it is infeasible to compute its discrete logarithm, using the asserted parameters g and p.

Currently, the private key for DSA should have at least the length of 160 bits, and the public key at least 1024 bits.

The size of q is fixed in the algorithm DSA (as per [32]) at 160 bits, while the size of p can be any multiple of 64 between 512 and 1024 bits inclusive. [32] does not permit primes p larger than 1024 bits. Along with some minor revisions, and reflecting advances in technology, [33] recommends that it is prudent to consider larger key sizes. It allows the use of 1024, 2048, and 3072-bit p, and the (p, q) pair lengths of (1024, 160), (2048, 224), (2048, 256), and (3072, 256). DSA produces digital signatures of length twice the size of q, i.e., of 320, 448, or 512 bits, respectively.

Also [33] adopted the RSA algorithm, as specified in [1] and [81] (version 1.5 and higher) for the computation of digital signatures, and the Elliptic Curve Digital Signature Algorithm (ECDSA), as specified in [2], with a minimum key size of 160 bits (producing digital signatures that are twice the length of the key size). ECDSA computations are designed in the arithmetic of certain special groups of points lying on carefully selected elliptic curves.

The idea of a digital signature described above faces some considerable inconvenience. The algorithms of asymmetric cryptography take a great deal of time. Encrypting (signing) large data incurs a large computational overhead. Such complications can be solved by using the cryptographic hash functions.

5.2 Cryptographic Hash Functions

This section presents one-way functions and their usage as cryptographic hash algorithms. These are widely used in everyday digital telecommunication world networking practice. Their design principles as well as cryptanalysis, i.e., methods

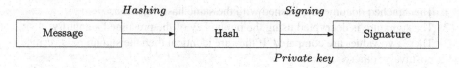

Fig. 5.2   Digital signature using a hash function

of breaking them, have been actively studied and experimented on for the last 2 decades, with some very interesting developments quite recently. This section gives the current (as of August, 2013) account. Three algorithms are presented and discussed in more detail: MD5, SHA-1, and SHA-3/Keccak.

The hash algorithms produce hash values (a.k.a. digests, or fingerprints) of messages. In general, the hash values are used to detect whether messages or files have been changed since the hash values were generated.[2] Examples of well-known usage include: Unix passwords storing, data validation, authentication of software packages, file identification in peer-to-peer networks, video file references on YouTube, implementations in widely used security protocols and systems like TLS, SSL, PGP, IPsec, Bitcoin, etc. Digital signature schemes provide one more example.

A document of any size is processed by a cryptographic hash function into some fixed-size (relatively small) hash in such a way that the transformation is computationally one-to-one. This means that the function does not need to be one-to-one (some different documents may get the same hash value), but it must be infeasible to find any two documents which get the same hash. In general, good cryptographic hash functions are designed in such a way that there is no formal proof of this property, and the security of widely used hash functions nowadays is based on the fact that so far no one has found any feasible algorithm able to construct two different documents with the same hash. In this respect the status of the problems of breaking currently good hash functions is the same as that of the factorization and discrete logarithm problems.

Digital signing using a hash function is a two-step process (Fig. 5.2):

1. The signatory processes the message to be signed into some fixed size form using a hash function.
2. The signatory transforms the hash with his own private key according to the signing algorithm.

This way one can sign data of any size, e.g., a one-sentence e-mail or a file of size 100 MB.

Hash functions are one-way functions. This means that in practice no message can be retrieved from its hash. It is not difficult to notice that this method of electronic signing prevents us from decrypting the document with a public key. It is necessary to attach a signed document to the data which form the digital signature on it. Then the signature is verified in the following three steps:

---

[2]For further reading, see Chap. 9 in [68].

1. The attached document is hashed with the same hash function.
2. The signature is decrypted using the public key of the presumed signatory.
3. These two values are compared. If they are identical then the signature is verified positively; otherwise not.

5.2.1 Classification of Hash Functions

In modern cryptography a hash function h is defined as an efficient algorithm taking any sequence of an arbitrary finite bit-length and returning a hash (or digest) that is a binary sequence of fixed bit length (typically between 160 and 512) such that:

1. preimage resistance—for any given hash, it is infeasible to find any input string which has this hash.
2. 2nd preimage resistance—for any given input x, it is infeasible to find any second input string x' which gives the same hash; i.e., given x, it is infeasible to find $x' \neq x$ such that $h(x') = h(x)$.
3. collision resistance—it is infeasible to find two different input strings x and x' such that $h(x) = h(x')$.

All cryptographic hash functions belong to one of two groups:

- hash functions without a parameter, i.e., whose algorithms take one input (a message);
- hash functions with a parameter, i.e., whose algorithms take two distinct inputs— a message and a secret key; called keyed hash functions.

Hash functions can be divided by usage into:

1. hash functions that are used to ensure integrity of data—MDCs (Modification Detection Codes).
2. hash functions that are used to verify the authenticity of a message—MACs (Message Authentication Codes). These functions have an extra parameter (a secret key).

In the modern cryptography paradigm hash function algorithms are public knowledge. Everyone can compute and check the hash in the case of a function without a parameter (a secret key), although to check the hash in the case of a function with a parameter one has to know the secret key.

Currently, the most often used cryptographic hash functions are SHA-1 (SHA stands for Secure Hash Algorithm) and SHA-2, which have been gradually replacing their ancestor MD5 (Message Digest). The function SHA-1 computes a 160-bit hash from a given bit string message.

All the MD/SHA-1/SHA-2 family algorithms are based on a very similar design principle. MD-5 computes a 128-bit message digest. In comparison with MD algorithms the drawback of SHA-1 is a smaller rate of coding: MD5 is approximately 20 % faster than SHA-1. SHA-1 gives a longer hash and executes more computations. SHA-2 is further enhanced: longer hash and still more computations.

Thanks to this, SHA-1 and SHA-2 are less susceptible than the MD5 algorithm to the brute force attack (searching the entire space) or differential cryptanalysis. Moreover, in MD4 and MD5 some weaknesses have been discovered which in some cases enable us to find collisions, i.e., two different messages with the same hash. There have been cryptanalytic attacks on SHA-1. Its credibility is not considered high now.

Breaking a hash function means showing that it does not have one of the above three defining properties, or any of them. In [100] three Chinese researchers published an effective method of finding two distinct messages with the same MD5-hash value. A pair of different documents with meaningful realistic contents and the same MD5-hash value were demonstrated in 2008, see [98].

The method finds also collisions in SHA-1 requiring an estimated 2^{69} SHA-1 evaluations, reduced recently to 2^{61} (see [97]). This is much faster than the birthday brute force attack, but still is not considered feasible with the currently available technology.

SHA-2 is a family of four hash algorithms: SHA-224, SHA-256, SHA-384, and SHA-512, with output hash of size 224, 256, 384, and 512 bits, respectively. It was published and specified by the US NIST Federal Information Processing Standard in 2001 (superseded by [45]). The longer hash is intended to make the algorithm harder to break.

Many experts claim that practical breaking SHA-1 is just a matter of time. For that reason more often the functions from SHA-2 are used. These have a much larger security margin, although their algorithms are derived from SHA-1. So far, the best known cryptanalytic results on them break only some of their much round-reduced variants: preimage resistance for 41 out of 64 rounds of SHA-256, collision resistance for 24 rounds of SHA-256, and preimage resistance for 46 out of 80 rounds of SHA-512; see [6].

5.2.2 Birthday Paradox and Brute Force

The birthday problem is the following: *How many people must be selected to have with probability greater than 0.5 at least two of them celebrating their birthday on the same day?*

For simplicity, we assume a year has 365 days. We ignore February 29, we ignore twins, and any seasonal irregularities in birth statistics. Possible small corrections reflecting those circumstances would not really make a significant change. The answer is: only 23. Despite an intuitive impression that many more must be required. That is why it is called a paradox.

The computations justifying the answer are not difficult. Suppose we number the participants of our experiment with $1, \ldots, 365$. We assume we start off with 365 persons. Thus every group of m participants can be identified with an m-element sequence of numbers. Such a sequence is called an m-element variation with possible repetitions from the 365-element set. There are 365^m such sequences (variations).

Consider the event opposite to the one we are interested in. That is, look for such groups of participants in which there is no pair with the same birthday. Sequences representing such groups are the m-element variations with no repetitions from the 365-element set. There are $\frac{365!}{(365-m)!}$ such sequences.

Therefore the probability of the event opposite to the one we are looking for is $\frac{(365-m)!\cdot 365^m}{365!}$. Already for $m = 23$ this number is less than 0.5. It is about 0.493. Thus the probability of occurrence of an event described in the paradox is bigger than 0.5. Notice that for $m = 22$ these numbers are about 0.52 and 0.47, respectively.

The birthday paradox has interesting consequences in cryptanalysis of hash functions. In general one can think of it in terms of probability theory. Consider an urn containing m hash values (balls numbered with all possible hash values of an n-bit hash function). One hash value (ball) is drawn randomly, its value is observed, it is then placed back in the urn (drawing with replacement), and the selection process is repeated. If m is sufficiently large, then with high probability a repeated element will be encountered after approximately $m^{\frac{1}{2}}$ ($\sqrt{m}$) selections. This result is applicable to all n-bit hash functions with $m = 2^n$. The process can be parallelized with a factor r speedup on r processors.[3]

Given an n-bit hash function h, the brute force method to search for a collision is by simply evaluating the function h at different inputs one-by-one chosen randomly (or pseudorandomly) until the same hash value is found twice. Due to the birthday paradox result, we can expect to obtain such a pair after approximately $(2^n)^{\frac{1}{2}}$ ($\sqrt{2^n}$) evaluations of h at different arguments on average.

In other words, for an n-bit hash function, there are 2^n different hash values. If these are all equally probable, then it would take approximately $2^{\frac{n}{2}}$ attempts to generate a collision using brute force. For example, if a 160-bit hash function is used, there are 2^{160} different outputs. If these are all equally probable, then it would take approximately 2^{80} attempts to find a collision using brute force.

5.2.3 MD5 Algorithm

The MD5 hash algorithm was introduced by Rivest [99] without mathematical proof that it is a good one-way cryptographic hash function. MD-5 is not recommended for use anymore for any purpose requiring collision-resistance, as its collision-resistance has been shown to be weak, as pointed out above. The algorithm takes a message in the form of a bit sequence $M = m_0, \ldots, m_{b-1}$ of any practical length b, and returns a 128-bit hash. Processing the message into a hash proceeds in four steps. The data in each step processed in 512-bit blocks divided into sixteen 32-bit words.

---

[3]For all technical details and discussion, see [68].

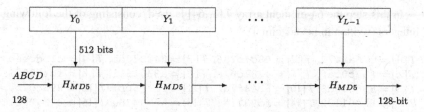

Fig. 5.3 The block scheme of processing the message in steps 2 and 3

- *Step 1*. The message is padded with additional bits in such a way that its length is 64 bits shorter than a multiple of 512 bits. The additional bits are appended even when the above mentioned condition is fulfilled, i.e., if $b \equiv 448 \pmod{512}$, where b means the initial length of the message. In such a situation the addition has length between 1 and 512 bits. First a single bit 1 is appended, then all zeros.

- *Step 2*. The remaining 64 bits represent the initial length of message M. If the initial length of M is bigger than 2^{64} (which is practically impossible: $2^{64} = 18446744073709551616$), then take its remainder modulo 2^{64}. As a result we get L 512-bit blocks $Y_0, Y_1, \ldots, Y_{L-1}$, where each block can be divided into sixteen 32-bit words.

- *Step 3*. The MD5 algorithm operates one of four variables A, B, C, and D, stored in four 32-bit registers according to the block scheme shown in Fig. 5.3 These variables have the initial values (written in hexadecimal):

$$A = \texttt{01234567}, \quad B = \texttt{89abcdef}, \quad C = \texttt{fedcba98}, \quad D = \texttt{76543210}.$$

- *Step 4*. In this step four auxiliary functions are used each of which takes three 32-bit words and outputs one 32-bit word. These are the following functions:

$$F(X, Y, Z) = (X \text{ and } Y) \text{ or } \big((\text{not } X) \text{ and } Z\big), \tag{5.1}$$

$$G(X, Y, Z) = (X \text{ and } Z) \text{ or } \big(Y \text{ and } (\text{not } Z)\big), \tag{5.2}$$

$$H(X, Y, Z) = X \text{ xor } Y \text{ xor } Z, \tag{5.3}$$

$$I(X, Y, Z) = Y \text{ xor } \big(X \text{ or } (\text{not } Z)\big). \tag{5.4}$$

These functions work on suitable bit blocks X, Y, Z according to the array:

X Y Z	F G H I
0 0 0	0 0 0 1
0 0 1	1 0 1 0
0 1 0	0 1 1 0
0 1 1	1 0 0 1
1 0 0	0 0 1 1
1 0 1	0 1 0 1
1 1 0	1 1 0 0
1 1 1	1 1 1 0

In this step the 64-element array $T[1..64]$ is used, consisting of the following integers (written in hexadecimal):

$T[\,1] = \text{d76aa478}$, $T[\,2] = \text{e8c7b756}$, $T[\,3] = \text{242070db}$, $T[\,4] = \text{c1bdceee}$,
$T[\,5] = \text{f57c0faf}$, $T[\,6] = \text{4787c62a}$, $T[\,7] = \text{a8304613}$, $T[\,8] = \text{fd469501}$,
$T[\,9] = \text{698098d8}$, $T[10] = \text{8b44f7af}$, $T[11] = \text{ffff5bb1}$, $T[12] = \text{895cd7be}$,
$T[13] = \text{6b901122}$, $T[14] = \text{fd987193}$, $T[15] = \text{a679438e}$, $T[16] = \text{49b40821}$,
$T[17] = \text{f61e2562}$, $T[18] = \text{c040b340}$, $T[19] = \text{265e5a51}$, $T[20] = \text{e9b6c7aa}$,
$T[21] = \text{d62f105d}$, $T[22] = \text{02441453}$, $T[23] = \text{d8a1e681}$, $T[24] = \text{e7d3fbc8}$,
$T[25] = \text{21e1cde6}$, $T[26] = \text{c33707d6}$, $T[27] = \text{f4d50d87}$, $T[28] = \text{455a14ed}$,
$T[29] = \text{a9e3e905}$, $T[30] = \text{fcefa3f8}$, $T[31] = \text{676f02d9}$, $T[32] = \text{8d2a4c8a}$,
$T[33] = \text{fffa3942}$, $T[34] = \text{8771f681}$, $T[35] = \text{6d9d6122}$, $T[36] = \text{fde5380c}$,
$T[37] = \text{a4beea44}$, $T[38] = \text{4bdecfa9}$, $T[39] = \text{f6bb4b60}$, $T[40] = \text{bebfbc70}$,
$T[41] = \text{289b7ec6}$, $T[42] = \text{eaa127fa}$, $T[43] = \text{d4ef3085}$, $T[44] = \text{04881d05}$,
$T[45] = \text{d9d4d039}$, $T[46] = \text{e6db99e5}$, $T[47] = \text{1fa27cf8}$, $T[48] = \text{c4ac5665}$,
$T[49] = \text{f4292244}$, $T[50] = \text{432aff97}$, $T[51] = \text{ab9423a7}$, $T[52] = \text{fc93a039}$,
$T[53] = \text{655b59c3}$, $T[54] = \text{8f0ccc92}$, $T[55] = \text{ffeff47d}$, $T[56] = \text{85845dd1}$,
$T[57] = \text{6fa87e4f}$, $T[58] = \text{fe2ce6e0}$, $T[59] = \text{a3014314}$, $T[60] = \text{4e0811a1}$,
$T[61] = \text{f7537e82}$, $T[62] = \text{bd3af235}$, $T[63] = \text{2ad7d2bb}$, $T[64] = \text{eb86d391}$.

The entries of the array T are determined from the formula

$$T[i] = E\left(2^{32} \cdot |\sin(i)|\right) = E\left(4294967296 \cdot |\sin(i)|\right),$$

where i is given in radians and $E(\cdot)$ means the largest integer not greater than the expression in brackets. Let $M[0, 1, \ldots, N-1]$ stand for 32-bit words of the padded messages L 512-bit blocks. In this case $N = 16 \cdot L$, and every block Y_q consists of 16 words $M[j]$, $j = 0, 1, \ldots, 15$. In this step each 16-word block Y_q is processed as follows:

for $q := 0$ to $L - 1$ do
for $j := 0$ to 15 do
$X[j] := M[16 \cdot q + j]$; (copy the next word into array X.)
$AA := A$; $BB := B$; $CC := C$; $DD := D$; remember the initial values of registers $ABCD$

Round 1. (Let $[abcd\ k\ s\ i]$ denotes of the operation

$$a := b + \left(\left(a + F(b, c, d) + X[k] + T[i]\right) <<< s\right).$$

Here $(B) <<< s$ means the 32-bit word obtained by the cyclic shift of word B of s positions to the left, the variables a, b, c and d mean also some 32-bit words, F is the function determined by formula (5.1), T is the array defined above, and $+$ denotes addition of 32-bit words without carrying (addition modulo 2^{32}).)

Do the 16 following operations (the order of the operation corresponds to the order of reading text in Indo-European languages (left to right and top to bottom)):

[ABCD 0 7 1]	[DABC 1 12 2]	[CDAB 2 17 3]	[BCDA 3 22 4]
[ABCD 4 7 5]	[DABC 5 12 6]	[CDAB 6 17 7]	[BCDA 7 22 8]
[ABCD 8 7 9]	[DABC 9 12 10]	[CDAB 10 17 11]	[BCDA 11 22 12]
[ABCD 12 7 13]	[DABC 13 12 14]	[CDAB 14 17 15]	[BCDA 15 22 16]

Round 2. (Let [abcd k s i] denote the operation

$$a := b + \big((a + G(b, c, d) + X[k] + T[i]) <\!<\!< s\big).$$

Here G is the function defined by formula (5.2), the other symbols are as in round 1.)

Do the following 16 operations:

[ABCD 1 5 17]	[DABC 6 9 18]	[CDAB 11 14 19]	[BCDA 0 20 20]
[ABCD 5 5 21]	[DABC 10 9 22]	[CDAB 15 14 23]	[BCDA 4 20 24]
[ABCD 9 5 25]	[DABC 14 9 26]	[CDAB 3 14 27]	[BCDA 8 20 28]
[ABCD 13 5 29]	[DABC 2 9 30]	[CDAB 7 14 31]	[BCDA 12 20 32]

Round 3. (Let [abcd k s i] denote the operation

$$a := b + \big((a + H(b, c, d) + X[k] + T[i]) <\!<\!< s\big),$$

Here H is the function defined by formula (5.3), the other symbols are as in round 1.)

Do the following 16 operations:

[ABCD 5 4 33]	[DABC 8 11 34]	[CDAB 11 16 35]	[BCDA 14 23 36]
[ABCD 1 4 37]	[DABC 4 11 38]	[CDAB 7 16 39]	[BCDA 10 23 40]
[ABCD 13 4 41]	[DABC 0 11 42]	[CDAB 3 16 43]	[BCDA 6 23 44]
[ABCD 9 4 45]	[DABC 12 11 46]	[CDAB 15 16 47]	[BCDA 2 23 48]

Round 4. (Let [abcd k s i] denote the operation

$$a := b + \big((a + I(b, c, d) + X[k] + T[i]) <\!<\!< s\big),$$

Here I is the function defined by the formula (5.4), the other symbols are as in round 1.)

Do the following 16 operations:

[ABCD 0 6 49]	[DABC 7 10 50]	[CDAB 14 15 51]	[BCDA 5 21 52]
[ABCD 12 6 53]	[DABC 3 10 54]	[CDAB 10 15 55]	[BCDA 1 21 56]
[ABCD 8 6 57]	[DABC 15 10 58]	[CDAB 6 15 59]	[BCDA 13 21 60]
[ABCD 4 6 61]	[DABC 11 10 62]	[CDAB 2 15 63]	[BCDA 9 21 64]

Compute the new value of the registers ABCD.

End of loop q.
Return ABCD.

The algorithm outputs 128-bit message digest M, that is the content of the·last computed registers $ABCD$. The MD5 algorithm is easy to implement on 32-bit processors, and computation is fast. It is a corrected version of the MD4 algorithm, in which some weaknesses were shown. The MD5 algorithm had been considered very strong until the work [100].

5.2.4 SHA-1 Algorithm

The SHA-1 algorithm, similar to MD5, was designed by the NIST in cooperation with NSA and published as a federal standard FIPS PUB 180 in 1993. The abbreviation SHA stands for: secure hash algorithm. The input is a message of any length less than 2^{64} (18446744073709551616) bits, and the output is a 160-bit hash value.

- *Step 1*. The message is padded in the same way as in the MD5 algorithm.
- *Step 2*. At the end of this message 64 bits are added, including the information about the length of the message before padding (Fig. 5.4). These bits are treated as a binary number, written in a processor convention used in Sun computers, where the most significant byte of the word is located in the first position (unlike in Intel processors), which probably speeds up the rate of processing. After this activity the message from which the hash is executed consists of n 512-bit blocks. Every block is treated as sixteen 32-bit words: $M = M[0], M[1], \ldots, M[16n-1]$. Then initialize the auxiliary variables h_1, h_2, h_3, h_4, h_5:

$$h_1 = 67452301$$
$$h_2 = \texttt{efcdab89}$$
$$h_3 = \texttt{98badcfe}$$
$$h_4 = 10325476$$
$$h_5 = \texttt{c3d2e1f0}$$

and take the following values for the constants $y_1, \ldots, y_4$:

$$y_1 = 5\texttt{a}827999$$
$$y_2 = 6\texttt{ed9eba1}$$
$$y_3 = 8\texttt{f1bbcdc}$$
$$y_4 = \texttt{ca62c1d6}.$$

- *Step 3*. This step is the main loop of the algorithm in which the n 512-bit blocks are processed. For $i = 0, 1, \ldots, n-1$ every block of sixteen 32-bit words is copied into the temporary memory $X[j] := M[16i + j], 0 \le j \le 15$ and expanded into an 80-word block: for $j = 16, 17, \ldots, 79$ do

$$\big((X[j] := X[j-3] \oplus X[j-8] \oplus X[j-14] \oplus X[j-16]\big) <<< 1\big).$$

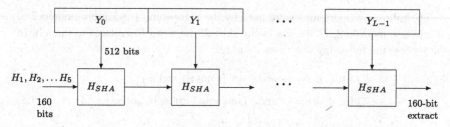

Fig. 5.4 The block scheme of processing the message in steps 2 and 3

The variables H_1, H_2, H_3, H_4, H_5 are initialized:

$$(H_1, H_2, H_3, H_4, H_5) := (h_1, h_2, h_3, h_4, h_5)$$

And variables A, B, C, D, E:

$$(A, B, C, D, E) := (H_1, H_2, H_3, H_4, H_5)$$

And the extended block is processed in four 20-step rounds:

- Round 1. For $j = 0, 1, \ldots, 19$ do

$$t := \big((A <<< 5) + f(B, C, D) + E + X[j] + y_1\big)$$

$$(A, B, C, D, E) := (t, A, B <<< 30, C, D)$$

- Round 2. For $j = 20, 21, \ldots, 39$ do

$$t := \big((A <<< 5) + h(B, C, D) + E + X[j] + y_2\big)$$

$$(A, B, C, D, E) := (t, A, B <<< 30, C, D)$$

- Round 3. For $j = 40, 41, \ldots, 59$ do

$$t := \big((A <<< 5) + g(B, C, D) + E + X[j] + y_3\big)$$

$$(A, B, C, D, E) := (t, A, B <<< 30, C, D)$$

- Round 4. For $j = 60, 61, \ldots, 79$ do

$$t := \big((A <<< 5) + h(B, C, D) + E + X[j] + y_4\big)$$

$$(A, B, C, D, E) := (t, A, B <<< 30, C, D)$$

After these rounds the auxiliary variables $H_1, \ldots, H_5$ must be updated:

$$(H_1, H_2, H_3, H_4, H_5) := (H_1 + A, H_2 + B, H_3 + C, H_4 + D, H_5 + E)$$

and we go on to process the next block.
- *Step 4.* The output is the concatenation of the final values of H_1, H_2, H_3, H_4, H_5.

The following operations were used by the algorithm: $+$ addition modulo 2^{32}, $\oplus$ addition modulo 2, $U <<< s$ cyclic shift of the word U s places to the left. In the process the following functions are used:

$$f(u, v, w) = (u \text{ and } v) \text{ or } \big((\text{ not } u) \text{ and } w\big),$$

$$g(u, v, w) = (u \text{ and } v) \text{ or } (u \text{ and } w) \text{ or } (v \text{ and } w), \qquad (5.5)$$

$$h(u, v, w) = u \text{ xor } v \text{ xor } w.$$

The presented algorithm gives a 160-bit hash, that is 32 bits longer than that of MD5, which is more secure. Both algorithms were designed for 32-bit processors. SHA-1 is easier to implement but its execution takes roughly 25 % more time than MD5.

5.2.5 Keccak/SHA-3

In 2007, the US National Institute of Standards and Technology (NIST) announced a public contest aimed at selection of a new standard for a cryptographic hash function. Similarities between the designs of SHA-1 and the more recent standard SHA-2 seem worrisome and NIST decided that a new, stronger hash function is needed. At the end of 2010 five finalists were nominated: BLAKE [7], Groestl [90], JH [16], Keccak [15], and Skein [40]. With perfectly transparent rules, the entire course of the SHA-3 competition was actively monitored by all concerned around the world, with all the submissions made available for international public examination and criticism, and Keccak (pronounced *catch-ack*) was announced the winner in October 2012, [73]. (For more on the SHA-3 competition, see http://csrc.nist.gov/groups/ST/hash/sha-3/.)

The NIST Selection Conclusion declared that *any of the five finalists would have made an acceptable choice for SHA-3 standard as excellent hash algorithms, providing acceptable performance and security properties*. NIST chose Keccak mostly due to its fundamentally new design that is entirely different and unrelated to the SHA-1 and SHA-2 constructions, making it a reasonable complement to the SHA-2 standard. It is unlikely that any single cryptanalytic attack would compromise both SHA-2 and Keccak simultaneously.

Keccak demonstrates also a remarkable entirely new kind of relatively compact nature. With its flexible construction parameters, it can operate on much smaller states, conceivably useful also as lightweight alternatives for so-called embedded or smart devices with limited resources (memory, energy, computational power) that connect to electronic networks but are not themselves full-fledged computers. Examples include sensors in future wide security systems and home appliances that can be controlled remotely.

As of writing (August 2013), NIST is in the process of standardization and specification of SHA-3, to update the Secure Hash Standard. According to its time-

Table 5.1 Preimage and collision attacks on the SHA-3 finalists with the highest number of broken rounds

Function	Attack	Broken	Rounds	Complexity	Reference
Blake-256	preimage	2.5	(14)	2^{241}	[63]
Blake-256	collision	1	(14)	practical	[50]
Gröstl-256	collision	3	(10)	2^{64}	[90]
JH-512	preimage	42	(42)	2^{507}	[16]
JH-256	collision	2	(42)	practical	[50]
Keccak-512	preimage	8	(24)	$2^{511.5}$	[13]
Keccak-256	collision	5	(24)	2^{115}	[34]
Skein-512	preimage	72	(72)	$2^{511.76}$	[56]
Skein-512	collision	14	(72)	$2^{254.5}$	[55]

line [72], a draft for public comments is to be announced by October, 2013, and the final SHA-3 US FIPS standard publication is expected by mid-2014. Although SHA-2 is still considered secure and recommended by NIST, SHA-1 is recommended only for some applications that do not require collision resistance, see [71].

Table 5.1 shows the cryptanalytic attacks against the SHA-3 competition finalists known so far. The attacks listed here are those with the highest number of rounds reached in a given class of the attack. The total number of rounds is shown next to the number of broken rounds.

The rest of this section presents the Keccak algorithm. (All details can be found in the original specification [15].)

Keccak uses the sponge construction [14]. Keccak has two main parameters r and c, called bitrate and capacity, respectively. The sum of these two parameters makes the state size, which Keccak operates on. In the SHA-3 proposal the state size is 1600 bits. Different values for bitrate and capacity give trade-offs between speed and security. A higher bitrate gives a faster function at the expense of a lower security.

For the variants proposed to the SHA-3 contest, the value of the parameter c is equal to the hash length multiplied by 2. For example, the SHA-3 candidate with 512-bit hash length is Keccak with $c = 1024$ and $r = 576$ ($r + c = 1600$). We denote the variants proposed as the SHA-3 submission candidates by Keccak-224, Keccak-256, Keccak-384, and Keccak-512. (The number at the end of the name specifies the hash length.)

The number r of message bits processed per block permutation depends on the output hash size. The rate r is 1152, 1088, 832 or 576, for 224, 256, 384 and 512-bit hash sizes, respectively (with 64-bit words). To ensure the message can be evenly divided into r-bit blocks, it is padded with a 1 bit, zero or more 0 bits, and a final 1 bit. A state can be visualised as an array of 5×5 lanes, where each lane is a 64-bit word, see Fig. 5.5. The initial 1600-bit state is filled with 0's.

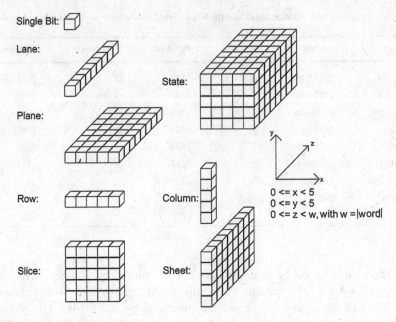

Fig. 5.5 Keccak construction terms

The state size determines the number of rounds in Keccak-f block permutation function. For the default 1600-bit state, there are 24 rounds. All rounds are the same except for round constants. Each round consists of the following 5 steps.

```
Round(A,RC) {
  Θ step
    C[x] = A[x,0] xor A[x,1] xor A[x,2] xor
    A[x,3] xor A[x,4], forall x in (0...4)
    D[x] = C[x-1] xor rot(C[x+1],1),
      forall x in (0...4)
    A[x,y] = A[x,y] xor D[x],
      forall (x,y) in (0...4,0...4)
  ρ step forall (x,y) in (0...4,0...4)
    A[x,y] = rot(A[x,y], r[x,y]),
  π step forall (x,y) in (0...4,0...4)
    B[y,2*x+3*y] = A[x,y],
  λ step forall (x,y) in (0...4,0...4)
    A[x,y] = B[x,y] xor ((not B[x+1,y]) and B[x+2,y]),
  ι step
    A[0,0] = A[0,0] xor RC
return A }
```

Here, index arithmetic on the first two indices x and y is performed modulo 5. A denotes the complete permutation state array and A[x,y] denotes a particular lane in that state. `B[x,y]`,`C[x]`,`D[x]` are 64-bit intermediate variables. The constants r[x,y] are the rotation offsets, while `RC` are the round constants. `rot(W,m)` is the usual bitwise rotation moving bit at position i into position $i+m$ in the lane `W`. ($i+m$ is calculated modulo 64, which is the lane size.) Θ is a linear operation that provides diffusion to the state. ρ is a permutation that mixes bits of a lane using rotation and π permutes lanes. The only non-linear operation is λ. Finally, ι XORs the round constant with the first lane.

Keccak follows the sponge two-phase processing. In the first phase (called absorbing), the succeeding message block is XORed into the state leading bits and permutation Keccak-f is applied. The absorbing phase is finished when all message blocks have been processed. In the second phase (called squeezing), the first r bits of the state are returned as building the output bits, interleaved with applications of the permutation Keccak-f. The squeezing phase is finished after the desired length of the output digest has been produced.

Chapter 6
PGP Systems and TrueCrypt

6.1 PGP System

PGP is a security software package developed in the USA in 1991 (and originally maintained) by Philip Zimmermann. It supports strong symmetric and public-key encryption and decryption for privacy, confidentiality and authentication of data and network communication, with digital signatures based originally on a web of trust certificates. Its services include key management, entity authentication, and digital signatures. The package incorporates the best modern cryptographic algorithms and protocols. There have been many versions of PGP; e.g., the open source OpenPGP standard specified by RFC 4880, and implemented as GNU Privacy Guard (GnuPG or GPG), with its variants GPG4Win and FireGPG for Firefox. There is a mobile web-based encryption service that uses a downloaded Java applet to encrypt and decrypt email in your browser. There are also commercial versions. PGP and Pretty Good Privacy are registered trademarks of the American software company PGP Corporation, now part of Symantec. The latter allows the public to download the source code for peer review, in this way maintaining public confidence in the product.

6.1.1 The Idea and the History of PGP

PGP was in some sense a response to the US government policy which wanted to relax the laws which guaranteed the privacy of different forms of interpersonal communication (traditional post, telephones and e-mails) in order to enable the police and other services to carry out surveillance of suspected criminals. American society became more sensitive to their rights guaranteed by the constitution. The public was afraid that the new technology could lead to abuse and the laws to prosecute the criminals can turn against ordinary citizens, e.g., during election campaigns.

Currently PGP is the most modern, well-known and commonly used cryptographic system all over the world. Even the most advanced computer users are satisfied with operating PGP.

C. Kościelny et al., *Modern Cryptography Primer*,
DOI 10.1007/978-3-642-41386-5_6, © Springer-Verlag Berlin Heidelberg 2013

The first commonly known and used PGP version was PGP 2.3a—the version available on the market since 1993. In this version, as in later versions until PGP 5.0, RSA was used as the asymmetric encryption algorithm, IDEA as the symmetric cipher, and MD5 as the one way function. The 2.3a version enabled generation and use of RSA keys of 1024-bit length. In subsequent versions of PGP the capability of the system was increased. New encryption techniques were added and the length of the encryption for generation and use was increased. Improvements in PGP 5 included a new asymmetric algorithm: the Digital Signature Algorithm, DSA (known also as DSS—Digital Signature Standard); new stronger symmetric ciphers: 3DES and CAST; and hash functions: SHA-1 and RIPEMD-160. The DSA algorithm was added because of patent restrictions on the RSA algorithm (the patent expired in 2000).

According to US export regulations (ITAR), which classified advanced encryption algorithms as military technology, it was not possible legally to export the PGP software from the USA. Those regulations limited only the electronic version of the software. The export of the printed source code (the algorithm) was not restricted by ITAR. That is why PGP Inc. released the full PGP source code in the form of a 14-volume book which was legally taken outside the USA and scanned by Ståle Schumacher, the former coordinator of the international version of PGP. It took about 1000 hours in cooperation with 70 people from across Europe. This procedure was conducted to avoid any accusation against Phil Zimmermann connected with PGP version 2.6.3i which was written in the USA and was used in Europe.

In 1998 the rights to the PGP software were bought by Network Associates Inc. (NAI). From then on PGP enlarged its capability. From an encryption program used mainly in e-mails, PGP transformed into a complex product which enabled the creation of private virtual encryption networks, the use of X.509 protocols and the encryption of logical disks.

In 1998–2001 the PGP software produced by NAI was a commercial product. It also supported other functions besides signing and encrypting data. Subsequent PGP versions included among other things software to secure a Windows system. In May 2001 Phil Zimmermann left NAI, because he disagreed with the corporation's use of PGP. In 2002 NAI announced the suspension of commercial support for PGP as encryption software. In August 2002 the PGP product line was finally sold by NAI to the newly established PGP Corporation.

Currently, the rights to the PGP software are owned by Symantec Corporation, which offers a wide range of products designed to ensure a suitable level of security of computer systems. Some of the proposed solutions are listed below:

1. *PGP Universal Gateway Email*—an application that provides centrally managed e-mail encryption in order to secure communication with customers and partners.
2. *PGP Desktop Email*—software that is used in desktop computers and laptops. It offers automatic e-mail encryption. The application works as a proxy server, and automatically detects keys and certificates of two e-mail encryption standards used globally: OpenPGP and S/MIME.
3. *PGP Universal Server*—an application that provides organizations with a single console to manage multiple encryption applications from the PGP Platform.

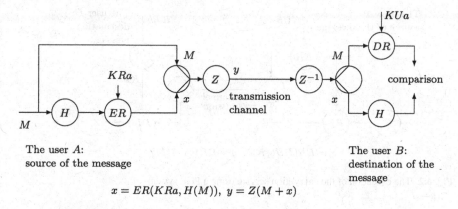

$$x = ER(KRa, H(M)), \quad y = Z(M + x)$$

Fig. 6.1 The execution of service authentication by a PGP system

4. *PGP Key Management Server*—a system that provides companies with tools to manage encryption keys. It enables centralized management of cryptographic techniques in a whole enterprise.

6.1.2 PGP Algorithms

In general a PGP system provides five services:

- *Encryption*. The messages are encrypted by the IDEA algorithm using a one-time session key, generated by the sender. The RSA algorithm and the public key of the recipient are used to encrypt the session key. The encrypted session key is enclosed in the sent cryptogram.
- *Digital signature*. Using the MD5 algorithm a digest is created, which is a compressed version of a message. The digest added into the message, is encrypted by the sender using their private key.
- *Compression*. Before sending or saving on a disk the message can be compressed using the ZIP program.
- *E-mail compatibility*. Messages can be independent from the e-mail system using a radix-64 conversion after encryption.
- *Segmentation*. To fulfil conditions which limit the size of e-mails, PGP can use the segmentation and defragmentation (desegmentation) on longer messages.

Discussing in detail these services, we use the following designations: *ER*—the RSA coder, *EI*—the IDEA coder, *DR*—the RSA descrambler, *DI*—the RSA descrambler, *Z*—the compression, Z^{-1}—the decompression, *H*—the MD5 hash function, *KRa*, *KUa*—the private and public keys of the user *A*, *KRb*, *KUb*—the private and public keys of the user *B*, *Ks*—the session key.

The execution of service authentication is shown in Fig. 6.1 The sender edits the message *M* and using the MD5 algorithm the sender creates a 128-bit digest

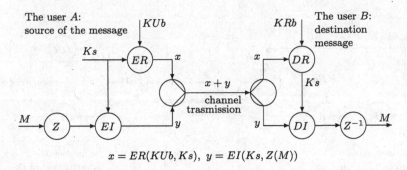

$$x = ER(KUb, Ks), \quad y = EI(Ks, Z(M))$$

Fig. 6.2 The execution of the encryption service using a PGP system

of that message. The encryption of the digest is executed using the RSA algorithm and the private key of the sender KRa. To the encrypted digest $ER(KRa, H(M))$ the message M is attached. After compressing the data, it is sent to the recipient.

At the receiving end the decompression of the data takes place, resulting in the message with the encrypted extract; and these two components are separated. The encrypted result of hashing the message M is decrypted by the public key of the sender, using the operation $DR(KUa, ER(KRa, H(M))) = H(M)$ and simultaneously the extract of the unencrypted message M is computed. Comparing these shortcuts determines the authenticity of the received message.

In a PGP system the method of executing a digital signature is a combination of the RSA and MD5 algorithms. Assuming the reliability of the RSA system, the recipient of the message has a guarantee that only the owner of the private key KRa can have created the extract $H(M)$ of the message M if the signatures received and reproduced based on the received message are the same.

The principle of the execution of the message encryption service using PGP system is illustrated in Fig. 6.2. The service encrypts messages to be sent by e-mail or saved to a disk. Encryption uses the IDEA algorithm with a 128-bit key working in the encryption mode with feedback with the initial vector in the form of the zero sequence. The key Ks is a one-time key generated randomly for each message and which accompanies the given message.

During the execution of this service the sender edits the message and then randomly generates a 128-bit number, which is the key Ks to the encryption and decryption of the message. The compressed message $Z(M)$ is encrypted, resulting in the message cryptogram $y = EI(Ks, Z(M))$. At the same time the key Ks is encrypted using the RSA algorithm: $x = ER(KUb, Ks)$. The data is sent to the recipient, beginning with x. At the receiving side the recipient decrypts the session key $Ks = DR(KRb, x)$, and then the compressed message $Z(M) = DI(Ks, y)$. The last stage of receiving the encrypted message is the decompression of the message M.

It is worth noticing that using the RSA system facilitates the distribution of the keys and guarantees that only the recipient can decrypt the key Ks of the cryptogram. That is why the PGP system proposes the usage of three kinds of keys for RSA:

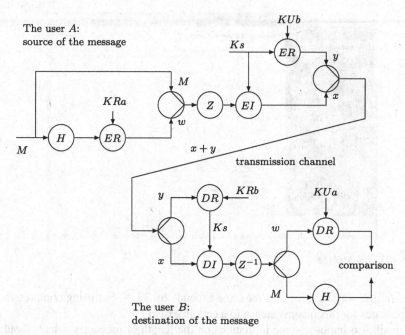

Fig. 6.3 The execution of the encryption and authentication service using a PGP system

- a casual key, 324 bits, possible to break using a lot of work,
- a 512-bit commercial key, probably possible to break by the NSA, with their fastest computers worldwide,
- a 2048-bit military key, impossible to break in the foreseeable future.

The most complicated service is the simultaneous authentication and encryption of a sent message. The scheme of the execution of this service is shown in Fig. 6.3 First the extract of M is calculated, that is $H(M)$. Then the calculated extract is encrypted using RSA and the private key of the sender: $w = ER(KRa, H(M))$. The encrypted shortcut is attached to the message M and the result is compressed. The received data is encrypted using the IDEA algorithm: $x = EI(Ks, Z(w + M))$, and to this is added the encrypted RSA system session key $y = ER(KUb, Ks)$; the result is sent to the recipient. At the receiving side the session key is recreated, using which the compressed data including message M and the encrypted extract are decrypted. Next the extract is decrypted, and is compared with the shortcut calculated at the receiving side, and it is determined whether the received message is authentic.

When sending the encrypted messages, some requirements imposed by e-mail systems must be observed. Almost every system demands that sent messages must use the 128-symbol ASCII code. Encryption results in a stream of arbitrary octets which usually extends beyond the range of such a code. To cope with these requirements, the PGP system changes the octet stream of the cryptogram into a printable octet stream, using the conversion called radix-64. Such a conversion means the exchange of every triple of adjacent octets into four printable symbols of ASCII

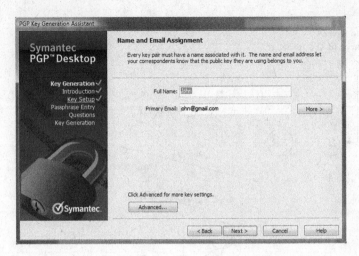

Fig. 6.4 Key generation

code. In this way the size of a message expands by 33 %, but using compression compensates for this inconvenience to a certain extent.

E-mail also imposes some limitations on the length of messages, which should not consist of more than 50 kilobytes. In such a situation every longer message must be divided into smaller parts and every part must be sent separately. The PGP system executes such a segmentation and defragmentation (desegmentation) automatically.

6.1.3 The Use of PGP

Below we briefly present the installation process and capabilities of the PGP system in its free version PGP^{TM} Desktop Version 10.2 for Windows offered by Symantec Corporation. The necessary installation files and information can be found at www. pgp.com. The installation process starts in a standard way, by running the file *PGPDesktopWin32-10.2.0MP3*.

Installation uses Wizard and can easily be performed even by beginners. At some point the system displays a dialog box asking whether encryption keys have been generated, or it will even find the keys, provided they have been generated and reported to one of the PGP servers.

In case the keys have not been generated, the system is capable of generating keys in different cryptosystems and of different sizes. Keys for the RSA algorithm may be up to 4096 bits long. During the key generation process we input, among other things, the applied encryption system (one has to remember that RSA is not supported by some older PGP versions). It is also possible to limit the lifetime of the key, e.g., for one year (see Figs. 6.4, and 6.5).

Next, we enter the password for our key. Let us pay attention to the security level of the given password that is signalled by the computer. The password should

Fig. 6.5 Key generation

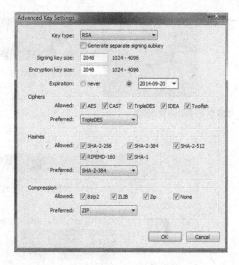

Fig. 6.6 Key generation

consist of at least eight symbols. It is recommended to include digits and other unusual characters. It should be emphasized, however, that not only do we have to ensure a high security level by providing a long and complicated password, but the password needs to be remembered perfectly, as forgetting it makes it impossible to apply the encryption keys impossible to be applied.

After the password is provided, the generator begins to generate encryption keys, starting with a public key and then generating a corresponding private key (Fig. 6.6). It should be stressed that generating long keys (i.e., longer than 2048) may take several minutes. In extreme cases it is even advisable to break the key generation process and then start it over again.

Fig. 6.7 Key manager

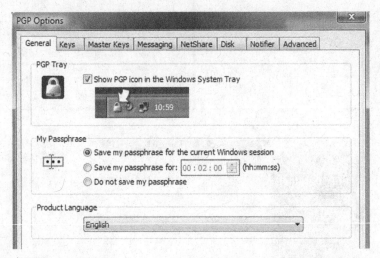

Fig. 6.8 PGP Options/General

When generated, public and private keys are stored in special files: *pubring.pkr* and *secring.skr*. After the generation process the generator finishes its work and suggests to restart the computer.

In order to manage encryption keys, the *PGP Desktop* file should be run, which makes the program display a dialog box (Fig. 6.7).

The dialog box lists all currently available encryption keys. They may be pairs of keys (private and public) or public keys of our friends, co-workers or business partners.

In the *Tools* menu an *Options* bookmark is available, which allows us to configure the encryption program system. Setting a suitable configuration is crucial for efficient and proper use of the program.

For example the *General/My Passphrase* section is responsible for the temporary automatic use of an unencrypted key. Options available within this section allow to store passwords to keys (during a whole session of cooperation with the program or temporarily, for example, for two minutes). Moreover, it is possible to set a requirement for typing the password each time when using a given encryption key. This option is the most secure (Fig. 6.8).

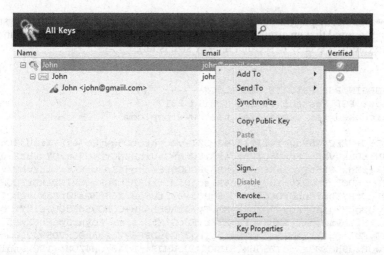

Fig. 6.9 Key manager

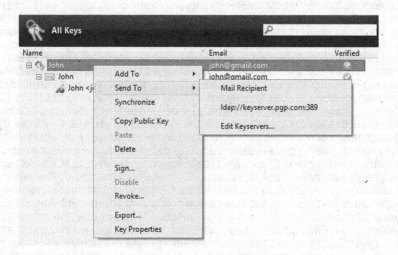

Fig. 6.10 Key manager

The PGP program allows us to export encryption keys outside the system. This is needed for two reasons. First, if we want to receive encrypted mail, we have to share our public key with others. Second, it may happen that we want to keep our private key somewhere else than on our computer (a CD, etc.).

In order to export an encryption key we can use the *Export* option when we simply click the key with the right mouse button (Fig. 6.9). The key can also be sent directly via e-mail by means of the *Send to/Mail Recipient* option (Fig. 6.10).

The software allows us to export both a public key and a pair of keys. The exported key is kept in a text file with a *.asc* extension.

Now, we can display its contents, e.g., using Notepad. Let us look at the key size. Keeping in mind that an arbitrary ASCII character is represented by eight bits in the binary system, it is easy to see that the key size is large.

-----BEGİN PGP PRIVATE KEY BLOCK-----
Version: PGP Desktop 10.2.0 (Build 2317) -
not licensed for commercial use: www.pgp.com

lQPGBE9E+dEBCAC5Vhwo14lITIE/eJD8ZI+vZcynrQtD8qwjSoI4zKVYiaU32tnK
PcXmJN5EDMk0vhRufFmnN5QIXhzJ49klYCngxGtUrhHZNCrD4U95m/OYx0ZhZl0h
ch3mIkgzMqxCFP56FYozaKSC3qLvhB89RGGC0PEeacoj4ZpAueRKir6lhzubT/vk
wVEFXDvvWDO7yRb79XymYu0juQsp6E1scj0fWlfkN9B5bFGRgqGx7WXAxBrFCQH9
K4D10YWCfP7Nbb7cnnNFOCa9UEWUO6qMC5wwP1fVS5s2X6853Gs1JnE5XuvebQI0
ZCs8r8bcq8H9gjAQ/nqyc9QzbP3iSlyTy/4rABEBAAH+CQMC35dK5QUJelCYY2bU
FVt+52ESfLhVrmQ5kfyAMrRwprneHTKbYE8oG1XtS5s/me7RdynrJpdHhFXxFz+b
M2pGeGyEDliQgfY2BeW+1wOMGW6er2UIFg2cG45DFK6PYcPeAhCCxVD594YSCGev
XL0F1wOEzd9HOEO9zSqcYZ3dbMT5lUKMWSUcVMJSipESA0/QM4ZUMi/TDQZPnnlt
PL1P0SgjWgtxMKVDLx64uocPJsVXEDzpJeARRDtnybCFTvz7RutAT50y/fYHmpky
aG/Czwi/IKPooP0GgIicSoJMS3wGDrKhgWADyolGEG/jwwmmO89A5/7wVAEi8kpK
qaJeyVrsEZkpDXm4bp0AGtN9KTm4vATlqMSentfVAgvekoYB29Jsdh54sJr1sXjF
ethet2l5vfLtfRT6DcWAL5VXryKhtjPFr9WWBkOTKF2zfSS1IG2Spn6VY7SdDgf5
vdOcKjVFd1cAea7g/JV331RN8LBb+hA/R5Ic2xtsPapqhtBm/C/CxlbAGWj4+aKv
HfaE0IgjGHQmn+1G88EukqpkB/sRiu1ZHnzthXG4tH8WRG6YtBwnrg6hRcQgQSm+
YLGSzBwStGE7uLTQbaAp5cxssL21AO+IbEmHbMock1//nUF2130Lb6LVoTB33H49
/gx7ERX6sfnL4vhNvopptBhxOw+WjLFZWbn68agQR2ybiwPN45NsD1/ZgNM85YFA
bhd9ROAsPrfIfADXL8hdVc2+/CE+xJ3HecnfS2OopGJ1z8sh4y4GpWDinEZKLCH0
j/+yPmqsWtXKIMhcz9t/Oiqd0iBaPKxYNx7KHaWSq1qiO+vKx1nKIz1Jl/1v2Zfj
LYwEFotshi5KxOYv8wcpCCMP+28cG8TH2krnCJOjN9DbPlSyGFjIOKE5gLiRYfRO
O8TTXeY/szgCtB9NaXJlayA8Y3J5cHRvZ3JhcGh5QGdtYWlpbC5jb20+nQPGBE9E
+dIBCADGUHUgcSE/MVp/zzvX3g5NXIEzPYJlIvgJBo2kJGJmvgeruHODEAF2sBX1
LhdHFWgaFn2fC4wdnOhQyx3+LOjb8TBdGu1CgHDhUYoWCe1nw1avywvrDZeJcTrs
E2N4Jpdfd+KvH13q8yH7PlJntFwIda2LSE0hFQpUR/ozL8JPyCLNr9LrDWO+1Xsm
6DWqJL7Pyf166GxPSrvVU1CE8L1FOOkYzoAmyZVwtp00okYEtSM/gU2F0usnJYR2
SX926hzoKX7VQt+PmuRYPY8xOrzbW6KXh2bDJfW+MKoR/sPLIAUQOEoe0MMYLIM6
mMkMqRyxrUDYOw+6HqvK+tkZ60H1ABEBAAH+CQMCfGrVlSCirUmYzNOyHsWzl61D
pAmgNOgEL2GUbWBBLBVYeXJ10U27+KZqamdh50b6tj4gQMHCobKRj9WmfB7TSH2O
SsqPsPsTrLjoJtwhDs5XUzJyz1Lv07io8jnMEf0EDR9D0JpXgz+nfY8dRYaUGiF7
c5c1Wlzyw65hrLQFcODeNtY2eHSQ6NS2QOIeFFa5lvyHYA+2E0XKVgLN521Kgn1T
bhy0lWQpuw/cnbLZdKfe7NS6m6QcWRUzYesbAX9yZ43DUOCGuU5h9IEXetZNxPdn
EkDvaj8zsXLtYm9TuVAq+a4P2UrFHI/aghx6dcSxvQv0DyFnS4ej8FdZZa6UGNGA
ZT39TEtRXBAA7TjQZk/4JXaMq8XV4oVgGgXPn25a11SrOL6n/qRNhippsRO6pEGd
Sza/+xgJzsWacrfgykPBQuqoaDHHyFDGYkN68J4I7+zU6lvcvPnvN0ZnGf+jq6DE
6PUSyDf47WcJj7LjxgHVNj/En5zQvepA54FDvMiljGwtcWvsU/QZ6ID9zNLPfOxc
pKC23ryt2Ziyo4mZD9fFf6/cowHReQU40YGr4ZW/SfYovM2k0DaL2ChIfHWfGE9y
aCeMsWTloGlXeLYJJNcvcALfdrGqmRaEjwKcS+48ude29ZP86+uU8v7qLnAzjeId
EXFXwSF+jIINi8U/+Q9j3FnS5Ds5BlzKW2aOcBAeEzX+T4kSlmusGI/TFhRh5nL6
LNpD81Yj3xe1lffoOe5Ei2v2alERECVCioJBecrgU6BFXok4gzROxPYj8KbPXkTH
JQbQ9mMkSFEslk1I5yEMBOC9fs8vNFrudyfMGX3yOzNTtqM4ndFzQNlr9EoFQ6s4
x9tPrvX+KWzbuumJb69+C/kzUb9E0YqwFSzdX5RtTgt6KPd3kAie4+qgk7kzHGOo
kiLE
=kx8E
-----END PGP PRIVATE KEY BLOCK-----

```
-----BEGIN PGP PUBLIC KEY BLOCK-----
Version: PGP Desktop 10.2.0 (Build 2317) -
not licensed for commercial use: www.pgp.com
```

mQENBE9E+dEBCAC5Vhwo14lITIE/eJD8ZI+vZcynrQtD8qwjSoI4zKVYiaU32tnK
PcXmJN5EDMk0vhRufFmnN5QIXhzJ49klYCngxGtUrhHZNCrD4U95m/OYx0ZhZl0h
ch3mIkgzMqxCFP56FYozaKSC3qLvhB89RGGC0PEeacoj4ZpAueRKir6lhzubT/vk
wVEFXDvvWDO7yRb79XymYu0juQsp6E1scj0fWlfkN9B5bFGRgqGx7WXAxBrFCQH9
K4D1OYWCfP7Nbb7cnnNFOCa9UEWUO6qMC5wwPlfVS5s2X6853Gs1JnE5XuvebQI0
ZCs8r8bcq8H9gjAQ/nqyc9QzbP3iSlyTy/4rABEBAAG0H01pcmVrIDxjcnlwdGcn
cmFwaH1AZ21haWlsLmNvbT6JAXIEEAECAFwFAk9E+dEwFIAAAAAAIAAHcHJlZmVy
cmVkLWVtYWlsLWVuY29kaW5nQHBncc5jb21wZ3BtaWllCAsJCAcDAgEKAhkBBBRsD
AAAABRYAAwIBBR4BAAAABhUICQoDAgAKCRCnWUFHBTNOTfyqB/wLm3SRzvFpzWA5
VigvmKEPbXT2Rh5oLpw2hGY13wuQsE1CuvIzw+oICunkSUEPuznq0dFr9mpMvA/r
Hr+zxqd+Ang9jZZHPS/VjGu8se7n1q3d3oW7H/8w7WDKer76bDWnUWV9q0yImjfb
0k0xwVguksPGydJrElI/BFcuTudhNZyna+6o4/YyiVqzpvWZiNuHRzVeTDdQMI0o
ayIrPxfrRuCHkomDJBeRHWZ9WaWY1rMJWF+wk10hxVYTUeW3muJzMMDBGzWeOHBa
Vas8Kp9i9UOPAUR1u3gx2VQkTe6F/enkNdHoILWcM2aDyqest0Wlj0boMFuSZkc3
mCNFF+SEuQENBE9E+dIBCADGUHUgcSE/MVp/zzvX3g5NXIEzPYJlIvgJBo2kJGJm
vgeruHODEAF2sBX1LhdHFWgaFn2fC4wdnOhQyx3+LOjb8TBdGu1CgHDhUYoWCe1n
w1avywvrDZeJcTrsE2N4Jpdfd+KvH13q8yH7PlJntFwIda2LSE0hFQpUR/ozL8JP
yCLNr9LrDWO+1Xsm6DWqJL7Pyf166GxPSrvVU1CE8L1FOOkYzoAmyZVwtp0OokYE
tSM/gU2F0usnJYR2SX926hzoKX7VQt+PmuRYPY8xOrzbW6KXh2bDJfW+MKoR/sPL
IAUQOEoe0MMYLIM6mMkMqRyxrUDYOw+6HqvK+tkZ60H1ABEBAAGJAkEEGAECASsF
Ak9E+dMFGwwAAAADAXSAEGQEIAAYFAk9E+dIACgkQX+Ea4xxSV5VSNgf/eWAxfG/g
L8HLHn0/vFcJnkSr0g5Wij2zs2shSu9U9Ajd4NO4vTtkoWb8h8Eeiu5FS8uX90dQ
dwutb65P97wu09N9MwvJXr/ok3uHAbZRLpCgOAEZ6jViqRBQ07vHL5hjU/vZKPlk
kB/xwztoGEN6z9P91Ui00xTkFGxMGWj0Zmm5VTsVHn2IGqLtkXmd1oVnREqvi/RW
S15kgINv8x0+anDjho7bFAbZT5oRtr0YsLD1ar0EKrnYWmlNWyGdyuIkUKEcUdbb
Fdf7Ktz0QsBq0ZEJnVasKjyRXcggEZp3eWcOLSCdRW6ZBHn+xJB1posHeP8fPnsL
VwTkPIE2PT7BaQAKCRCnWUFHBTNOTS3CCACE7TKgRNP7ojQDKJLSzimWOxHK5c0Y
bqEj+kqF16X+ammS6JaN/mJZFwTgNpp2oN0cnfVzufia50QOOM0qM9vGZL220QVo
rdQKPAtTSA9X/fV3WWnbgbLmehE8SMOfD6EZYcXN0WP5g6Caj1T6P416HD3GNnbI
Lpvy2puAbBTysq0iq6IVN32ETNtf77Q+7K4MQik617CiP+3eUHj0X7KNEGnTfqbO
KmzBOhycuL62AEodu7uzX76g1KXh9GvRJE3m7cj3wBwnvFnecFqw7XRV2pRxM86q
YpYJStGxYaEIUI3eENVegtRQ6CnX4h1H29DOu5fKweYH5xGKOs7HMidv
=S1KX
```

```
-----END PGP PUBLIC KEY BLOCK-----
```

   In this way, exported keys can be stored on any memory devices or sent via e-mail.

   If we want to know the public keys of other users with whom we wish to communicate in an encrypted way, then the keys need to be downloaded by clicking *Import* in the menu *Keys*. Launching this option allows us to add a new key to our resources (keyring). This can be realized by indicating the location where the key in question is stored (this may be a file sent to us by someone else). Import/export of keys from/to other computers is also possible by copying the afore mentioned special files *secring.skr* and *pubring.pkr*.

   After several such operations we are able to encrypt messages with the obtained keys.
```

Fig. 6.11 Properties of the key

Fig. 6.12 The *silent.txt* file

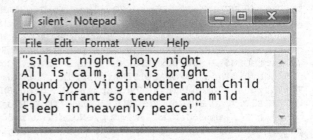

We can learn about the properties of a given key by selecting it and clicking the option *Properties* in the menu *Keys* (Fig. 6.11).

A dialog box with information about settings and properties of the key is displayed. Using it we can check which algorithm encrypts the key, its size, its lifetime, when it was created, etc. We can also see the key fingerprint (the numerical value of the key transformed by a hash function) given in its hexadecimal representation or as a text (using the appropriate set of words).

The PGP program allows us to encrypt files of any format. Since the process of encrypting and signing text files is simple, we present it below.

In order to encrypt a file displayed in the window of a given folder, we click its icon with the right mouse button. Next, we choose *PGP* and then *Secure* from the options.

The file *silent.txt* we will encrypt contains the following text in the ASCII code (Fig. 6.12):

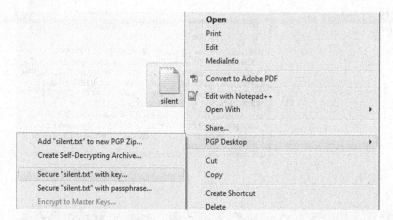

Fig. 6.13 Secure option

Fig. 6.14 Key selection dialog box

After running the *Encrypt* option (Fig. 6.13), the PGP program starts to encrypt the file.

It displays a dialog box (Fig. 6.14), in which we have to input the key with which the document should be encrypted. The upper part of the box contains the keys we know.

The file encrypted in this way is saved in a special format chosen from among options for the output file. The text contents of the file is changed to a cryptogram (Fig. 6.15).

This file can be decrypted (provided we have the private key symmetric to the one with which we encrypted the plaintext) by selecting the file and clicking the appropriate option *PGP—Decrypt/Verify*.

Fig. 6.15 Cryptogram of *silent.txt*

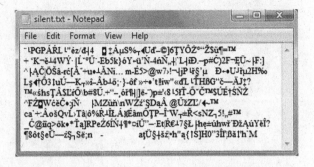

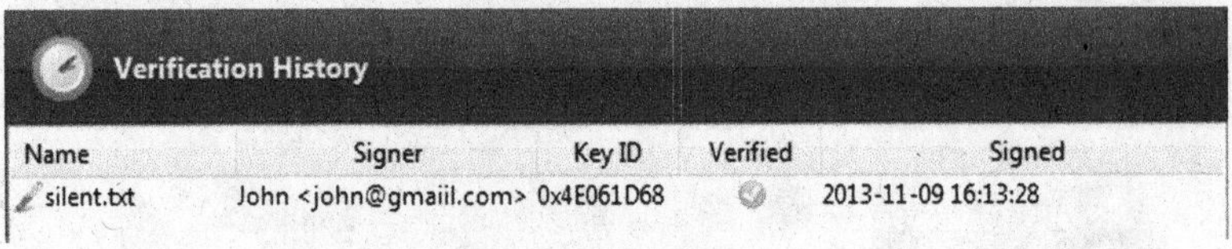

Fig. 6.16 Positive verification of the signature on the file *silent.txt*

After this is done, we need to type the password for the key used for encryption in the displayed dialog box.

If the document is encrypted with a key for which we do not have a symmetric one, the program informs us about the failure of decryption.

The PGP program enables electronic signing and verification of files of any format. Since signing a text file are simple, below we describe the processes. To sign a file displayed in the window of an appropriate folder, we have to click on its icon with the right mouse button. Then we select *PGP* and *Sign* from the options.

After selecting the option *PGP—Sign* the program asks first with which key (a private one according to principles of asymmetric cryptography) we want to sign the message (in case there is more than one key available) and it requests the appropriate password for this key.

Verification of the signature is executed by, among other things, double clicking on the file or selecting the appropriate option from the menu.

Let us notice that together with the confirmation of the authenticity of the signature the date of its creation is also displayed (Fig. 6.16). Recall that verification of the file is possible provided the signed file is located in the same folder as the file containing the signature. If the main file is missing, the system informs us about the failure whenever we try to verify the signature.

If we change the contents of the already signed file, the signature will be considered invalid (Fig. 6.17).

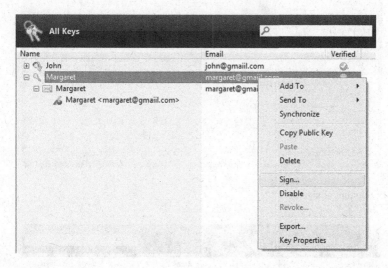

Fig. 6.17 Negative verification of the signature on the file *silent.txt*

Fig. 6.18 Key for signing

6.1.4 Web of Trust and Key Certification

The PGP system supports certification of encryption keys. This is achieved by building a web of trust. One can use only those keys that have been signed by trusted participants. Certification is performed by signing a given public key with a key of another trusted person. The user who is signing the key must determine whether they trust the other user or not.

In order to sign somebody's key, we have to import it to our keyring and select the *Sign* option from the *All Keys* menu (Fig. 6.18).

In the dialog box we confirm selection of the key used for certification (signature). By clicking the option *More Choices*, we can additionally configure the certificate. Available options include *Exportable* for export of the signature along with the key (this option is recommended, as it is very important for creating an adequate trust chain), *Non-Exportable* for no export opportunities, and determining timelife limits for the certificate in question (Fig. 6.19).

Each key can be certified many times. If we want to create a large mutual trust group, then each entity can certify keys of the other users from the group (Fig. 6.20).

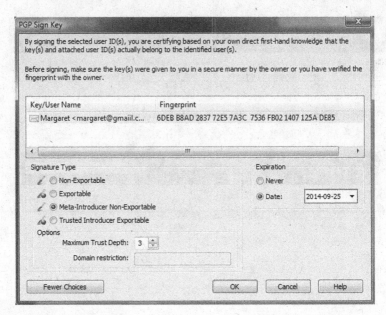

Fig. 6.19 Options of signing

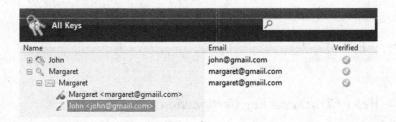

Fig. 6.20 Key signed (certified) with other keys

6.2 FireGPG and Enigmail

Another example of a program to encrypt or sign data is FireGPG. Although this system is not developed any more, since it was discontinued in 2010, this subsection presents its brief description. It is still quite popular, with over half a million registered users in 2010, especially among Linux users. This is a free plug-in to the Mozilla Firefox browser. It uses a GnuPG module to encrypt, decrypt, a digital signatures, and verify documents using different cryptosystems. FireGPG lets you work on any text in your browser and offers additional options of data security when using a Gmail account.

To use FireGPG, the GPG module must be installed in the system. It is available in versions for different operating systems. In the case of systems from the Linux/MacOS family it is enough to download and install a suitable package from the page http://www.gnupg.org/download/, in case of the Windows system it is enough to install the program WinPT from the page http://gpg4win.org/download. html. After this stage FireGPG can be installed.

The FireGPG installation is very similar to ordinary installation of additions to the Firefox browser. For it to work properly make sure you have a correct path to the GPG module (in your browser go to menu *Tools* → *FireGPG* → *Options*). If a prompt shows the lack of the GPG module the path must be written manually into the FireGPG options. When the Firefox extension is configured correctly, it is necessary to generate your pair of asymmetric keys: public and private. In that case the GPG module (Windows system) is run. The creator appears which helps you to create your own set of keys. After writing your personal details you should receive information about the correct program operation, which saves all the keys in a so-called key store. GPG provides intuitive and easy management of the key store. In order to export the public key, choose (*Tools* → *FireGPG* → *Export*)from the extension options. A window with your public key appears which can be copied and made publicly available.

As in other similar programs you can send to people messages encrypted by their own public keys. In order to do this it is necessary to import to FireGPG the appropriate keys (*Tools* → *FireGPG* → *Import*). This extension can also find a block with a public key on any website and import it. If the import of the key is successful you will receive an appropriate confirming message.

To send an encrypted message, mark the text in your browser, press the right button of the mouse, and choose the option *FireGPG* → *Encrypt*. A window appears where you should choose a suitable public key in order to encrypt. After this the message gets encrypted.

If you have an e-mail account on a Gmail server, FireGPG offers additional functions and push buttons, for example during typing an e-mail you can encrypt the message or sign it digitally. If someone e-mails you a message encrypted with your public key, it is enough to mark the cryptogram and choose in FireGPG the option *Decrypt*. FireGPG offers an easy way to sign messages digitally and verify the signatures of other messages. In order to sign a given message using your own private key it is enough to mark the text: from the menu choose *FireGPG* → *Sign*. To verify the signature of another person (another private key), you must mark the text and from the hand menu choose the option *FireGPG* → *Verify*. When the window appears you can choose the public key of the sender. The verification ends with an appropriate message on the authentication of the digital signature.

Various OpenPGP-compliant programs are available. Enigmail is one of those more important. It is a client plugin to Mozilla/Netscape e-mail. It has similar functionalities to those of PGP and FireGPG described above. It enables the users to write and receive email messages encrypted or signed with the OpenPGP standard. It is an opensource software based on GNU General Public License and the Mozilla Public License. Its installation is very simple, see [52].

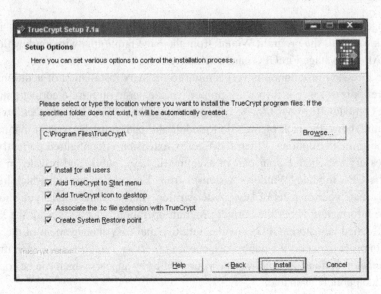

Fig. 6.21 Setup of TrueCrypt

6.3 TrueCrypt

TrueCrypt is today one of the best commonly available applications used to protect data from being read by unauthorized persons. The system secures the data by encrypting it using one of three algorithms: AES, Serpent, and Twofish, or even a combination of them. It is worth recalling that these algorithms are considered very strong. This means that no other method has been found so far to break the code than to find the correct password by brute force or a dictionary attack. It is free open-source software which can compete very well with commercial applications for data protection. TrueCrypt enables us to create encrypted files of any size, however limited to the capacity of the medium, and also enables us to encrypt a disk partition. From the fifth version, the program makes it possible to encrypt a system partition. TrueCrypt is available for Windows and Linux systems and from the fifth version also for Macintosh. Its basic functions, namely the formation of encrypted volumes and the encryption of a partition, are available for all platforms, however the Windows version has the best functionality. A wizard helps the user to install the program and the process is not difficult even for a beginner. During the installation you can choose one of two options: the standard installation or creation of a directory where you can store the portable version of the program. (The portable version of the application can be used on computers running Windows.) The standard installation is recommended if the user installs the program on their own computer. This choice is essential if the partition or the system disk is encrypted. To install the program you can decide (see Fig. 6.21) whether:

1. the program is available for all users,
2. a program shortcut is created in the Start menu,

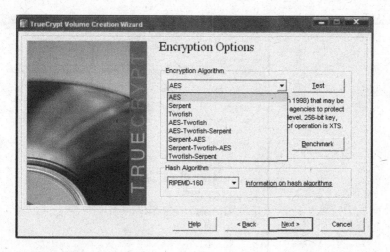

Fig. 6.22 Encryption options

3. a program shortcut is created on the desktop,
4. files with .*tc* extension are assigned to TrueCrypt,
5. a file including the system settings before the installation of TrueCrypt is created.

The portable mode is useful for all who want to have access to encrypted containers (files with data) from different computers or on computers where they do not have the authority to install the programs. If you choose the portable version of the installation it is only possible to choose the folder where the application files will be stored.

6.3.1 Formating the TrueCrypt Volume

TrueCrypt offers two forms of data encryption. A file can be created to fulfil the container function for data or you can encrypt the whole partition. The encryption of the system partition is a version of the second form however much modified so we can say it is a third form of encryption. Container-files are ideal if during our work we need to copy data between partitions and disks or to other computers. Then instead of entering the password and copying the files from an encrypted partition, you can copy the entire container-file.

As has been mentioned the AES, Serpent and Twofish algorithms are offered for use in encryption (Fig. 6.22). You can choose to encrypt using different sequences of these algorithms (using first one, then another, etc.). This can result in a very high (in practice, even unnecessary) level of security and at the same time in overloading the computer processor. To see how the computer can cope with the different encryption methods choose the option *Comparative Test*. This test can be performed in the RAM memory if we want to have the results independent of the speed of the hard

Fig. 6.23 Test vectors

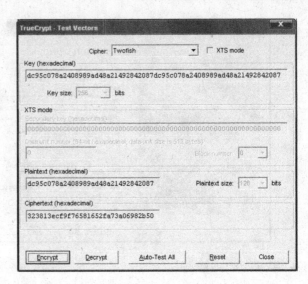

disk. After the test, you can compare how fast-our processor encrypts using the individual algorithms.

When you select an algorithm, it is worthwhile to take into account the results of the test (Fig. 6.23)—current drives have real transfers exceeding 100 MB/s, but the use of very strong encryption methods can slow down the computer. Although the latest processors can encrypt your data faster, remember that speeds should be halved, if you want to move or copy the data from one encrypted partition to another. In this case, the processor will have to decrypt first and then re-encrypt. Furthermore, this process can load the processor and decrease the power of the computer during the reading/writing of data from and to the disk.

After selecting the encryption algorithm a password must be chosen (Fig. 6.24). It must fulfil two conditions: first, it must be long. Of course, this is a protection against the brute force method of code-breaking. The password-breaking program checks passwords one after another, in most cases in alphabetical order. Taking into account that the password can consist of uppercase and lowercase letters, digits and special characters, if you extend the password by only one character it will increase the time needed to break it a few dozen times. For example, if a very fast computer is able to check 100000 passwords in a second, then breaking a five-character password will take 22 hours, a six-character one 90 days, and a seven-character one—more than 20 years. Second, the password should be rather complicated in terms of linguistics. The second method of finding passwords, known as a dictionary attack, uses the fact that many users to make their life easier choose easy to remember passwords, that is, for example, words or short sentences, names, names of places and things. Such words are easier and faster to find than random strings even if they are longer. Different words and sequences of words are checked in a specially prepared database called the dictionary.

The file format of the volume and its size must be fixed (see Fig. 6.25). You can also define whether you want to create a dynamic volume—then the specified

Fig. 6.24 Volume password

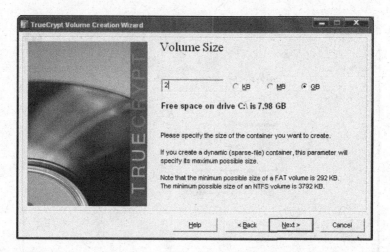

Fig. 6.25 Volume size

size will be the maximum size of this volume, but if you store less data its size will decrease. However this option should not be used because it affects in a negative way the power of the encryption process (see Fig. 6.26). After defining all the parameters you can start formatting the volume. If you use an existing file, the wizard will warn again that the operation will lead not to encryption but formatting the file into *a pure volume*. This is necessary because it can help to avoid tragic mistakes.

When a volume is mounted, its icon appears as another drive in My Computer (Fig. 6.27). You can now work with it as with any other partition. All you need to do now to encrypt the file with data is to copy the file into the newly created partition.

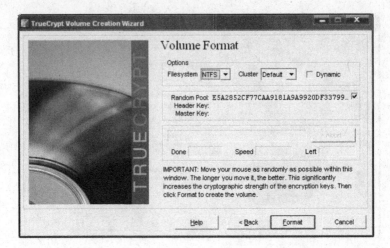

Fig. 6.26 Volume format

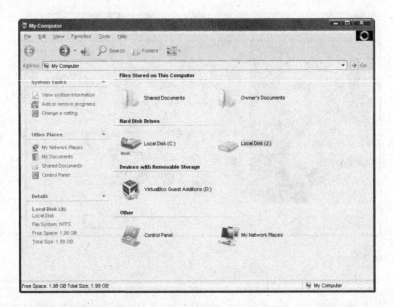

Fig. 6.27 View of the My Computer window

This file is automatically encrypted during copying. If you want to move it just copy it and the process goes the other way.

When you finish working with the volume choose the option *Dismount*—the partition will disappear from the above list and from My Computer, and the volume will become impossible to read (Fig. 6.28).

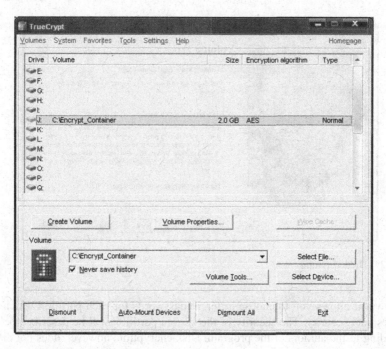

Fig. 6.28 Dismounting volume

6.3.2 Encrypting a Partition

A disk partition can be encrypted in order to limit the risk of an unauthorized access to its data. A password-protected partition can be invisible in the structure of the disk files. Reading any data from the partition would be possible only when it is activated with the appropriate password. Encrypt the partition before you save any data there—during encryption the whole content of the partition is formatted. If you want to encrypt a partition with files and folders move them first to another location. Only after you encrypt and mount the partition can you store data on it. This allows you to encrypt partitions of external and internal disks, pendrives and other memory devices.

One of the most important functions of TrueCrypt is the possibility to encrypt the root partition where the operating system is installed. This allows you to have more privacy than in the case of the encryption of a partition with data, especially if the system partition contains applications and temporary files, which happens in most cases.

Nowadays TrueCrypt also allows you to encrypt the entire disk containing the system partition. The only disks that can be encrypted totally are those with the operating system.

Disk partitions should be encrypted in the traditional way—this prevents the difficulties that can occur when you change the operating system on the encrypted disk,

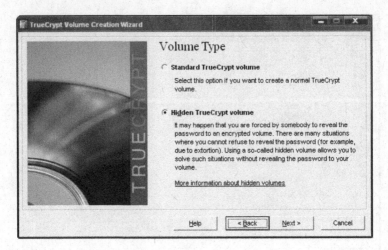

Fig. 6.29 Hidden volume

moreover it allows you to choose different passwords for each partition which increases data security. The security of the system partition will be described below
according to the authors of the program. Disk encryption, however, does not differ
too much and should not cause many difficulties for those who decide to protect
data in such a way.

6.3.3 Forming a Hidden Volume

Sometimes a user or a computer owner will be forced to give the password to secured
data. Such a situation occurs very seldom to individuals, only when a crime happens,
but sometimes an employer can insist on disclosure of a password. The TrueCrypt
authors have taken such a situation into consideration. You can try to prevent it by
creating a so-called hidden volume (Fig. 6.29).

Hidden volumes are created in standard volumes, so such a volume must be created first. Keep in mind one thing—you must not raise suspicions that a hidden
volume exists; the standard volume should consist of some neutral data which can
be revealed without any regret. When you choose the size of the standard volume
you have to take into consideration not only the data which will be hidden but also
the data which will be placed outside the hidden part. It is templity to compare the
hidden volume to *a small safe with a combination lock placed in a larger safe*—so
if you want to get the data from *the small safe* you must force open *the lock to the
larger safe*. Nothing could be further from the truth! If a container with a password
that can be broken in 20 years will consists of a hidden volume with a password
that can be broken in five minutes, to get the data from the hidden partition will
take someone who knows about it … just five minutes. This is because to reach the

hidden volume you do not have to break the password to the standard volume. The latter is only *a cover*, but not an additional protection for the hidden volume.

6.3.4 Work with Hidden Volumes

The operating system sees the effects of TrueCrypt the way an outsider sees the work of an artist who creates a masterpiece of surreal black and white blocks, scattered around the room. Only the author of the work knows which blocks are a part of the work, and which lie on the floor for "future use". If you ask an artist to write some information using their own cipher then only the artist will be able to read, it-more, only the artist knows which blocks form the cipher, and which do not. In a situation where in one room there is only one artist, there is no problem. It is worse when two artists use the same laboratory and different codes. The problem is that one artist can destroy the work of the other without realizing it.

The same happens with TrueCrypt volumes. If in the basic volume there is a hidden one even the external volume will not realise that—so during editing of the standard external volume there is a danger of overwriting hidden data. The application is protected against such a situation by a function called Hidden Volume Protection.

6.3.5 The Usage of Keyfiles

TrueCrypt lets you enhance the security of system files by using keyfiles (Fig. 6.30). A keyfile can be any file on your computer, or a medium, e.g. a pen drive. The key file forms a second line of security of your data, after the password. The password is of course obligatory, while an additional indication of the file is not (generally a well-constructed password should be enough).

The idea of a keyfile lies in the fact that TrueCrypt reads part of it and uses it as a password. Deciphering the file then becomes impossible without a password and an indication of the keyfile; both elements consist of a mechanism for protecting the volume. There can be many keyfiles (then a fragment from each volume is taken). The lack of even one ruins the chances of decrypting its content. This can be very useful in certain situations. There can be many examples—for example, students who finish school encrypt the only copy of pictures from the last school trip in the volume, created on the basis of as many keyfiles as there are students. Each student receives a keyfile. The volume is duplicated on CDs—everyone gets a copy of the encrypted pictures, but no one will be able to use it until they all meet again.

The necessity to gather all the keyfiles, however, as it can be seen clearly from the example, has a fundamental fault—we must assume that none of the files is lost, damaged, or modified (the first megabyte of the file counts). Furthermore, since any file can become a keyfile, there is a risk that the location of the file could simply be forgotten.

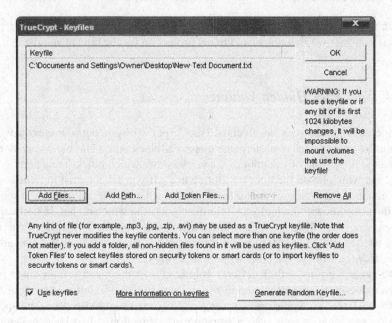

Fig. 6.30 Keyfiles

The best way to use a keyfile is to save it on any storage medium (CD, pen drive, memory card, memory of a mobile phone) and put it in a safe place. You can also use one keyfile for many volumes. This method prevents it from being lost and even though technically it should be considered as less safe, it is probably the most convenient. We advise you against storing a keyfile and a container on the same medium, especially if there are only files stored on it—the reasons are rather obvious.

6.3.6 Summary

TrueCrypt is a powerful encryption tool, which gives its users lots of options in the field of data security. It is a comprehensive application that allows creation of a single container-file as well as encryption of an entire partition (including the system partition). The program is considered to be very stable and reliable—practically no one reports the program hangs, let alone loss of data (excluding the user's mistakes).

TrueCrypt cooperates with the user to secure the data. It has great potential, but should be wisely used: the effectiveness of the program depends on the user—the choice of a strong password and also the keyfiles. The program warns the user to take all necessary precautions. Some precautions will influence the effectiveness of the data security and some can prevent its loss. The risk of losing information is minimal when the warnings and instructions are applied.

TrueCrypt is available free of charge. More importantly, the authors of the program make it clear on their web site that they do not have the slightest intention to commercialize it (as happens with many popular free programs). In the FAQ section on the TrueCrypt official website the question was asked *Will TrueCrypt be open-source and free forever?* The answer is *Yes, it will. We will never create a commercial version of TrueCrypt, as we believe in open-source and free security software.*

The advantages of the program:

- the program is free,
- it has the strongest current encryption algorithms,
- it is available for various operating systems (Windows, Linux, Mac),
- keyfiles can be used,
- the high stability of the program,
- it is portable—it can be run from a USB flash drive
- the ability to encrypt a disk or a system partition,
- clear interface,
- there are warnings and messages to prevent accidental mistakes,
- very good documentation on the official website.

The disadvantages of TrueCrypt:

- need to create and memorize the longest and most complex passwords,
- there is a risk of data loss in case you forget your password (or if a keyfile is lost),
- the load on the computer processor during the encryption/decryption of information,
- time-consuming operations, especially formatting large partitions (in some extreme cases, this process may take longer than a day, on average a dozen minutes).

Chapter 7
Public Key Infrastructure

This chapter briefly looks at a PKI network security infrastructure and its basic services: entity authentication, message integrity, and confidentiality. It presents a PKI structure, its basic components, and the tasks of Registration Authority (RA), Certification Authority (CA), key repositories, certificates and Certificate Revocation Lists (CRLs).

7.1 Public Key Infrastructure and Its Services

Every year more and more people become users of the Internet. Each of them uses data accumulated on the network and exchanges information with other people using well-known services such as e-mail or WWW. Sometimes, when you communicate with a person you are intentionally misled about their identity. Many people are not aware of how important it is to verify the identity of the sender or recipient of a message or other web services. This fact is often used by intruders.

Cryptography and its latest achievements appear extremely helpful in this case. You already know the advantages of asymmetric cryptography which enables electronic signatures. Data which is transmitted or accumulated can be signed electronically. With a signature you should not have any problems with identification of the data's author or a message originator. If you know the author's public key you can easily verify the signature's authenticity.

A risk, however, is that a phisher can impersonate the relevant person or institution and replace the public keys. To avoid this type of action a Public Key Infrastructure was invented. Its main purpose is to ensure the authenticity of private and public keys in a given sector.

7.2 Modern Web Threats

When you have your own pair of asymmetric keys and want to exchange some electronically signed information with another person, you must each make public

C. Kościelny et al., *Modern Cryptography Primer*,
DOI 10.1007/978-3-642-41386-5_7, © Springer-Verlag Berlin Heidelberg 2013

keys accessible to the other. You may do so using a web site, an e-mail or any other form of electronic exchange.

A threat is that intruders can replace the transmitted public keys by their own. Unknowingly using an inappropriate public key causes incorrect authorization of the partner you communicate with. A Trusted Third Party is one of the possible ways to make the information exchange system reliable and appropriately secure. Its main function is to confirm the authenticity of public keys owned by users communicating in the system.

A TTP can also inform us about any change of the keys in case of loss or theft. This is why the idea of a Public Key Infrastructure was born. The three main components of the structure are:

- a Registration Authority (RA) verifies and registers the user's personal data,
- a Certification Authority (CA) issues digital certificates which testify to the authenticity of a given person and their public key. Certification is preceded by the applicant's identification process,
- a Repository of certificates, keys and Certificate Revocation Lists (CRLs).

7.3 Trusted Third Party, Certification Process

The idea of a PKI system is based on digital certificates issued by a CA. These certify the authenticity of asymmetric cryptographic keys owned by a given person.

A digital certificate is an electronic document containing data which bind a person and keys for generating an electronic signature and verifying its authenticity. This gives the opportunity to verify the identity of a given pair of keys' owner (a legal person, a server, a website or a computer device). Detailed rules for building certificates are specified by international standards. One of them, and currently the most widely used is the X.509 standard.

Each certificate meeting the X.509 standard requirements contains the following fields:

- a version number—defines the version of the certificate format,
- a serial number—the unique serial number of the certificate,
- an algorithm identifier—defines the algorithm used for signing a certificate and the algorithm parameters,
- a drawer—contains the name of the Certification Authority which issued the certificate, and its duration of validity—stated as two dates; the certificate is not valid before the starting date and after the expiry date,
- a person (user)—defines the person who received the certificate,
- public key—contains the user's public key and defines the algorithm used by this key,
- the signature of the Certification Authority—each certificate is electronically signed by the Certification Authority it was issued by,
- a hyperlink to a website where one may download the CRL list.

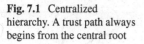

Fig. 7.1 Centralized hierarchy. A trust path always begins from the central root

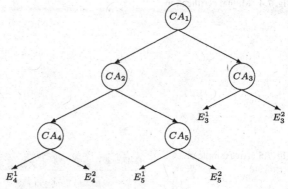

Fig. 7.2 Separate sectors, each with its own certification authority

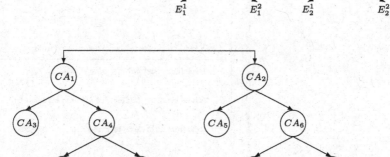

Fig. 7.3 Multiple rooted tree

Since an Intruder can create a virtual Certification Authority you should ask the question: who testifies the authenticity of this kind of institution? It appears that Certification Authorities also need authentication. They are certified by other authorities specially assigned to this purpose by relevant legal and technological provisions in a given country. Finally it is obvious that the root Certification Authority certifies itself.

The Certification Authorities' hierarchy, appointed by law as we mentioned before, forms what is usually called a certification path. Below a few possible schemes of certification paths are presented—Figs. 7.1, 7.2, 7.3 and 7.4, cf. [68]. Notation used in depiction: CA_n—certification authority, E_n^m—end user.

The certificate shown in Fig. 7.5 (a printscreen from Internet Explorer) was issued by Comodo Client Authentication and Secure Email CA for some e-mail address. It provides information about what CA issued the certificate, for whom, and

Fig. 7.4 Mutual certification

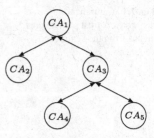

Fig. 7.5 An example of a
certificate

its lifetime window. The button *Install the certificate* makes a local copy of the certificate and places it in the relevant folder.

The *Details* tab (Fig. 7.6) contains all fields required by the certificates protected
for a chosen certificate: its serial number, etc. Choosing each of the elements you
may verify the information (e.g., a public key) or copy this information to a file.

Verification of a certificate consists of tracing its trust path, to a root authority
which is authorised by the relevant provisions. The authority certifies itself. The
Certification path (Fig. 7.7) shows us the certification path and the certificate status. Signature verification consists remotely verifying the consecutive signatures
along the path chain of certificates. This action continues until the CA reaches a
so-called trust point. The trust point is specified by national policy and it is usu-

Fig. 7.6 Tab *Details*

ally a self-signed certificate of the Main Certification Authority. The chain begins with a subscriber's certificate and ends with a certificate of the Main Certification Authority. If a certificate has expired or been canceled, a person who receives a digitally signed message is automatically informed about the certificate expiry. The information about the certificate expiry appears in the certification trust path.

EU law recognizes the concept of advanced electronic signature and qualified certificate. They have different legal effects. An advanced signature based on a qualified certificate has legal effects completely equivalent to a handwritten signature. Below a brief characterization of qualified certificates is presented. Qualified certificates were introduced and defined by [39].

The validity lifetime of a qualified certificate is restricted to a maximum of two years. A qualified certificate must contain the following fields:

1. the certificate's serial number,
2. an indication that the certificate was issued as a certificate qualified to be used according to a specified certification policy,
3. the subject providing certification services, the subject issuing certificate, and the country where the subject is located, as well as a subject's identification number in a registry of qualified subjects providing certification services,
4. name and surname or a nickname of the certificate's owner. Usage of a nickname must be clearly indicated,

Fig. 7.7 Tab *Certification Path*

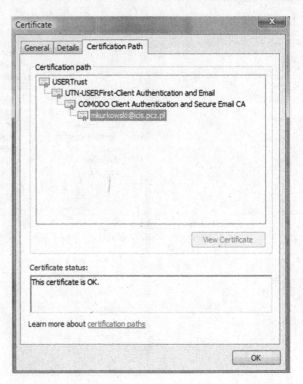

5. the public key,
6. the certificate's lifetime dates,
7. the CA's electronic signature,
8. the liability value of a transaction in which the certificate can be used, as stated by the certification policy or an agreement.

A qualified certificate is revoked when its private key gets compromised, or is lost. A qualified certificate can be suspended even if one only suspects the private key might have been compromised.

7.4 PKI

The main task of a PKI, with its digital signature and the above-described certificate systems, is to enhance the system security.

Figure 7.8 presents an exemplary PKI environment. Its most important component is the main Certification Authority. As we have already seen there may be many certification authorities but usually each of them, if it is required by law, is certified by the main authority. Each certification authority performs the role of a trusted third party.

The Policy Management Authority (PMA) is usually a group of specialists who create the rules under which certification services are provided by Certification Au-

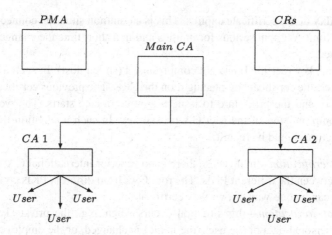

Fig. 7.8   An example of PKI structure

thorities. Certification policy is prepared and provided to recipients of the services in order to build their trust. The policy defines inter alia the duties and responsibilities of the Public Key Infrastructure's users, types of certificates and their fields of application. The main CA is a trust point for all participants in a given PKI. The CA's public key is used directly or indirectly for signing all certificates in a given structure. The main CA also signs certificates issued for other PKI structures (cross certification). The list of the CA's subjects is theoretically unlimited. In each PKI structure there are certificate repositories (CRs) in which certificates, Certificate Revocation Lists and Authority Revocation Lists are stored. The repository must be available to all individuals who wish to use the security services available in applications operating in the PKI structure. Registration Authorities (RAs) exchange essential information between the users and Certification Authorities, taking on some of their administrative functions.

The following are the most important functions of every PKI.

Registration—the user asks the Registration Authority to issue a certificate. The applicant should submit some information, e.g., name, the domain name, IP address. The CA verifies the submitted data, and verifies the authenticity of the handwritten signature on the application to issue the certificate.

Certification—after positive identification, the CA issues the certificate and gives it to the applicant. The certificate goes to the public repository and is available to all interested parties.

Generating the keys—the user can generate a correct pair of keys on his own or use the CA service. In the case of generating the keys (on his own) the public key is sent to CA in order to conduct the certification. If one uses the services of the CA the keys are delivered in a secure way, e.g., on a secure chip card.

Key renewal—each pair of keys and the certificate need to be renewed periodically. This is one of the methods which improves the security. There are two cases, when you have to exchange your pair of keys:

- The validity of the certificate expires. This is a common situation connected with the time limit. Without serious formalities and in a short time the change of keys takes place.
- The private key (certified) has got compromised (stolen, lost). In such a case the CA cancels the certificate by placing it on the CRL. The previous certificate loses its validity and the procedure to issue a new certificate starts. The worst case is the compromising of the root CA private key. In such a situation the whole infrastructure should be rebuilt.

Mutual certification—in this case there is no superior international CA; the trust is shared between the different PKIs. The root CAs from different PKIs certify each other. This can be one-way or two-way certification.

Certificate revocation—this situation occurs when, e.g., the private key is revealed, or personal data of the user (the name) is changed, or the employee leaves the firm where he was given the certificate. The method uses the CRL, periodically published in the repository where the certificates are stored. Every certificate has its own unique serial number. The CRL contains the list of identifiers of all canceled certificates and the timestamp.

Recovery of a key—in some PKIs there is an option to store some pairs of keys with access to them in case of key destruction. The most important feature is to ensure that the private keys can be recovered only by the owner.

Most software used today to secure computer systems enables cooperation with PKI. These standards include:

- SSL (Secure Sockets Layer)—uses private keys and PKI to encrypt data. It is used for example by Internet Explorer and other browsers. Many websites use SSL to secure the privacy of such data as credit card numbers. Formally, websites which use the SSL protocol start their domain names with *https* instead of *http*.
- S/MIME (Secure Multipurpose Internet Mail Extensions)—is a secure extension of the popular e-mail standard MIME. The goal of the S/MIME project was to enable the transmission of messages ensuring privacy.
- SET (Secure Electronic Transaction)—allows secure transactions to be carried out without direct contact with the Internet, using credit cards. It is supported by the two biggest credit card organizations VISA and MasterCard, and also by IBM. SET extends the opportunities of SSL by introducing the identification of the other side—the client. The protocol contains the identification mechanisms of two parties. The possibility for a salesman to see the number of a credit card is eliminated—encrypted credit card numbers are transferred directly to the organization responsible for the service.
- IPSec (IP Security)— ensures the confidentiality of packet exchange on the level of an internet protocol. IPSec has two modes of encryption: Transport and Tunnel. The Transport mode encrypts only part of the packet data and leaves the headers untouched. More secure is the Tunnel mode which encrypts the packet data and the headers. For the correct working of IPSec, public key exchange is required.

7.5 Certificates, Keys and Management

This section presents installation, configuration and management of certificates in the Windows system. In particular, we examine the revocation of certificates and the basic tasks of the repository, where the lists of revoked or suspended certificates are made public.

7.5.1 Generating and Installing the Certificates

There are many vendors offering certificate services on the market. Each of them enables different kinds of public key certificates to be downloaded. Among unqualified certificates there are free certificates, which can be downloaded by any person who has his/her own e-mail account. Below we present the process of downloading such a free certificate and its configuration in the browser.

Generating and installing your own free certificate from some chosen CA begins with downloading and installing the root certificate of the CA.

How a certificate is generated and downloaded from the CA's website depends to some extent on the selection of the CA. Various procedures can be applied. Sometimes this can be as simple as just downloading a form filled in on-line. Below we present a more elaborate, but much more secure process consisting of six steps. It includes a kind of verification of the user's identity.

On the CA's website find and select the Certificate of CA Main Office. In the dialog window to download the files you can select Open, and then confirm with the OK button. On the screen the window Certificate Manager appears. Then you install the certificate in the operating system. Select the option Install the certificate. Using the default settings of the repository, accept the next steps in the following windows of the wizard. In the last window called the Certificate Manager Import Wizard select Finish. The computer reports the correct installation of the certificate. In the window Certificate Manager you can see the installed certificate by choosing the tab Main trusted certificates drawers. Then in the same way you install the UC Certificate class I. To generate your own certificate using the internet service you have to configure your e-mail program. The process of generating and installing your own certificate consists of six stages. Generating the certificate you begin by finding a suitable certificate among those offered by the Center and selecting the Download the certificate button (the offer for individual clients). Notice whether it is free or paid.

- Stage 1. You fill in all the fields on the form according to the instructions. Before going to the next Stage check that the form has been filled incorrectly.
- Stage 2. Finishing Stage 1 causes the completed form to be sent to the CA. The CA then sends to your e-mail address a message containing the address of a web page where you have to go in order to continue the certification. The CA checks the authenticity of your electronic address. To continue the process of generating the certificate you choose the address which is added to the message.

- Stage 3. In the open dialog window type your password.
- Stage 4. In order to send the correct application you have to use the digital signature on the application using encryption keys, which you can generate by selecting the Generate keys button. The keys are generated by your Web browser. Two windows appear. In the first one there is the question whether to set up the private and public key. The public key will be sent by e-mail. In the second window there is the question whether to sign the form using the private key. The keys are generated and the application to issue the certificate is sent.
- Stage 5. The CA sends a second e-mail to your electronic address, to tell you from which address you can download the certificate. Open your inbox, read the message, and then go to the given WWW address. At this point let us give some details about generating, storing and managing the certificates and encryption keys. The encryption keys are made by yourself, as a recipient of the certification service, or the CA. If the keys are generated and submitted to the CA, the public key is given to the CA with the application to issue the certificate in a format which confirms its authenticity and the fact that the recipient has a certificate of appropriate private key. If the keys are generated by the CA, they are transferred to the user who wants the certificate. Notice that the keys generated during the registration process are given on a chip card. Keys which were generated outside the chip card are sent in encrypted file in an appropriate format. A vital fact is that when the key is generated by the CA, the quality of the key parameters is verified by the application of the CA; in the case of keys submitted by the user, the CA does not verify the quality of the keys. You are responsible for the quality of your keys.
- Stage 6. On again visiting the website of the CA you start installing the certificate by selecting Install the certificate.

After installing the certificate a dialog window appears which informs you about the status of the installed certificate. If you want to see the installed certificate, e.g., in MS Outlook Express, you have to choose Tools from the main menu, choose Options and the tab Content (Fig. 7.9).

Next, you choose digital Identifiers and overlap Personal (Fig. 7.10). You choose the Advanced button. In the displayed window you can see the detailed information about the generated certificate.

7.5.2 Configuration of Certificate

In order to configure the certificate, open MS Outlook Express, in the main menu choose *Tools—Accounts*.

Then, choose the tab *Mail* and check with one click your own account, and click the *Properties* button (Fig. 7.11).

On the screen there is a window where you have to select the tab *Security* (Fig. 7.12). In the window you have two sections. The first one: Signing certificate is responsible for signing e-mails, the second one is responsible for encrypting

Fig. 7.9 Options—Content

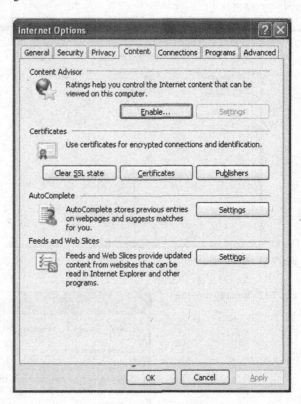

Fig. 7.10 Certificates

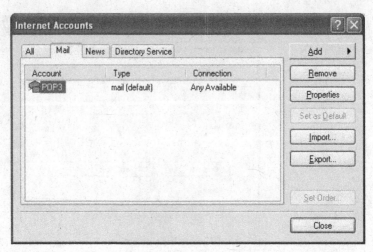

Fig. 7.11 Accounts

Fig. 7.12 Security properties

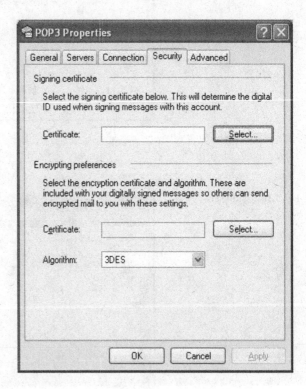

the messages. If in both cases the fields are empty, click the button *Select* in the first section. The window *Selection* of the certificate appears.

In the *Selection* dialog window of the certificate you check your own certificate (Fig. 7.13) and confirm with the *OK* button. Next, click the *Select* button in the

Fig. 7.13 Selecting
certificate

second section and do the same activities as in the first section. Your certificate is
now properly configured.

Access to the certificates of other people is essential to encrypt the e-mails to
them and also to verify their electronic signatures. There are several options to get
the certificates (the public keys) of other people. Below we present each of them.

The easiest way to obtain the certificate of another person is to receive a signed
message using the digital key of the sender. MS Outlook Express on getting the
message automatically adds the certificate of the sender to your address book (on
condition that the sender is added to the address book).

The other way to obtain the certificates of other people is to import the certifi-
cates and store them on your disk using Certificate Manager. In the main menu of
MS Outlook Express select *Tools* and click *Options*. Next, in the tab *Security* click
Digital identifiers. On the screen you will see the window of the Certificate Manager.
Click the *Import* button, and in the newly opened window of Certificate Manager
Import Wizard click *Next*.

In the next step, write in the access path of to the files with certificates or click
the *Scan* button (Fig. 7.14) and mark the file with certificates. Next, click the *Open*
button. In order to go to the next window, click the *Next* button.

The next dialog window lets you choose the repository (Fig. 7.15), where you
will store your certificate.

You have two possibilities: the first allows the computer to choose the repository
automatically on the basis of the certificate's type; the second allows you to choose
the repository yourself. You can use the second option by clicking the round field
of Place all the certificates in the following store, and choose the *Browse* button
(Fig. 7.16). You choose the repository and click the *OK* button. In order to finish
the installation, click the *Next* button. In the dialog window you will see all the
information about the imported certificate. Then, click the *Close* button.

You can also use an LDAP server to import the certificates. You can use this
method when you know the address or the name of the LDAP server which stores
the certificate of the person with whom you want to correspond. The certificates of
people who used the service from the Certification Center are available on the server.

Fig. 7.14 Certificate import

Fig. 7.15 Container

Fig. 7.16 Certificate Import
Wizard

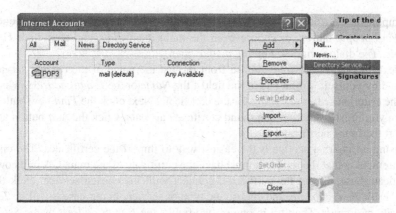

Fig. 7.17 Internet Accounts

Fig. 7.18 LDAP creator

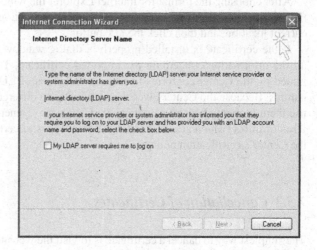

To import certificates from the LDAP server you first have to configure it in your e-mail program. From the main menu choose Tools and click the option *Accounts* (Fig. 7.17). In the window which appears on the screen, click the tab *Directory Service* and click the *Add* button, Directory Service.

On the screen there will be the dialog window of the Internet Connection Wizard, where you write the name of the LDAP server (Fig. 7.18).

In the next window the wizard asks you if you want to check the e-mail addresses using directory services. Click the window *Yes*, and then the Next button. The next window informs you about the correct configuration of directory services, and by clicking the *Finish* button you end the installation. Then, marking the appropriate LDAP server in the dialog window Internet accounts you click the *Properties* button. In the newly opened window you click the tab *Advanced* and the section *Search*. In the field *Search base* you write the required parameter of search characteristics for the given LDAP server. Click the *OK* button, finish settings and close the window.

To import the certificates from the LDAP server, open the address book and click the *Find people* button, or choose from the main menu *Edit*, and then click *Find people*. The dialog window *Finding people* opens.

Next, in the field *Search*, choose from the list the name of the catalog service defined by yourself. Fill in one of the fields: the *Name* or the *E-mail address*, which are the criteria used in searching for the certificate. Next click the *Find* now button. When you finish searching, the found certificate appears. Click the *Add* button and import the found certificate.

Using an internet service is the easiest way to import the certificates. The only requirement is that the recipient must have the certificate of the main CA in its own certificate base. To get the certificate, connect with the chosen service, click the link *Verify the certificate*, and choose the type of service. In our case it will be *Test security of e-mails*. Then fill in one of two fields: the *E-mail address* or the *Serial number*, and click the *Check* button.

After choosing the format for Internet Explorer the window opens with the question, what you want to do with this file. Choose the option *Open* this file with the current location, and then click the *OK* button.

If the certificate is installed properly a dialog window appears which presents all the information concerning the imported certificate. The profile of certificates issued by the Center conforms to recommendations of EU Law on electronic signatures. Because the Center gives the certificates to different subscribers, who may use them in many areas of activities, the Center may generate certificates with different profiles (which are defined for different types of certificates) as regulated by the Center's certification policy.

7.5.3 Cancellation of Certificates

The simplest way to cancel a certificate is to visit the website of the Center and click the link Cancel the certificate.

In the displayed window, you can choose the type of service, and type in your e-mail, the password and the reason for cancellation; you then click the *Cancel the certificate* button. The next window informs you about the cancellation of the certificate and about the publication of your certificate on the list of canceled certificates. The lists of canceled and suspended certificates are stored in a special repository. The repositories of information use a directory system. The recipients of certificate services can have certificates issued, access the lists of suspended and canceled certificates and also electronic documents which are currently and previously in force about the Certification Code of Conduct and the Certification Policy. The repository is managed by the Center. Certification Authorities publish certificates, and the lists of suspended and canceled certificates in the Repository.

The Center allows publication of information in the Repository, in accordance with proper Certification Policy and valid legislation. The list of canceled and suspended certificates published in the repository consists of:

- the number of the list,
- for qualified certificates—indication whether the list was published according to the certification policy and certificates issued according to this policy,
- the date and time when the list was published as specified by the certification policy, mainly the publication date of the next list,
- the number of every suspended or canceled certificate, and the indication whether it was suspended or canceled,
- the date and time each certificate was suspended or canceled, as specified by the certification policy,
- an electronic certificate of the Certification Center.

Chapter 8
Cryptographic Protocols

This chapter gives some examples of cryptographic protocols that are interesting and important from practical, theoretical, historical and didactical points of view. It also presents the problem of the correctness and security of such protocols. It is now known that several important cryptographic protocols, which were still in use not so long ago, had some significant faults. It is worth analyzing them in order to understand how surprising, at the first glance, attacks can be and how obvious they become after the analysis. We are going to look at the very instructive history of some versions of the Needham-Schroeder protocol for entity authentication in computer networks—a story that illustrates very well all the most important issues. Methods for verifying protocols (not only cryptographic ones) have been an area of active research and practical applications in both academia and industry. One can learn more about it from the website http://www.lsv.ens-cachan.fr/spore devoted to cryptographic protocols.

Cryptographic protocols—algorithms that realize goals important for providing security of electronic transactions and documents being sent—are widely applied in computer networks, particularly in public key infrastructure systems during data exchange. Such protocols are widely applied as essential components of large systems, such as commonly used communication systems. As examples of such protocols consider Kerberos, SSL and Zfone.[1]

In general, a *protocol* is a concurrent program run on computers (or just on processors) working together. Such programs carry out concurrent processes (sometimes called parallel or simultaneous—in contrast to sequential processes, i.e., those whose program instructions are executed sequentially on one processor). One can consider such processes as some number of sequential processes communicating with each other from time to time by data (parameters) exchange or by using common resources. Cryptographic protocols are those that use encryption.

A cryptographic protocol can also be defined as a concurrent algorithm, determined by a sequence of actions performed by two or more entities, that allow one

---

[1] A lot of information about cryptographic protocols can be found in [79, 92].

C. Kościelny et al., *Modern Cryptography Primer*,
DOI 10.1007/978-3-642-41386-5_8, © Springer-Verlag Berlin Heidelberg 2013

to realize a specified goal, with certain actions being performed by means of cryptographic algorithms.

A protocol specification should contain:

1. the number of entities participating in the protocol,
2. the nature of their participation,
3. the aim of the protocol,
4. the actions of which the protocol execution comprises.

The main goals that should be achieved by cryptographic protocols can be:

1. mutual authentication of communicating entities,
2. confidentiality of sent information,
3. integrity of sent messages,
4. session key distribution.

Actions performed by the entities during a protocol execution can be divided into internal and external ones. By external actions we mean those involving mutual transmission of information between the entities. Specification of these actions must define a definite source (sender) of each piece of information, a receiver (recipient) of the information and of course its content, indicating respectively which parts of the information have to be encrypted and how. Internal processes are all the other actions that each entity performs on their own during the protocol realization. These include, for example, generating new confidential information, encryption and decryption of cryptograms, comparing parameters or performing mathematical operations on parameters held locally.

Applying protocols in security systems must fulfill several requirements:

1. each user has to know the protocol and execute in the correct sequence all the actions of the protocol,
2. each user has to agree to use the protocol,
3. each action of the protocol must be precisely defined, so that the users cannot be confused about the method or the order of their executions.

8.1 Examples of Cryptographic Protocols

An important type of cryptographic protocols are systems of entity authentication which identify and verify the identity of the participating entities (users, agents, parties, servers, processors, etc.) working in real networks. It would be hard to overestimate the role of these systems in data protection, security of network transactions, and construction of trust models, especially for large distributed open networks with easy access from any location. In general, in order to confirm someones identity, an ID and a password/PIN are used. This method is not very reliable. Data transmitted without any protection from a remote device can easily be intercepted (eavesdropped). Even an encrypted password can be captured and reused in its encrypted form. As an alternative, biometric methods, possibly combined with identification cards, can be used. However, these are neither widespread, so far, nor cheap.

Challenge-response protocols make remarkable examples of protocols designed specifically for reliable entity authentication. Their general idea consists in verifying a party's identity by sending her specially constructed unforgeable information encrypted with her public key. If she can decrypt it and send it back, then without any doubt this is an entity who knows the private key that corresponds to the public key with which this information was encrypted. The password is sent back encrypted (with a different key), therefore it is not disclosed. The interested reader can find comprehensive information concerning authentication protocols in [68]. Below, we will discuss in detail several versions of the entity authentication protocol proposed by Needham and Schroeder [69]. The X.509 standard [83] contains an interesting protocol of the similar class.

Other commonly applied protocols are those for establishing a secret cryptographic key used for further encrypted exchange of information. The most popular protocol for exchanging and establishing session keys is Kerberos (version 5, see [68]). In fact, it uses as its basis the original Needham-Schroeder protocol, enhanced by, among other things, the so-called timestamps, i.e., the possibility of affixing an exact date to a message being sent. Other commonly used protocols are Internet Key Exchange (IKE) [53] and, the charmingly named Wide-Mouth Frog [92]. More and more often similar protocols are applied in electronic payment systems. As examples one can see the Internet Keyed Payment (IKP) protocol [12] and the Secure Electronic Transaction (SET) standard [93].

Beside entity authentication, an important objective of the protocols is to secure documents (e.g., those containing sensitive data of a transaction or a contract) against unauthorized modifications. Protected information may concern conditions of services, descriptions or prices of commodities, personal or company data. Usually, several (at least three) entities take part in communication: a customer, a seller, and a credit card issuer.

8.2 Reliability

Since cryptographic protocols are usually relatively short and simple, an informal reasoning is often applied in order to justify their reliability and to convince all their users that the protocols meet the declared goals. However, when a protocol can be performed simultaneously (concurrently, in parallel) several times and its executions can interleave on the same computers and the role of some entity may alternate in different executions (she may act as an initiator or as a responder), then the analysis of such a protocol gets very difficult. Asynchronous composition and interleaving runs are complicated enough, additionally one has to take into account the analysis of individual entities' knowledge at various stages of each run of the protocol. In other words, knowledge about private keys and freshly sent/received information has to be taken into considerations.

Some of the presented protocols, seemingly correct, turned out to have flaws. The problem lies in possible protocol runs or their interleavings which were unexpected by the authors of these protocols. Such behaviours or interleavings of behaviours are called attacks. However, an attack does not always mean a discrediting error and a complete compromise of the considered protocol.

For this reason, there is the challenging motivation for researchers and engineers to develop methods to verify protocol correctness. This is a non-trivial task, since it is not easy to define formally the objective of verification and the property of correctness. Different protocols are used for different purposes and are specified in different languages. Therefore, it is not clear whether one formalism could describe all possible cases. Let us mention only that the first methods in this area concerned verification by means of specially constructed deduction systems, called BAN authentication logics (Burrows-Abadi-Needham [23]). Since the early 1990s, they have been used to detect flaws in entity authentication protocols. However, it has turned out that even positively verified protocols may still be vulnerable to attacks. Over the last two decades, researchers from numerous academic and commercial centers have been extensively developing methods for cryptographic protocol analysis with the aim of constructing tools for automatic or semi-automatic verification of the basic properties of such protocols, as well as tools for their systematic design and validation. One of the most interesting verification methods is the technique called model checking. This issue will be the presented in the next sections.

8.2.1   The Needham-Schroeder Protocol

In 1978 Needham and Schroeder [69] published a pioneering paper in the area of authentication protocols. Its authors presented an idea of using cryptographic techniques to solve the problem of entity authentication in network communication. They also proposed schemes of authentication protocols that use symmetric and asymmetric cryptography.

In what follows, symbols A and B denote the identifiers of two users who wish to communicate securely with each other. The symbol S stands for a server—a third party that is fully trusted by the users. By $E_{K_A}(X)$ we mean a ciphertext containing a message X encrypted with the public key of user A, while $E^{K_A}(X)$ denotes the respective ciphertext encrypted by A's private key.

The entity authentication protocols use so-called nonces, i.e., unique and nonrepeatable large pseudo-random numbers generated and used for only one execution of a protocol or communication session. The term *nonce* is an abbreviation of **number used once**.

The randomness of these numbers aims to ensure that no one has ever known or used any of them before, and in practice (i.e., with a sufficiently high probability) it is unfeasible for anybody to reconstruct the used nonce. In this sense it is said that the information is fresh. Such numbers will be denoted by N_A (a nonce generated by A) and N_B (a nonce generated by B). Typically, a nonce serves as a time-variant parameter to prevent unauthorized or undetectable replay.

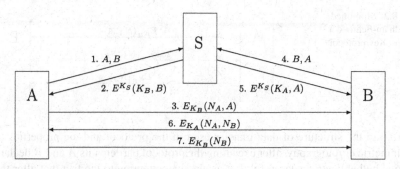

Fig. 8.1 Entire Needham-Schroeder Public-Key protocol

Here $A \rightarrow B : X$ denotes A sending the message X to B. In our considerations it is often assumed that sending a message is equivalent to the receiver receiving it.

In the Needham and Schroeder protocol three entities take part: A, B and S. The server S is the third entity fully trusted by the two others. User A initiates the protocol. The goal to be achieved after the protocol execution is a mutual authentication of entities A and B, i.e., the mutual confirmation of their identities. The external actions performed by the participants during the protocol execution are listed in the following scheme (and illustrated in Fig. 8.1).

1. $A \rightarrow S : A, B$.
   User A begins by sending its identifier and the identifier of B to S (indicating willingness to communicate with B).
2. $S \rightarrow A : E^{K_S}(K_B, B)$.
   S sends to A the public key of B together with B's identifier encrypted with the private key of S. User A receives the information and gets B's public key.
3. $A \rightarrow B : E_{K_B}(N_A, A)$.
   A generates its nonce N_A and sends it together with its own identifier to B, encrypting everything with the public key of B.
4. $B \rightarrow S : B, A$.
   B sends its identifier together with the identifier of A to S, requesting A's public key.
5. $S \rightarrow B : E^{K_S}(K_A, A)$.
   S sends the public key of A, encrypted with the private key of S, to B. The latter receives the information and gets the public key of A.
6. $B \rightarrow A : E_{K_A}(N_A, N_B)$.
   B generates its own nonce N_B and encrypts it together with the obtained number N_A with A's public key. Then B sends the so-prepared ciphertext to A, who decrypts it (being the only one who is able to do it). A compares the number received from B with its nonce N_A and gets the number N_B.
7. $A \rightarrow B : E_{K_B}(N_B)$.
   A encrypts the nonce N_B with the public key of B and sends it to B. B decrypts the ciphertext (being the only one who can do it) and compares the number sent by A with its own N_B.

Fig. 8.2 Simplified
Needham-Schroeder
Public-Key protocol

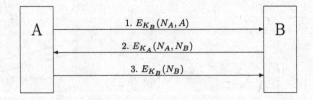

Due to the structure of data transfer used in the protocol and the properties of asymmetric cryptography, after executing the protocol participants A and B declare mutual authentication successful. Let us also pay attention to the fact that after the protocol execution both users can also be sure that they are the only holders of the numbers N_A and N_B and they can use them as identifiers of the current session in further communication.

Let us notice that the above protocol can be simplified. Assuming that each user already knows the public key of the other entity, the protocol can be presented in three steps (Fig. 8.2):

1. $A \rightarrow B : E_{K_B}(N_A, A)$
2. $B \rightarrow A : E_{K_A}(N_A, N_B)$
3. $A \rightarrow B : E_{K_B}(N_B)$

The story of this protocol is very instructive. It was used in practice in its original version for 17 years. However, in 1995 it turned out that the protocol can be broken. Gavin Lowe, a professor at the University of Cambridge, presented an attack on the protocol, i.e., a run of it that does not fulfill the aim of the protocol, namely mutual authentication. See [64].

The attack is performed by an intruder denoted by I. Below we present the attack given by Lowe. After its execution one of the entities is deceived as to the identity of another participant.

$\alpha 1. \quad A \rightarrow I : E_{K_I}(N_A, A)$

$\quad \beta 1. \quad I(A) \rightarrow B : E_{K_B}(N_A, A)$
$\quad \beta 2. \quad B \rightarrow I(A) : E_{K_A}(N_A, N_B)$

$\alpha 2. \quad I \rightarrow A : E_{K_A}(N_A, N_B)$
$\alpha 3. \quad A \rightarrow I : E_{K_I}(N_B)$

$\quad \beta 3. \quad I(A) \rightarrow B : E_{K_B}(N_B)$

The above run consists of two simultaneous interleaving executions of the protocol. Steps α correspond to communication of an honest user A with an intruder I, who impersonates A (we denote it by $I(A)$) during steps β. In the step $\alpha 1$, A starts communicating with I. The latter, however, abuses A's confidence and improperly uses the nonce N_A, given to I by user A, in order to start a session with B (the step $\beta 1$). According to the protocol, B sends a ciphertext $E_{K_A}(N_A, N_B)$ to I (believing it is A). Of course, I is not able to decrypt this ciphertext, since it does not know the private key of A. Therefore, the intruder forwards the message to A (the step $\alpha 2$). Unaware that anything is wrong, A decrypts the ciphertext, obtains the number N_B, encrypts and sends it to I (the step $\alpha 3$). Now, I is able to decrypt the message and knowing the value of N_B sends it to B (the step $\beta 3$). After that, B is convinced he is communicating with A, while in fact B exchanges information with the intruder I. In further conceivable communication, the intruder may use the numbers N_A and N_B, for example, to deceive B. An attack like this, using an honest user's information is called a replay attack.

A fixed version of the protocol, also developed by Lowe in [64], is as follows:

1. $A \rightarrow B : E_{K_B}(N_A, A)$
2. $B \rightarrow A : E_{K_A}(N_A, N_B, B)$
3. $A \rightarrow B : E_{K_B}(N_B)$

The modification affects the second step. Simply adding the responder's identifier B to the ciphertext $E_{K_A}(N_A, N_B, B)$ excludes the possibility of its deceptive use by a potential intruder. This, as it may seem, easy correction defends the protocol from the attack presented above and from any attacks known previously. The Needham-Schroeder protocol revised by Lowe has successfully passed all correctness tests invented so far. At the same time, this version of the protocol is the favorite toy example tested in the best academic and corporate research centers by new programs and tools for cryptographic protocol verification.

8.3 Needham-Schroeder Symmetric Key Protocol

Needham and Schroeder also proposed a protocol in which entities establish symmetric keys for use in the current session. Moreover, the protocol needs to provide mutual authentication. Let us suppose that A and B do not know each other. In particular, they do not know each other's public keys; however, they can take advantage of a trusted entity (represented usually by a server, not necessarily a human). Before communication each participant specifies a cipher and a secret key used for secure communication with the server. The protocol is as follows:

1. $A \rightarrow S : A, B, N_A$
2. $S \rightarrow A : E_{K_A}(N_A, B, K, E_{K_B}(K, A))$
3. $A \rightarrow B : E_{K_B}(K, A)$
4. $B \rightarrow A : E_K(N_B)$
5. $A \rightarrow B : E_K(N_B - 1)$

User A requests a session key from the server in order to start communication with B. Therefore, A sends to the server its name (identifier), the identifier of B, and a fresh nonce generated by A. This nonce will later allow A to verify whether the response of the server is a repetition of any previous request. The server generates a key and prepares an encrypted package consisting of the nonce generated by A, the identifier of B, the key, and the same key along with the identifier of A (the so-called ticket)—both encrypted with the secret key of B. The whole package is sent by the server to A, who is the only one able to decrypt this message. However, user A cannot decrypt the ticket, which is forwarded by A to B. The latter is informed that A wants to start a communication session. B obtains the symmetric key to be used in the session. In order to find out whether A is still alive and whether A is ready for communication and has the right key, B sends its own nonce encrypted by the key just proposed by A and verifies that A is able to decrypt it, transform and encrypt this nonce.

Thus, A and B have established a one-session key. Moreover, they know that the communicating entities are really A and B. This knowledge follows from the assumption that they are the only ones who are able to decrypt the key encrypted by the trusted third party. Furthermore, they know that all information being sent is fresh, i.e., A knows that the information obtained from the server constitutes a reply to its last request to establish communication with B. Since user A has proven that it knows the shared session key, this is known to B. Nonetheless, the protocol is currently considered as incorrect. Why? In the practice of encrypted communication, it is assumed that the key is established once in a session and it stays undisclosed during this session only. Everlasting secrecy is not assumed. First, the key may happen not to be strong enough and insufficiently resistant to possible future attacks, and thus it could be broken through extensive computations. Secondly, no user has full control over its own computer. For instance, in case of a disk failure a computer may be serviced in a repair center and it may turn out that a session key used several weeks ago lies in a swap file. Security of communication channels is usually based on the fact that knowledge of used key that was already applied is useless—the exchange of messages is over and a potential new session should use a new key.

Let us look more closely at the above protocol. In step 3 A sends to B a session key K encrypted with the key K_B, which is not known to A. Let us suppose that the intruder I was able to find some traces of an old session some time after it had taken place; for this session I knows both the ticket with the encrypted key and the key itself. Moreover, let us assume that I can impersonate A in the network. I can now repeat the protocol twice, starting with step 3:

3. $I(A) \rightarrow B : E_{K_B}(K, A)$
4. $B \rightarrow I(A) : E_K(N_B)$
5. $I(A) \rightarrow B : E_K(N_B - 1)$

In step 3 the encrypted key along with the identifier of A to B. Then user B considers this to be an attempt of A to start a new communication session, so in step 4 B wants to check that the receiver also knows the session key. B cannot verify whether A or I is the receiver of the message and the holder of the session key. Therefore, B gets deceived. The key being repeated twice does not make B suspicious—for at least two reasons. First, B does not keep *used* session keys. On the contrary, the possibility of reusing them is risky and dangerous, so they should be deleted immediately after being used. Secondly, the former execution of the protocol could have been unfinished. It may have happened that A had wanted to communicate with B, but the session was not established. Maybe there were some disturbances, maybe A changed its mind, maybe, finally, there was not enough time for communication.

And now B does not know whether such a session key has ever been proposed or used.

What can we do about it? For example, introduce timestamps.

8.4 Timestamps

Nonces are used in order to provide a kind of marker of each execution of a protocol. Nonetheless, nothing prevents us from repeating or resuming the protocol after a long break—the notion of time does not occur in the above protocol at all. In order to avoid a replay attack one can assume that cryptographic keys are not fixed once and forever, but they have some definite lifetime. When the time expires the keys have to be *refreshed*, i.e., generated once more. Usually this is done by a server of a specialized service provider, called a trusted third party. The generated key can be equipped with the exact date and time of its creation and a certificate including all important information, for example the lifetime window. Issues concerning synchronization of the clocks of the participants who use such dated keys can be solved, for example, by special technical components supplied by the service provider.

A timestamp is a sequence of characters denoting and recording the actual date and exact accurate time at which a certain message was created, modified, stored, or sent. A digital timestamp can be appended automatically to a message file. The problem is that the local system administrator can reset the system clock to any value he or she likes. One can generate timestamps that have nothing to do with the actual *real* time that the message is processed. Trusted timestamping is a reliable service which sets the actual exact time in such a way that no one can alter it without detection once it has been recorded, provided that the timestamper's security and integrity is never compromised. Usually, the service involves management infrastructure to collect, process and renew timestamps, together with publicly available digital timestamp certificates, revocation lists, and verification procedures. The most accurate timekeeping devices are atomic clocks, which are accurate to seconds in many millions of years, and are used to calibrate other timekeeping instruments.

A message being timestamped does not have to be released to anybody to create a timestamp. It suffices to timestamp its hash (fingerprint) value. In the cryptographic protocol context, timestamps are typically used for marking freshness of protocol step messages, preventing replay of old ones. That is why nonces were introduced above as a kind of time-relevant parameter. In some cases, a time-relevant parameter can be just the numbering of events. Then a date-and-time format is not necessary.

See [3, 8, 37, 102] for basic security requirements for effective use of trusted timestamps as a reliable time source that is provable to any interested party.

The most famous and currently most often used in practice authentication protocol that uses timestamps (timed entity authentication protocol) is Kerberos (see [68]). We present it in detail in Sect. 8.6. Here, we only point out that timestamps can play a role similar to the nonces in the Needham–Schroeder protocol.

1. $A \rightarrow S : A, B, N_A$
2. $S \rightarrow A : E_{K_B}(K, L, A), E_{K_A}(N_A, B, K, L)$

3. $A \rightarrow B : E_{K_B}(K, L, A), E_K(A, T_A)$
4. $B \rightarrow A : E_K(T_A)$

In Kerberos in step 3 A sends to B an encrypted timestamp T_A, according to A's local clock, and the key K with its lifetime L. An essential enhancement concerns attaching to the key its date and lifetime. A sends to B not only the ticket meant for them, but also an encrypted timestamp according to A's local clock. B checks that the key is valid according to both their clocks. By sending back a modified version of A's message, B proves the possession of the session key. The protocol can be extended by elements included in the Needham-Schroeder protocol, i.e., by the possibility of mutual exchange of nonces meant for verifying identities. The Kerberos protocol allows us not only to prevent the replaying of a part of the protocol after a long time, but also enables us to repeat the end of the protocol while the key is still valid with no need to establish a new connection with an independent server.

8.5 Key Exchange Public-Key Protocol

Finally, let us describe a hypothetical protocol, which can be easily broken and fixed in a simple way. It is hypothetical since its drawback is obvious and thus the protocol has never been proposed in serious applications. Anyway, it is instructive. The protocol assumes that users A and B have never communicated before. When discussing the Needham-Schroeder protocol, we assumed that both A and B have public keys of the other entity exchanged in a secure way and acknowledged by the Certification Authority. In the case of this protocol, A gets the public key of B and sends to the latter a suggested session key encrypted by B's public key.

1. $B \rightarrow A : K_B$
2. $A \rightarrow B : E_{K_B}(K)$

This way they establish a key K for one session. A drawback of the protocol lies in the baseless trust of A that the received key was really sent by B. The protocol can be broken by the following man-in-the-middle attack:

1. $B \rightarrow I(A) : K_B$
2. $I(B) \rightarrow A : K_I$
3. $A \rightarrow I(B) : E_{K_I}(K)$
4. $I(A) \rightarrow B : E_{K_B}(K)$

I is an active intruder set between the users A and B. The intruder may eavesdrop and intercept the message sent from B to A and replace it with some fake information pretending it is from B. The user A gets the public key of I being convinced it is the key of B. A sends a session key K to B, which is again intercepted by I who can decrypt and send it to B adequately encrypted as a message from A. This allows I to get the session key and to continue eavesdropping the communication between the users. Furthermore, if all further messages are captured by the intruder, then I can modify them.

In order to prevent such attacks, one can apply certificates. If A cannot obtain the public key of B via a trusted channel, they have to rely on a certificate issued by a trusted certification authority.

8.6 Kerberos System

Kerberos is a security system designed at MIT (Massachusetts Institute of Technology) for verifying identities of users or devices in a client/server network environment. It was developed in the late 1980s within the test project Athena. Its specification can be found in the memo RFC 1510.

This system allows encryption of transmissions and identification services, which provide access to servers via the password system. Kerberos is considered a reliable external identification system, mostly executed on a special computer which is neither a server nor a client. This computer is called the authentication server. Kerberos is usually implemented as a part of security systems, as it itself does not provide all necessary security functions. The system is used for security reasons during remote login and, in addition, it facilitates access to the system by avoiding separate logins to each server.

The passwords of all users are stored in a central database by the authentication server, which issues special references needed by the users in order to access the servers that are within its domain. This domain consists of all users and servers that are monitored by the authentication server. Since all identification procedures are entirely assigned to the latter, the application server does not execute them but relies on user references. There is some always risk associated with the transmission of a key during every process of communication that requires encryption. The Kerberos system secures key distribution, encrypting them when communicating with both clients and servers. Such a key is called a session key. The authentication server operates in a specific space called a domain, within which the security strategy is determined. The domains can trust each other, i.e., once a user is accepted by one of the domains no other authentication is required. In other words, it is assumed that a server belonging to another domain carries out identification and verification procedures properly. The name of the protocol originates from the fact that it offers three levels of protection: it authenticates communicating parties, authenticates sent messages, and allows their encryption. The inspiration for the name came from the Greek mythological character Kerberos (or Cerberus), the monstrous three-headed guard dog of Hades. We can distinguish three subprotocols:

1. the authentication protocol, which enables mutual authentication of parties sharing a secret key,
2. the key distribution protocol, which enables confidential distribution of secret session keys among users,
3. the single-signature protocol, which enables replacement of weak keys (passwords of users) by strong random cryptographic keys.

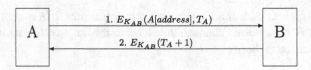

Fig. 8.3 Simplified version of the Kerberos protocol

8.6.1 Description of Kerberos Components

In the following example, a trusted party acts as a server called the Authentication Server (AS) and as a server that assigns tickets—the so-called Ticket Granting Server (TGS). By $E_{K_{AB}}(A[address], T_A)$ we mean a package from a user A containing the name of this user, possibly its address, and a timestamp encrypted with a secret key shared by users A and B. The symbol N_A stands for some pseudo-random number of A; the lifetime is a suggested validity period of the session key. The timestamp is denoted by T_A.

The authentication protocol enables mutual authentication of users. It is assumed that users A and B wishing to run the one–way or mutual authentication procedure share a secret key K_{AB}. Figure 8.3 illustrates a simplified version of the protocol.

In order for A's identity to be authenticated by B, the user A prepares so-called authentication package which includes: its name (possibly its address) and a timestamp T_A. The package is encrypted with the key K_{AB} shared by A and B, and then it is sent to B. The latter decrypts the received package and checks whether it really contains the name of A. If the address of the sender is included in the package, then it is possible to verify whether this address corresponds to the address from which the message was received. Next, user B checks the validity of the package (if it has not expired) by comparing the timestamp with the current time. If mutual authentication is required, then the user B executes an established operation on the timestamp obtained from A (increases it by a specified value), encrypts the result with the key shared with A, and sends it to the latter. A decrypts the received message, checks whether the timestamp was modified by the set value. Executing the protocol above, the entities verify each other identity. The authentication protocol is based on the assumption that the parties performing the protocol share the secret key K_{AB}. If this assumption is not satisfied, then the protocol cannot be executed. If the user A were able to send the secret key K_{AB} to user B via a trusted channel, then the problem would be solved. In order to send a secret session key, the key distribution protocol is used.

The key distribution protocol (Fig. 8.4) assumes that in the network there exists a trusted computer, which serves as a center of key distribution and key generation (denoted below by C). Each user shares with the center a secret key, called the primary key of the user (for A it is K_{AC}, for B—K_{BC}). When user A wants to communicate with user B, A sends to the key distribution center a request to generate a session key for them.

The center generates a key K_{AB} and two messages: the first one, denoted by C_{AB}, is called the certificate, while the second, denoted T_{AB}, is called the ticket.

Fig. 8.4 Key distribution
protocol

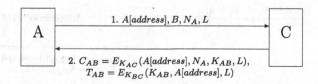

The certificate contains, among other things, the session key K_{AB} intended for users A and B, and it is encrypted with a key K_{AC} shared by A and the center. The ticket includes K_{AB}, and it is encrypted with a key shared by B and the center, namely K_{BC}. These two messages are received by A. Then, applying the authentication protocol, the user A decrypts the certificate using its main key K_{AC} and they get the session key K_{AB} from the certificate. A prepares an authentication package for B, encrypting it with the session key K_{AB}, and sends it along with the ticket obtained from the center. Now, the user B is able to decrypt the ticket with its main key K_{BC} and to get the session key K_{AB}. Therefore A and B may share a secret key and it is possible to carry out an authentication process.

In the key distribution protocol, a request for session key generation, which is sent by A to the center, contains, beside the names (and possibly addresses) of users A and B, some random number N_A and a suggested lifetime of the session key L. Such a solution is meant for protection against replay attacks. The idea is to prevent an intruder impersonating the center from sending to A a certificate that has already been used by the real center and intercepted by the intruder. Each request of A has to be answered with a certificate containing the same number that is included in the request. Since each user may send several requests for a session key, data sent in the certificate includes the name of the end-user. The username included in the certificate informs A which request has been answered with this certificate. The latter also contains the lifetime of the session key. The ticket sent to A (and ultimately to B) contains, among other things, the name of A. The user B can compare this name with the name included in the authentication package. The situation with the address is analogous. Moreover, the ticket contains the session key K_{AB} and its lifetime.

A single sign-on protocol (Fig. 8.5) is used in order to replace weak keys (usually passwords readily used by humans) by strong random cryptographic keys. The protocol is based on sharing of a secret password by all the users. This may be, for example, a shared key (e.g., K_{AAS}). The server knows the passwords of all users and shares the secret key with the TGS. The task of the authentication server is to generate keys for users who share these keys with the TGS. The protocol works analogously to the key distribution protocol. The user A requests the authentication server to generate a key for them and the TGS. The authentication server generates a key K_{ATGS} and sends it as one of the components of the certificate C_{ATGS} of the TGS encrypting it with the key of A. The key K_{ATGS} is included also in the TGS ticket T_{ATGS}, which is encrypted with a key K_{ASTGS} shared by the authentication server and the TGS, and sent along with the certificate. The remaining information sent within the protocol is used in the same way as in the case of the key distribution protocol.

Fig. 8.5 Single sign-on
protocol

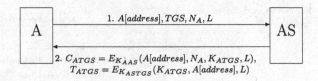

1. $A[address], TGS, N_A, L$

2. $C_{ATGS} = E_{K_{AAS}}(A[address], N_A, K_{ATGS}, L)$,
$T_{ATGS} = E_{K_{ASTGS}}(K_{ATGS}, A[address], L)$

Now, after having encrypted the certificate with its key, the user A shares the secret key K_{ATGS} with the TGS. By means of this key A encrypts the authentication package and sends it to the TGS along with the ticket T_{ATGS} and a request for B's ticket to the server. In this way the user A is authenticated by the TGS. Since the ticket T_{ATGS} is used by A in order to obtain a ticket to the server from the TGS, it is called a ticket granting ticket (TGT). It is worth mentioning that the password is not sent through the network from a client to the server, which increases the system security.

8.6.2 Example of Application of Kerberos

Authentication and authorization processes of the Kerberos system consist of the following steps:

1. The first step of a user is to obtain an appropriate TGT. At this point the user is verified. It requests from the authentication server a TGT. The server encrypts the TGT with a key that is based on the user's password.
2. When the user gets a reply, it must provide the password which allows decryption. Only an authorized user can do this, thus the whole procedure identifies it.
3. After decrypting the reply the user stores a copy of the TGT. It requests from the TGS access to a specific server, proving its credibility by sending the identifiers of the server, the user and the TGT.
4. The TGS decrypts the TGT and checks its contents. If the information is correct, the TGS creates a special ticket for the requested server and encrypts it with the key that is known to this server. Thereafter, it introduces a new key, which is now based on the user's password, and sends the ticket to the user.
5. The user decrypts the answer from the TGS obtaining the server ticket and the session key. Next, the server ticket along with the user's identifier are sent to the appropriate server. The identifier is encrypted within the server ticket, as well.
6. The server decrypts the obtained ticket and compares the included user's identifier with the identifier sent by it. If the identifiers are identical, then the user gets access rights.

The ticket to the server also contains the session key, which is separately sent to the user. Now both entities of the communication session possess the proper encryption key and they can use it for exchanging information, keeping it confidential. The authorization process can be extended by requesting from the user a timestamp from a device that resembles a credit card. The identifier (ID token) is synchronized with the server and its value is displayed by the device. The user enters this value at log in. The original version of Kerberos applies techniques of symmetric encryption. Some producers, however, implement similar public key schemes.

Kerberos was designed to operate in a particular environment, where it worked, and was used to authenticate users working on workstations for individual entities applying resources provided by large and secured servers. However, many computers operating on the Internet are multi-user systems. In the case of such systems some problems arise. One of these is associated with the necessity of storing keys and tickets in the operating system—in a multi-user environment these are exposed to some risk related to the presence of other users in the system. Another problem concerns diskless workstations. This means keys and tickets must be sent through the network in plaintext, in order to keep them on the outer disk. Transmitted data are vulnerable to interception by an intruder. When dealing with other environments, some modifications should be carried out in order to adapt the system to specific features of work. Kerberos Version 5 went through implementation on various types of computers and different operating systems. Among them there are Sun computers running Solaris, HP9000 machines running HP-UX, IBM PowerPC with the AIX system, Macintosh computers and PCs with MS Windows.

8.7 Verification of Correctness of Cryptographic Protocols

In this section we will briefly present the most important ideas and problems concerning verification of correctness of cryptographic protocols, i.e., verifying whether they really do what their author and users expect. Nowadays, methods of verifying software correctness form a wide area of practical and theoretical computer science. Often, even with the best of intentions, it is hard to imagine all possible runs of a program.

When dealing with reliability (correctness) of cryptographic protocols, we assume that applied ciphers are absolutely reliable (secure). Furthermore, we also assume that no one is able to read an encrypted document unless they have a proper key. Cryptographic protocols often make use of the fact that the relevant information has been created recently. It is said that the information is fresh. As indicated above, freshness is ensured, e.g., by generating a new nonce each time. Again, when verifying protocols we assume that an intruder cannot guess a recently generated nonce. The use of timestamps is associated with numerous technical problems, such as the necessity of reliable clock synchronization. Protocols that apply timestamps are more difficult to verify. Actually, all verification methods known until very recently consider timestamp values, i.e., the time of transaction, as yet another number used once. Their order expresses, in some sense, the flow of time.

In order to verify cryptographic protocols, we may apply general-purpose tools for software correctness verification that are intended for all programs, not necessarily for cryptographic or concurrent ones. An overview of such tools can be found, for example, in [9]. However, the complexity and the importance of the problem usually require the use of specialized tools. In general, there are four methods of verification:

- (real and virtual) system testing,
- inductive methods,
- axiomatic (deductive) methods,
- model checking.

Testing does not usually apply to cryptographic protocols, but the other methods do. It is worth recalling that verification need not prove correctness of the protocol. It can indicate examples of failures or flaws in the analyzed protocol, preferably by giving an instance of interleaving correct performances of the protocol which result in misleading one of the entities as to the identity of the other party. Such an interleaving is then an example of a successful attack on the protocol.

A formal definition of the property of correctness is already difficult. For instance, since the aim of a protocol is to confirm identity, then this should be covered in the protocol specification. The point is that such a formulation is given in an everyday conversational language and there is no way in sight of expressing this property in any formal language. But only formalized properties can be a subject of formal verification.

8.7.1 Axiomatic (Deductive) Method

The axiomatic method consists of constructing a specially designed formal deductive system, called logic, whose language allows us to specify a protocol to be verified and its operation scheme as a set of axioms. At the same time, it allows us to specify properties of the protocol which we want to verify. The objective is to derive the properties from the assumed axioms by means of the deduction rules of this system. The first such system was formulated in [23] by Burrows, Abadi, and Needham. After their names it is called the BAN logic or the authentication logic. The main construct in this logic is the belief modality. It allows us to formalize the correctness property of an entity authentication protocol, i.e., the correctness of the statement *if A has executed the protocol with B, then A believes in (or is convinced about) B's authentication*, and the converse one.

After early successes it turned out, however, that these methods do not always allow us to find possible flaws in the studied protocols. The famous Needham-Schroeder protocol was positively verified by the original BAN logic. However as the reader knows from Sect. 8.2.1, five years later Gavin Lowe found an effective attack on this protocol. For this reason the BAN logic along with its advantages and drawbacks is the subject of intensive investigations in numerous academic and commercial centers all over the world (see [60]).

One of the disadvantages of the original BAN logic was the lack of sound and complete semantics of the language of this logic, i.e., the semantics in which the formulas are true if and only if they are theorems of this logic. Without a complete semantics users of the BAN logic were not able to prove formally that some formula is not derivable from another one in this system. In general, such a proof consists of constructing a model in which the first formula is false while the second one is true together with all the axioms of this logic. The first complete and decidable BAN-type logic was presented in [60].

8.7.2 Model Checking

Model checking consists of constructing a mathematical model for the program (protocol) in question and proving in a formal mathematical way, preferably automatically or semiautomatically, that all possible executions of the program and their interleavings do not have undesired properties. One such method concerns checking whether no state with an undesired property is reached. For this purpose, it is specified what we mean by a mathematical model, in which language and by the use of which symbols and syntactic constructs the properties of the program (protocol) are expressed, and what it means that a formula in this language is true or satisfiable in the model. Usually, the methodology of model theory, basic concepts of which were introduced by Alfred Tarski in the 1920s and 1930s, is applied.

In model checking methods a temporal logic language is usually applied, which allows us to use constructs like *in the next step* or *sometime in the future*, etc. One of the studied formulations of the correctness property is the following one: *if A executed the protocol with B, then the latter finished all B's actions within this protocol*. Another property concerns confidentiality: *none of the nonces is captured by an unauthorized entity (i.e., an entity that does not know a proper cryptographic key)*. A model is generally built over the set of states of all possible interleavings of protocol executions. The biggest problem of model checking involves an exponential explosion of the number of states which are reachable by the modeled system. Usually we deal with such an enormous number of states that it is infeasible to examine all of them one by one. This is mostly due to the huge amount of possible information that can be generated and sent by a potential intruder. The computational complexity of model checking is generally exponential with regard to the parameters of a verified protocol, and especially with regard to the number of its participants and performed steps.

8.7.3 Inductive Method

The inductive method was proposed by Larry Paulson. In this method all possible traces of protocol runs are taken into consideration. A trace is a sequence of steps of type A *sends a message M to B*. The number of possible traces is infinite, since there is no restriction on their length. Our aim is to prove that some interesting property is valid for all traces of the protocol by means of mathematical induction. If we succeed, then the protocol satisfies this property. An unsuccessful attempt to prove the property may indicate a bug in the protocol. In this approach, as in the others, it is assumed that a potential intruder is not able to decrypt an encrypted message without knowing a proper key. We only examine whether the protocol itself does not reveal what it should not or whether it does not mislead one of its participants. An intruder is not able to decrypt the message, but it is able to prepare any message on the basis of information held, even one that the protocol does not expect. For example, the protocol requires generating a fresh random number, while the intruder prefers to apply the number that was used in another session. It is also assumed that the intruder is able to guess the names of participants of the protocol, the space of these names being too small to base the security of the protocol on their security. However, the intruder is not able to guess keys or random numbers generated for the use of one session. The inductive method is applied, among others, due to the availability of good tools for automated theorem proving by mathematical induction. This method was successfully used to analyze real and complex protocols such as TLS (Transport Layer Security/Secure Sockets Layer) [78] or SET (Secure Electronic Transaction) [11].

8.7.4 Results

Interesting results obtained by model checking were published by a team from Carnegie Mellon University (USA) led by Edmund Clarke. The model checker they implemented revealed a new attack on a single authentication protocol, a very simple and seemingly credible one. Here is the protocol (taken from Woo and Lam [105]):

1. $A \rightarrow B : A$
2. $B \rightarrow A : N_B$
3. $A \rightarrow B : E_{K_{AS}}(N_B)$
4. $B \rightarrow S : E_{K_{BS}}(A, E_{K_{AS}}(N_B))$
5. $S \rightarrow B : E_{K_{BS}}(A, N_B)$

In the first step A starts a session by sending its identifier (i.e., the name, the address, the IP or the ID number, etc) to B. In the second step B replies by sending a freshly generated large nonce N_B to A. Then A sends this nonce back to B, but now it is encrypted with a symmetric key known only to A and the trusted server S. B appends A's identifier to the obtained message, encrypts it with a symmetric key known only to B and S and sends it to the latter. The server encrypts everything, as it knows both keys, and sends A's identifier and the nonce N_B to B encrypting both with the key shared with B. In this way A confirms its identity. Now B knows that it is communicating with A since only A and the server know the key K_{AS}. The server is a third party fully trusted by the other participants.

Below we present an attack on this protocol published in [24].

1. $I(A) \rightarrow B : A$
2. $B \rightarrow I(A) : N_B$
3. $I(A) \rightarrow B : N_B$
4. $B \rightarrow I(S) : E_{K_{BS}}(A, N_B)$
5. $I(S) \rightarrow B : E_{K_{BS}}(A, N_B)$

In this case only B is an honest participant in the protocol. An intruder impersonates A and the server S. We denote this by $I(A)$ and $I(S)$. As a result, B is convinced that A participated in the session, while in fact A did not. It turns out that the flaw lies in the formulation of the third step of the Woo-Lam protocol. Since, according to the authors of the protocol, B does not know the key K_{AS}, it does not know what this information should look like. B is not able to verify it in any way. In particular, B does not check that the received number is identical with the number sent. The intruder can use this opportunity simply by replaying the information that it got in the second step. B believes that this is the information expected from A, so B executes the fourth step of the protocol. This means that B appends the ID of A in front of the message and sends it to S encrypted with the key shared by B and the server. In fact, this is precisely the information that B expects from the server. The intruder intercepts it and sends it back to B, impersonating the server S.

According to the authors of [24], this attack was found by their model checker in just a few seconds. Their program got as an input a list of participants and actions that can be executed by A, B and the server S. The protocol was implemented as a sequence of actions that can be performed by its users. The initial knowledge of the intruder covers the identifiers of all users, including the server, and the symmetric key shared by the intruder and the server.

8.7.5 Summary

Model checking requires methods to be developed for the essential reduction of the state space explosion. It is necessary to specify an equivalence relation which would allow us to identify at least some potential information not affecting the property of correctness. Restrictions concerning the complexity of information sent seem unavoidable. For this purpose various common knowledge logics are studied. Exponential growth of the number of states is also caused by adding a new user of a protocol. It is not clear whether proofs of correctness of a protocol with few users can be generalized.

The possibility of decomposing an analyzed protocol into some smaller components is an intriguing one. Also the other way round, the possibility of building a model of a protocol from its components provided that the conjunction of the specifications of smaller segments implies the specification of the whole protocol is interesting. For example, let us consider a protocol of electronic transactions, which requires authorization of the entities' identities, exchange of a session key, authorization of each bank transfer order, etc. The desired decomposition is not easy; what is more, it is not always possible. In order to verify such a protocol it is necessary, among other things, to define precisely the goals of the protocol. As an example of such a complex protocol one can take a relatively new protocol of e-mail delivery with acknowledgment receipt, which applies a protocol of multi-party secure information exchange (see [10]).

Nowadays, the most interesting challenge is to apply model checking techniques to other classes of cryptographic protocols. In particular, these include schemes for electronic voting, electronic auctions, an electronic purse, and electronic card software. They all need, however, a more sophisticated modeling language and a formalized specification language of much greater expressive power.

Chapter 9
Cryptographic Applications for Network Security

This chapter provides an overview of selected practical applications of crypto-graphic techniques, presented in the previous chapters, in electronic network and data security protection. It outlines examples of various threats occurring in open telecommunication networks (such as the Internet) and the most well-known examples of software systems for data security, privacy, protection and security of electronic mail. The most popular systems are similar to PGP (see Chap. 6). Some alternatives to it are provided by S/MIME, employing the asymmetric RSA, or the older protocol PEM (Privacy-Enhanced Mail). The system EDI (Electronic Data Interchange) for private data exchange between corporations, each of which possibly running different internal software, is shown. It is followed by the SSH and SSL protocols, as mechanisms protecting data transferred via public computer networks, e.g., over the Internet. Their basic practical functionalities are presented. Authenticated key transport can be considered a special case of message authentication with privacy based on digital signatures. These are currently the most often used in practical security systems for computer networks exposed to eavesdropping and data interception.[1]

9.1 Application of Cryptography to Internet Mail Systems Security

9.1.1 PEM

PEM (Privacy Enhanced Mail), the email system with the highest level of privacy, was one of the first standards for securing email. This term was defined by the IETF committee (Internet Engineering Task Force) in RFC 1421–1424, as a method for

---

[1]More on these and related topics can be found in [91].

C. Kościelny et al., *Modern Cryptography Primer*,
DOI 10.1007/978-3-642-41386-5_9, © Springer-Verlag Berlin Heidelberg 2013

7-bit text encryption. Most often it is used in connection with the internet SMTP protocol (Simple Mail Transfer Protocol), but also other email protocols (e.g. X.400). The main characteristics of PEM are:

- It is not limited to a definite server or software and allows cooperation between many different systems.
- It is compatible with a simple insecure email.
- It enables the security of email privacy in newsgroups.
- It is compatible with the different methods of key management.
- It is compatible with many protocols, email systems and email applications.

PEM supports all the essential email security functions: security and privacy, authentication, message integrity, undeniability, key management.

Sending a PEM message takes place in four stages:

1. Standardization—the transformation of the message from the format of the email program into the standard PEM format, which is recognizable on each platform.
2. Insertion of the information which enables us to check the cohesion of the message and the authentication of its author.
3. Encryption (optional).
4. Transmission coding (optional).

Receiving the PEM message is a complicated operation, so every implementation does it instead of the user. Receiving the message consists of 5 stages:

1. Decoding—the reverse of coding if it was used in the message.
2. Decryption—if the message was encrypted then it must be decrypted.
3. Checking the cohesion and the authenticity of the message.
4. Transformation from the PEM format into a suitable form of the recipient email program.
5. Disposal of the message—the recipient decides about the form of the saved message (encrypted, encoded).

9.1.2 S/MIME

The S/MIME alternative system of email security is the extension of securing mechanisms of the MIME popular email standard (Multipurpose Internet Mail Extension). MIME, defined in 1992, is the standard used to send different types of data via email. Traditional emails include only text. MIME specifies the standard means of coding different data, e.g. binary files, multilanguage alphabets, pictures, sounds and files written in special forms (e.g. compressed files). This standard enables us to use a special set of fonts in emails. The original specification of the S/MIME project allowed us to send the messages without sharing their secrecy. Because the new standard is the extension of a previous one it is easy to integrate it with existing products to send the emails.

Fig. 9.1 Microsoft
Outlook—Option

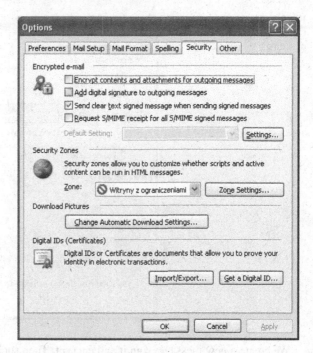

S/MIME lets us sign the messages in two ways:

- Placing the signature in a separate part of the MIME format. It lets the recipient, who does not have the S/MIME standard, read only the content of the message.
- Placing the signature and the message in one part of the MIME format. Changing one sign of the signature makes it impossible to verify it and the removal or the space merging at the beginning of the message causes a digital signature sent in this self-contained way to be useless.

S/MIME permits different cryptographic methods, the most important symmetric algorithms are RC2/40 and 3DES. The S/MIME standard enables us to sign and also encrypt the message using the RSA algorithm.

The S/MIME standard is promoted by the RSA Data Systems enterprise, and VeriSign Certification Center creates suitable PKI infrastructure for this system.

At the end of 1997 the IETF committee considered the acceptance of the S/MIME system as the internet standard for ensuring email privacy, but abandoned this idea because of the license policy of the RSA enterprise. One example of the S/MIME protocol usage is the Microsoft Outlook program. In the application choose from menu: *Tools → Options... → Overlap: Security* (Fig. 9.2). We can select by clicking to encrypt and sign our email with the attachments. Choosing the push button *Settings* we can change our security (Fig. 9.2). We choose the format of the confidential message as S/MIME and the suitable encryption algorithms. We can define some profiles of a different security level and then in an easy way choose from a drop-down list, visible in Fig. 9.1.

Fig. 9.2 Microsoft
Outlook—Option, the change
of settings

We create a new message, sign it and encrypt. Then such a message is sent. The recipient having an appropriate certificate can read the message.

9.1.3 MOSS

Together with the MIME standard, which enables us to send binary attachments by email, the value of the PEM system was decreased. PEM was extended and a MOSS (MIME Object Security Standard) protocol appeared. It is compatible with PEM and also serves binary attachments of the MIME standard. But its implementation and usage is not easy. More popular is the S/MIME standard, which is implemented in most cases by email users.

9.2 Security of Document Interchange

Every firm tries to improve and optimize work by using computers and different software. Computerization of a firm is not easy. There are many firms specializing in writing programs which ensure bookkeeping, invoicing or records storage.

But it helps only inside the company. It is very difficult to have a presence in the electronic market because this requires contact with other firms with other software. Everyone knows some email services reduce the time for sending information from one firm to another. These services do not ensure the security of data and do not guarantee its correctness.

In such a way arose the need to develop a system which can be used to connect some firms, independently from the local system. EDI, Electronic Data Interchange, thus originated.

9.2.1 EDI

This product is a system for electronic commercial information interchange in the form of orders, invoices, and consignment notes. It is used in a client-seller system. It enables us to send orders directly into supplier computers. It coordinates the delivery and generates the invoices. It works on the principle of saving the message and sending it into the proper recipient as in the case of email. Using an EDI system reduces the cost of work and decreases the number of mistakes during the exchange of documents in person. This system is implemented in firms connected with distribution, bookkeeping, finance, production, storage, transport and shipping.

The first versions of the EDI system would define standard documents, which forced the users to generate their own personal forms. New versions enable us to create any documents using simple tools. The system users can operate on different versions of the internal software. EDI changes automatically the document format of the sender into the standard one. The client version is changed from the EDI standard into the one required in the firm. In the USA, DISA (Data Interchange Standards Association, Inc.) deals with the standardization of electronic data interchange. The page http://www.disa.org is a compendium of useful information about EDI and its structures. Information about the specification of the standard is at http://www.x12.org. X.12 is the American document standard covering air transport, requests for loans, consignment notes, bills. In 1979 the American National Standards Institute designated the ASC X.12 committee (Accredited Standards Committee) as responsible for the EDI standards development. X.12 ensures the compatibility and transferability of documents between different system platforms. The documents sent from home PC computers are smoothly read by mainframe or Macintosh systems. The international standard for electronic data interchange is UN/EDIFACT (United Nations/Electronic Data Interchange for Administration, Commerce and Transport). EDI INT is the suitable standard for the Internet.

Most corporations noticed that the cost of EDI implementation in the Internet is smaller than building their own large systems. The Internet serves as a place for exchanging commercial information. The costs of installation are lower and most businesses have Internet access. As a result smaller businesses, which traditionally found the costs of EDI implementation to be too much, can now economically use this facility to conduct transactions with their partners where before it would only have been possible via email.

9.2.2 OpenEDI

ISO (International Organization for Standardization) and IEC (International Electrical Committee) created the Open-EDI committee. The aim of the committee is to help with business contacts over the Internet and to ensure suitable security. Open-EDI uses the Internet as the electronic platform for business information interchange. Thanks to modern standards they eliminate the need for the conversion and the translation of sent documents. The Internet helps to reduce the implementation of both costs and equipment to businesses. Despite the reduced cost and reduction of equipment required, the Internet delivers a very high value service. The diversity of the applications offers many possibilities. By email the inquiries can be sent, and then new contacts can be made.

Most systems develop integration with the Internet but face the difficulty connected with the transferability of the documents and the standards between the previous users of EDI and others with whom they had no contact. There are services which ensure the appropriate conversion. The most common conversion is the SMTP email protocol. The fast growth of technology leads to the unification of the standards.

9.2.3 OBI

Another solution can be OBI (Open Buying on the Internet). It is a protocol compiled by American Express and Supply Works in order to carry out WWW transactions in real time. Microsoft, Netscape, Oracle, Open Market and many others support this specification. The aim of this project is to reduce the cost and to improve the customer shopping experience by improving the level of service. Using the OBI protocol gives many benefits like EDI. The structure of the documents and the methods of sending the data use the EDI X12-850 specification. Transactions require electronic authorization, so the firms receiving the orders can verify their authenticity.

9.2.4 Swift, Edifact

Some specific standards have arisen for proper lines of business. The best known is SWIFT (Society for Worldwide Interbank Financial Telecommunications)—the interbank settlement system. In Europe the ODETTE standard appeared (Organization for Data Exchange by Teletransmission in Europe) because of the car industry. The United Nations decided to continue the EDI standard based on a uniform pattern for different business documents. The blocks of combining information should always be put into specific places in documents, and information fields should be filled in according to the Trade Data Elements Directory. In 1986 working group No. 4 RKG/ONZ, which deals with this technology, for the first time used the name United Nations Electronic Data Interchange for Administration, Commerce and Transport, the UN/EDIFACT or EDIFACT for short. EDIFACT concerns only the message structure not the transmission. It uses 5 basic tools:

1. the syntax of the EDIFACT standard,
2. the guidelines of the message construction,
3. the dictionary including unambiguous defined notions connected with trade transactions,
4. the dictionary of defined segments and messages,
5. the principles of the physical interpretation of the electronic document.

The EDIFACT message is a great matrix consisting of the sets of data elements, corresponding line or the section of a sent document. The data elements are quantitative or qualitative values of a given element. The advantage of EDIFACT is the fact that there is a great number of segments inside the message which enable the usage of one type message for many documents. The EDIFACT messages have 6-digit symbols connected with the English sounds of the message names (e.g., IFCSUM, Forwarding and Consolidation Summary). They are divided into such groups (e.g., IFTM, International Forwarding and Transport Messages) as trade, the needs of customs administration, and container trade. The EDIFACT standard serves every field of economic life and it is really the international and universal standard.

Electronic Data Interchange requires a platform which will link the computer systems of the firms participating. One option is the VAN network (Value Added Network). VAN can link firms from certain economy sectors, and there can be national VANs or global VANs. More often businesses stop using VANs in favour of the Internet.

9.2.5 EDI in Practice

EDI is the system where the application of the sender takes the information from its own database, places it encoded in a proper structure, and sends it through the telecommunications network to the recipient. The application of the recipient receives, translates and sends the content of the message to its own database. The computer systems of the sender and the recipient can be different and it is important to read and interpret the sent structure. To properly use Electronic Data Interchange it is important to define the structure of the electronic message. The message includes all the data of a traditional document, arranged in a proper form. When the structure of this message is settled we have the following steps of message interchange (Fig. 9.3).

1. In the internal system of the A firm there is the set of data. Appropriate software generates the intermediate form, the so-called internal message.
2. The internal message is converted into the arranged standard of the data interchange and ensured using suitable translating applications.
3. The translated message is sent into the system of the B firm.
4. The message in the EDI standard is changed into a proper intermediate form interpreted by the system of the B firm.
5. The internal message is fetched by the application of the B firm.

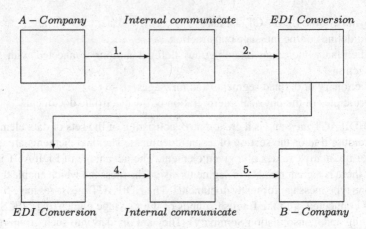

Fig. 9.3 The circulation of the document using the EDI standard

All stages are executed automatically, the duration of sending the message is incomparably shorter than the traditional form of a document interchange.

9.3 Computer Network Security—SSH and SSL Protocols

This subsection presents SSH (Secure Shell) and SSL (Secure Sockets Layer) protocols as the network information security mechanisms. It describes the protocols' operating principles and their practical implementations.

9.3.1 Introduction

Servers in the environment of TCP/IP protocols provide services through the ports. Protocol ports are labeled with integers from 1 to 65535. When a connection is established between two computers, a so-called socket is created on both machines. The socket is closely associated with the port number assigned to the application. A socket may be compared to a telephone and a port to a telephone number. The most popular services have fixed permanent numbers and software companies agree in this respect. The most common ports are: 80, http (WWW) server; 21, FTP server; and 22, SSH server.

An architecture which is often used on the Internet is the client-server architecture. In this method the server provides services to a number of clients, therefore it is characterised by a respectively high efficiency. Clients are those that use HTTP services or display WWW sites, and servers accomplish their requests and provide relevant sites. Servers are able to accomplish different types of services. They make calculations, store files, verify logging into a system, or they act as a print server.

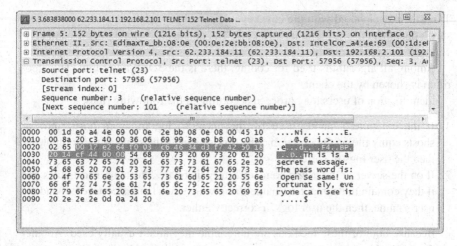

Fig. 9.4 TCP/IP frame telnet protocol

The Internet allows us to connect with and use remote computers and servers. Until recently the most common method was to use the telnet protocol based on port 23. The method is based on a client-server architecture. A user who wants to connect is a client (telnet application), a computer which provides this service is a server (telnet daemon). The service used to be very popular but it has one disadvantage. The user name, password and transmitted text are unencrypted; so, a potential phisher may capture this information. Figure 9.4 shows a captured TCP/IP frame of the telnet protocol. Everyone can see the content of a message in this way.

9.3.2 Idea of the SSH Protocol

A service extended by the ability to encrypt connections is the SSH protocol using port 22. The user who establishes the connection is the client (SSH application is required), a remote computer is the server (SSHD daemon is required).

There are two versions of SSH available. It is important to note that the protocol versions are not compatible with each other. The SSH Communications Security Company (http://www.ssh.com) does not recommend the use of SSH1 for security reasons.

The SSH1 protocol assumes that the server accepting SSH connection possesses a unique RSA key (host key). Its length is 1024 bits. An additional key (server key), the length of which is 768 bits, is generated at the time of starting the SSH daemon. This key is reproduced periodically after each use. The client connecting with the server receives a pair of keys. On the grounds of the host key, the client verifies the server identity (checks if the obtained key is in the local database—if not, the client fetches the key). Then a random 256-bit key (session key) is generated.

This key is enciphered with the host key and server key and sent to the server. The server deciphers the key with its own keys. The obtained session key is used to code connections symmetrically.

Among all algorithms used for coding, there is the 3DES algorithm. The algorithm is chosen by the client.

Identification of users may proceed according to the following rules:

1. If the computer's name, used by the client to log in, is in hosts.equiv or shosts.equiv file on the server and the user's name is the same as the computer's, then the user logs in correctly.
2. If on the server in the user's home directory there are .rhosts or .shosts files and if they contain the computer's name (from which the client is connected) and the user's name, then the user logs in correctly either.

Because both of these methods are unreliable they aren't usually used. Another method of authentication is a mechanism which uses the public key. On the server there is a list of public keys which are used for connecting. The client determines the key which is used to authenticate its credibility. If the key is on the list, the server generates a random value and enciphers it with the key. If the client receives the same value after deciphering then its credibility is authenticated. To make the authentication algorithm usable, one must copy the public key to a relevant file of the home directory on a remote machine.

Another well-known authentication method is to use an agent program. If the user wasn't authenticated with any of the previously mentioned methods, a password is required.

SSH-2 version has been significantly improved in comparison with the SSH-1 version. In the new version it is possible to use any data encryption methods and four different ways to identify the user, while SSH1 supports only a fixed list of several encryption methods and two different ways to recognize the user (RSA key and the usual password). Secure Shell was designed to secure remote terminal connection and transmission of confidential files. This protocol can tunnel any TCP sessions through a single Secure Shell encrypted connection (Fig. 9.5).

Tunneling allows us to protect the communication of other applications and protocols without modifying the applications themselves. We use it to transmit data packets through networks using protocols different from the broadcasting and receiving network. Thus we create a virtual channel running through the area of the intermediary network. Using tunneling, we still may use applications which do not enable an adequate level of security, such as e-mails, in a safe way. SSH-2 is an open and well-documented standard. SSH-2 protocol supports the strongest encryption algorithms. It provides data integrity through Hash Message Authentication Codes (HMAC). However, the use of a public key infrastructure compatible with the X.509 standard and public key certificates provides security at the appropriate level. In the case of using certificates there is no need to replace the SSH public key separately in each of the servers, the server must only trust the CA which issued the certificate.

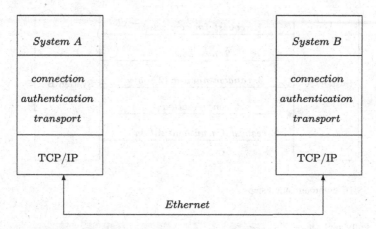

Fig. 9.5 SSH-2 connection

SSH-2 protocol consists of three elements:

1. transport layer protocol, which is responsible for server authentication, confidentiality and integrity,
2. users authentication protocol, which is responsible for client authentication to the server,
3. connection protocol which divides the encrypted tunnel into several logical channels.

User authentication can be carried out on the basis of the given user name and password or with the use of the public key. The last login is carried out with the use of the RSA asymmetric encryption algorithm. The client generates a pair of keys and then connects to the server and downloads the public key of the server. This key is compared to an internal keys database of previous connections. Detection of key inconsistencies generates a warning enabling interruption of a connection. Then the client gets his public key over to the server, generates a random number, and encrypts with his private key and a public server key. After receiving such an encrypted number, he deciphers it with its private key and the client's public key. A number obtained in this way is known only to the client and the server. It is used as a key to encrypt further communication with the use of symmetric algorithms such as IDEA, DES, 3DES. This solution is reliable and less burdensome to use.

1. The client sends a request to the server (Fig. 9.6).
2. The server sends the client its public key (host key). The client checks its local database to find such a key (at the first connection to the server the key is added). The client is informed if a particular database server has a different key.
3. The client generates a random 256-bit number used to encrypt the connection and selects the encoding algorithm. The encrypted key is sent to the server.
4. The server decrypts the key item and sends a confirmation to the client.
5. The client sends an authentication request.

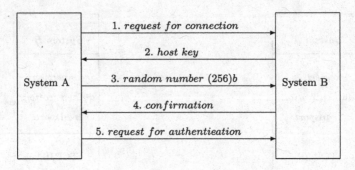

Fig. 9.6 SSH-2 communication steps

Fig. 9.7 Putty application

The SSH protocol descriptions (commercial version) can be found at http://www. ssh.com or http://www.ssh.org, and the free equivalent openssh at http://www. openssh.com or http://www.openssh.org.

9.3.3 Using the SSH Protocol

If we want to connect to the server from a computer with an operating system from the Unix/Linux family, we carry out the command: *ssh-l user* serwer.pl??

SSH is an application running in text mode, we call it with the -l user parameter by giving the user name to our server and the server name or IP address. In the Windows environment we can use the free application Putty (Fig. 9.7).

Fig. 9.8 Warning

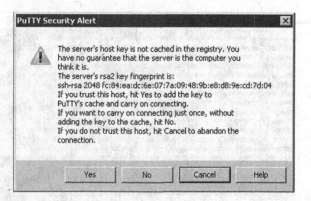

Logging in for the first time to a remote computer without its public key, we receive a message about the possibility of downloading the key with a warning that if a user is not sure of its authenticity the connection may be terminated (Fig. 9.8). After downloading the public key one can log in safely (Fig. 9.9).

Figure 9.10 shows the record of the connection's text version. At the beginning the application introduces itself, announces which of the SSH versions operates: application operates SSH-1 version (1.5 record) and SSH-2 (2.0 record). Then reads the configuration and connects to a remote server (mp) on 22 port. When the connection is established, a negotiation between the client and the server starts. The version of the protocol is determined and then keys exchange and number generation starts. After accepting the keys, one is ready to log in to a remote system.

In Fig. 9.10 we see a single TCP/IP frame with a message record in the SSH protocol. The whole message is encrypted, we cannot get to know its content, only the sender and the recipient.

9.3.4 Construction of SSL Protocol

SSL is a protocol used in WWW, which is responsible for authentication and confidential sessions between a client and a WWW server. All sent information is encrypted. S-HTTP (Secure-HTTP) is a protocol which encrypts only on the http level (Hypertext Transfer Protocol).

SSL was designed by Netscape which gave it to IETF (Internet Engineering Task Force). SSL and S-HTTP often appear in electronic trade because they protect against wiretapping and forgery. The SSL protocol uses mechanisms which enable mutual authentication of browsers and servers, and later encryption of data during communication sessions, and digital signatures.

The procedure of verification allows correct identification by the WWW server and a check of the client's authorization. Verification mechanisms require digital certification which is strictly based on the PKI infrastructure.

Both the browser and the server must be compatible with an appropriate SSL version. Usually the client is interested in confirmation of the server authenticity

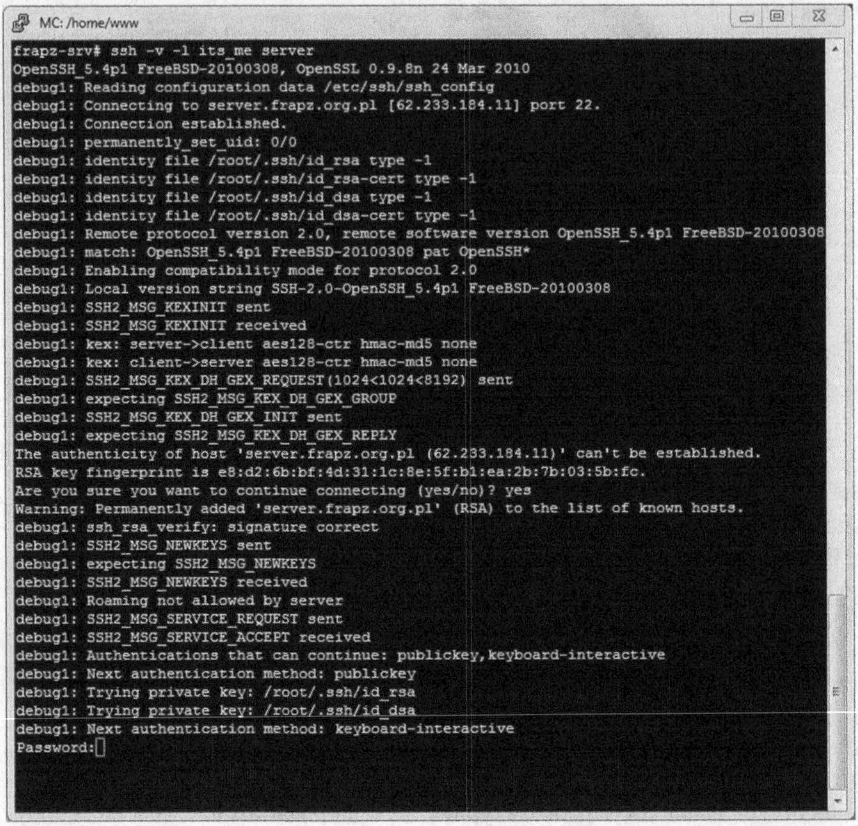

```
MC: /home/www                                                    □ ▣ ▨

frapz-srv# ssh -v -l its_me server
OpenSSH_5.4p1 FreeBSD-20100308, OpenSSL 0.9.8n 24 Mar 2010
debug1: Reading configuration data /etc/ssh/ssh_config
debug1: Connecting to server.frapz.org.pl [62.233.184.11] port 22.
debug1: Connection established.
debug1: permanently_set_uid: 0/0
debug1: identity file /root/.ssh/id_rsa type -1
debug1: identity file /root/.ssh/id_rsa-cert type -1
debug1: identity file /root/.ssh/id_dsa type -1
debug1: identity file /root/.ssh/id_dsa-cert type -1
debug1: Remote protocol version 2.0, remote software version OpenSSH_5.4p1 FreeBSD-20100308
debug1: match: OpenSSH_5.4p1 FreeBSD-20100308 pat OpenSSH*
debug1: Enabling compatibility mode for protocol 2.0
debug1: Local version string SSH-2.0-OpenSSH_5.4p1 FreeBSD-20100308
debug1: SSH2_MSG_KEXINIT sent
debug1: SSH2_MSG_KEXINIT received
debug1: kex: server->client aes128-ctr hmac-md5 none
debug1: kex: client->server aes128-ctr hmac-md5 none
debug1: SSH2_MSG_KEX_DH_GEX_REQUEST(1024<1024<8192) sent
debug1: expecting SSH2_MSG_KEX_DH_GEX_GROUP
debug1: SSH2_MSG_KEX_DH_GEX_INIT sent
debug1: expecting SSH2_MSG_KEX_DH_GEX_REPLY
The authenticity of host 'server.frapz.org.pl (62.233.184.11)' can't be established.
RSA key fingerprint is e8:d2:6b:bf:4d:31:1c:8e:5f:b1:ea:2b:7b:03:5b:fc.
Are you sure you want to continue connecting (yes/no)? yes
Warning: Permanently added 'server.frapz.org.pl' (RSA) to the list of known hosts.
debug1: ssh_rsa_verify: signature correct
debug1: SSH2_MSG_NEWKEYS sent
debug1: expecting SSH2_MSG_NEWKEYS
debug1: SSH2_MSG_NEWKEYS received
debug1: Roaming not allowed by server
debug1: SSH2_MSG_SERVICE_REQUEST sent
debug1: SSH2_MSG_SERVICE_ACCEPT received
debug1: Authentications that can continue: publickey,keyboard-interactive
debug1: Next authentication method: publickey
debug1: Trying private key: /root/.ssh/id_rsa
debug1: Trying private key: /root/.ssh/id_dsa
debug1: Next authentication method: keyboard-interactive
Password:[]
```

Fig. 9.9 Logging

before entrusting her credentials. One-way authentication is enough to download the key to encrypt the session, while its time complexity is much lower.

During the contact between the client and server, the client receives the certificate confirmed by the signature of the CA. To open the certificate the user uses the public key of the CA. The public key of the website received from the transfer is used to encrypt data towards the server. One of the SSL subprotocols is a protocol of the SSLHP handshake (SSL Handshake Protocol) which provides an identification service and negotiates the method of encryption. Another SSL subprotocol is a protocol of the SSLRP record (SSL Record Protocol) which is responsible for the packing data to be encrypted. The first protocol works in the application layer and the second one in the layer of the OSI presentation.

The phases of connection using the SSL protocol:

1. Establishment of communication with a server by a client.
2. Negotiations about operating encryption algorithms, identity certificates and other data and agreement of mutual set of operating algorithms.

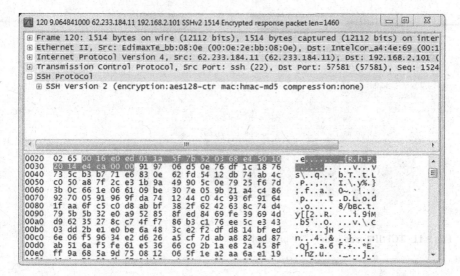

Fig. 9.10 TCP/IP frame

3. Verification of server identity on the basis of received information. (In the above points the asymmetric cipher is chosen from the mutual set.)
4. Exchange of session keys, generated at random.
5. Beginning of transmission encrypted by generated keys.

In order to encrypt tunneled data in SSL the asymmetric cipher is used, agreed during the initial data exchange. The encryption key is generated at random for every connection.

SSL guarantees:

- Privacy—connection is encrypted,
- Authorization—the client and the server determine their own identity,
- Integrity of sent data—by the checksum.

A description of the SSL protocol (commercial version) is available from http://wp.netscape.com/eng/ssl3/. Its free equivalent is OpenSSL http://www. openssl.org/.

9.3.5 The Use of SSL in Practice

When do we use a coded connection? The SSL protocol is one of the methods offering encryption for the security of financial transactions. Transactions using SSL are fast and transparent for the users. We often encounter this solution while using credit cards during logging into an e-bank. Today most banks have WWW interfaces which allow us to use bank resources. We purchase products by electronic transac-

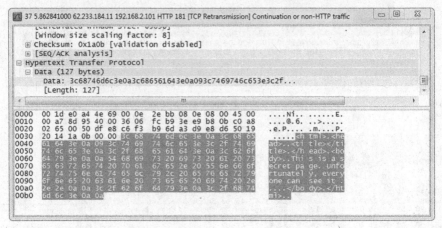

Fig. 9.11 TCP/IP frame with HTTP protocol

tions. Such solutions appear also in systems which need verification/logging of the users.

1. During SSL connection the browser's WWW address starts from https://; and initiates the connection on port 443 of the server instead of 80.
2. In the Internet Explorer browser in the right part of the status bar there is a small closed yellow padlock. If we stop the cursor above the padlock, the information of the length of the asymmetric key is highlighted. After clicking on the padlock we can see the certificate of the server authorisation.
3. In the browsers from the Netscape family the padlock is all the time shown in the left part of the status bar, during the SSL connection the padlock is closed.

Most servers use 128-bit keys. Current versions of the browsers support such encryption.

The security consists of these elements: strong cryptographic algorithms and well-designed protocols. The experts agree that SSL from the cryptographic point of view is very good. The weakest link is unfortunately the human. SSL informs the user about its state using the lock icon. The closed lock means that the browser is connected with some server. The task for the user is to verify the certificate of the server. There are some dangers which can violate the security of SSL and these are attacks on the service of the domain names (DNS). If the cyber-imposter imitates the name of the computer from the URL into an IP address which is under her control, and if she receives a certificate from one of the CA's, she may provide services at an appropriate level of security, while the user would have no idea what happened.

The following two figures show intercepted TCP/IP frames. In Fig. 9.12 use of the SSL protocol is visible and the data are incomprehensible—encrypted. Figure 9.11 presents the use of the HTTP protocol, where data is sent as plain text. If a user decides on unencrypted connection, the user should be aware of the risk of data interception.

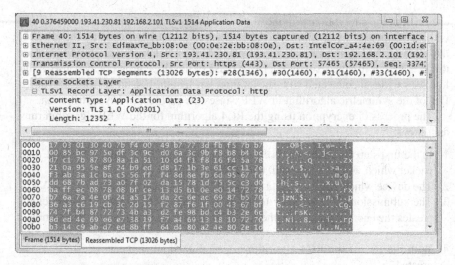

Fig. 9.12 TCP/IP frame with SSL/TLS protocol

9.4 Wireless Network Security

In traditional computer systems connected with a wired the data is sent using wiring. In order to send the data it is necessary to connect physically any computer to a proper network link. The security of such connections was discussed in previous chapters.

In this subsection the use of cryptography for security in wireless networks is presented. Such a network includes a client's station and access points. Direct wireless connection between two computers which are client stations is possible. In such a case there is peer-to-peer or ad-hoc connection. Wireless transmission of data is executed using radio waves. Wireless networks which fulfill the 802.11 standard use radio waves at frequency 2.4 GHz or 5 GHz to send data. Because of the properties of such waves the data sent by a network of type 802.11 can be intercepted by radio from a distance by any attacker. Such a person does not have to use any machines for radio transmission. This is a reason why wireless transmission should use cryptographic security means. Basic mechanisms which ensure the security of wireless networks are the protocols WEP, WPA, WPA-PSK and WPA2. Their basic versions are presented here.

9.4.1 WEP Protocol

The 802.11 wireless network standard assumes the use of the WEP encryption protocol. Such a protocol was designed to ensure the security of sent data and especially its confidentiality. The WEP protocol is used during authentication of communicating entities and in order to support the confidentiality of transmission. The protocol uses symmetric encryption with the algorithm RC4 presented previously. Since this is the asymmetric key stream cipher it is required that the key used by the client is the same as the key used by an access point. Unfortunately, the required length of the RC4 key is 40 bits. Usually in practical use of the WEP protocol, because of the low security level connected with such a short key length, 104-bit keys are also used. Use of the symmetric algorithm in WEP causes the problem of key distribution.

The process of encryption using the RC4 algorithm for the WEP algorithm runs as follows:

1. In the first step the checksum is calculated (Integrity Check Value), from the data packet which will be encrypted. CRC-32 algorithm is used.
2. The device which sends the data generates a 24-bit random initial vector (IV).
3. The submission of this vector together with the secret key at a proper length creates the encryption key for the RC4 algorithm, used to encrypt the data transmission.
4. With the use of the RC4 algorithm a pseudorandom sequence $RC4(IV, k))$ is created.
5. The packet of sent data is encrypted with calculated checksum $(M, ¢V(M))$.
6. After the encryption process we receive a cryptogram

$$C = (M, ICV(M))A(RC4(IV, k)).$$

7. To encrypt the data the IV vector and the whole pair (IV, C) is added and the sum is sent to the wireless network.

In order to decode the message the recipient has to know the secret IV vector and the k key. The key is added in the explicit way to a cryptogram.

Despite wide usage, the WEP protocol has some essential weaknesses excluding it from algorithms which can be recognized as secure. The faults allow very quick, effective attacks on networks protected by this algorithm.

It is proved that the used length of the initial vector is too short and there is a danger that many sent packets use the same vectors. The calculations show that it is enough to have 5000 packets and the IV vector repeats itself with 50 % probability. Additionally, because of faults in the software of some access points, the keys can be written as casual ASCII character strings which results in a space reduction of admitted keys to about 2 million keys. Of course this means that a network protected with such a key is open to brute-force attacks.

For many years there has been free software available on the Internet to monitor wireless transmission within a few minutes in order to get a proper set of information which can be enough to break the protocol. The discussed method was compiled by specialists from Technische Universitaet Darmstadt.

9.4.2 WPA Protocol and Its Modifications

Because of the very weak security of the WEP protocol, the WPA protocol was proposed (WiFi Protected Access). This protocol was designed to cooperate with authentication servers according to the 802.1X standard. There is a possibility that WPA can work in a mode *Pre-Shared Key*, in which every user can give a password (the same for everyone). During the work of the protocol the data is encrypted as in WEP using an RC4 cipher but with a longer 128-bit key and a 48-bit initial vector. The enlargement of the length of these parameters means that the time needed to break the code significantly increases. In order to increase the level of security, WPA requires dynamic change of keys using the TKIP protocol (Temporary Key Integrity Protocol). Besides the changes of encryption parameters and authentication in the WPA protocol the algorithm for calculating the checksum is strengthened.

On 24 June 2004 another standard of the 802.11i wireless network was published. The WPA2 protocol consisted of two basic modifications:

1. the algorithm of the calculating checksum was strengthened,
2. the RC4 cipher was replaced with a new symmetric encryption standard.

In practical wireless networks another variety of WPA protocol is used, WPA-PSK (Pre-Shared Key mode). The passwords used in this variety can consist of 63 characters of ASCII code or 64 hexadecimal numbers. In the case of passwords used from ASCII character strings the length of the password is decreased from 506 bits to 256 bits using a hash function. While choosing passwords remember that the process of authentication can be overheard and data received in such a way can be used in off-line analysis. Because of this, while choosing the passwords, avoid a character string which can be guessed using the dictionary method.

It is worth noticing that the WEP protocol does not give any protection in a wireless network. Using the WPA2 protocol is safer. While using the WPA-PSK protocol remember about possible brute-force and dictionary attacks; that is why you should choose a long key (at least 8–10 characters) which does not rely on phrases from the dictionary.

References

1. ANSI X9.31. Digital Signatures Using Reversible Public Key Cryptography for the Financial Services Industry (rDSA) (1998)
2. ANSI X9.62. Public Key Cryptography for the Financial Services Industry: The Elliptic Curve Digital Signature Algorithm (ECDSA) (1998)
3. ANSI X9.95. Trusted Time Stamp Management and Security, USA (2009). https://www.x9.org/news/pr050701
4. Agrawal, M., Kayal, N., Saxena, N.: PRIMES is in P. Ann. Math. **160**(2), 781–793 (2004)
5. Anderson, R.J.: Security Engineering: A Guide to Building Dependable Distributed Systems, 2nd edn. Wiley, New York (2008)
6. Aoki, K., Guo, J., Matusiewicz, K., Sasaki, Y., Wang, L.: Preimages for step-reduced SHA-2. In: Advances in Cryptology—Asiacrypt 2009. Lecture Notes in Computer Science, vol. 5912, pp. 578–597. Springer, Berlin (2009)
7. Aumasson, J.P., Henzen, L., Meier, W., Phan, R.C.W.: SHA-3 proposal BLAKE. http://www.131002.net/blake/
8. Barker, E.: Recommendation for Digital Signature Timeliness. NIST Special Publication 800-102, National Institute of Standards and Technology, USA (2009)
9. Basin, D., Wolff, B.: Theorem Proving in Higher Order Logics. LNCS, vol. 2758. Springer, Berlin (2003)
10. Bella, G., Longo, C., Paulson, L.C.: In: Basin, D., Wolff, B. (eds.) Theorem Proving in Higher Order Logics. LNCS, vol. 2758, pp. 352–366 (2003)
11. Bella, G., Massacci, F., Paulson, L.C.: Verifying the SET registration protocols. IEEE J. Sel. Areas Commun. **21**(1), 77–87 (2003)
12. Bellare, M., Garay, J., Hauser, R., Herberg, A., Krawczyk, H., Steiner, M., Tsudik, G., Waidner, M.: iKP—a family of secure electronic payment protocols. In: Proceedings of the 1st USENIX Workshop on Electronic Commerce (1995)
13. Bernstein, D.J.: Second preimages for 6 (7? (8??)) rounds of Keccak? NIST mailing list (2010). http://ehash.iaik.tugraz.at/uploads/6/65/NIST-mailing-list_Bernstein-Daemen.txt
14. Bertoni, G., Daemen, J., Peeters, M., Van Assche, G.: Cryptographic Sponges (2012). http://sponge.noekeon.org
15. Bertoni, G., Daemen, J., Peeters, M., Van Assche, G.: Keccak sponge function family main document. http://keccak.noekeon.org/Keccak-main-2.1.pdf
16. Bhattacharyya, R., Mandal, A., Nandi, M.: Security analysis of the mode of JH hash function. In: FSE 2010. Lecture Notes in Computer Science, vol. 6147, pp. 168–191. Springer, Berlin (2010)
17. Biham, E., Shamir, A.: Differential cryptanalysis of DES-like cryptosystems. J. Cryptol. **4**(1), 3–72 (1991)
18. Biham, E., Shamir, A.: Differential cryptanalysis of the full 16-round DES. In: Crypto. Lecture Notes in Computer Science, vol. 740, pp. 487–496. Springer, Berlin (1993)

19. Biham, E., Boneh, D., Reingold, O.: Breaking generalized Diffie–Hellman modulo a composite is no easier than factoring. Inf. Process. Lett. **70**, 83–87 (1999)

20. Biham, E., Dunkelman, O., Keller, N.: A new attack on 6-round idea. In: FSE 2007. Lecture Notes in Computer Science, vol. 4593, pp. 211–224. Springer, Berlin (2007)

21. Bos, J., Kaihara, M.E.: Playstation 3 computing breaks 2^{60} barrier: 112-bit prime ECDLP solved (2009). http://lacal.epfl.ch/112bit_prime

22. Bresson, E., Chevassut, O., Pointcheval, D.: The group Diffie–Hellman problems. In: SAC'02: Revised Papers from the 9th Annual International Workshop on Selected Areas in Cryptography, pp. 325–338 (2003)

23. Burrows, M., Abadi, M., Needham, R.: A logic of authentication. ACM Trans. Comput. Syst. **8**(1), 18–36 (1990)

24. Clarke, E., Marrero, W., Jha, S.: Using state space exploration and a natural deduction style message derivation engine to verify security protocols. In: IFIP Working Conference on Programming Concepts and Methods (PROCOMET) (1996)

25. Break DES in less than a single day, Copacobana Rivyera Project. http://www.sciengines.com/company/news-a-events/74-des-in-1-day.html

26. Copeland, J.: Notices of the AMS, vol. 58, pp. 1540–1542. AMS, Providence (2011)

27. Cormen, T.H., Leiserson, C.E., Rivest, R.L., Stein, C.: Introduction to Algorithms, 3rd edn. MIT Press, Cambridge (2009)

28. Crandall, R., Pomerance, C.: Subexponential factoring algorithms. In: Prime Numbers: A Computational Perspective. Springer, Berlin (2001)

29. Levy, S.: Crypto: How the Code Rebels Beat the Government Saving Privacy in the Digital Age. Penguin, Baltimore (2001)

30. Cryptographic Key Length Recommendation. BlueKrypt. http://www.keylength.com/en/compare/

31. Diffie, W., Hellman, M.E.: New directions in cryptography. IEEE Trans. Inf. Theory **22**(6), 644–654 (1976)

32. FIPS PUB 186. Digital Signature Standard (DSS), Federal Information Processing Standards Publication 186, US NIST (1994)

33. FIPS PUB 186-3. Digital Signature Standard (DSS), Federal Information Processing Standards Publication 186-3, US NIST (2009)

34. Dinur, I., Dunkelman, O., Shamir, A.: Collision attacks on up to 5 rounds of SHA-3 using generalized internal differentials. Cryptology ePrint Archive. Report 2012/672 (2012). http://eprint.iacr.org

35. Directive 1999/93/ec of the European Parliament and of the Council of 13 December 1999. Official EU Journal L 13

36. distributed.net Project. http://www.distributed.net/DES

37. Electronic Signatures and Infrastructures (ESI); Policy requirements for time-stamping authorities. ETSI TS 102 023 v1.2.2, European Telecommunications Standards Institute, Technical Specification (2008)

38. Erskine, R.: The Poles reveal their secrets: Alastair Denniston's account of the July 1939 meeting at Pyry. Cryptologia **30**(4), 294–305 (2006)

39. EU Directive 1999/93/EC on a Community framework for electronic signatures. Official Journal L 013, P. 0012–0020, Annex II, 19/01/2000

40. Ferguson, N., Lucks, S., Schneier, B., Whiting, D., Bellare, M., Kohno, T., Callas, J., Walker, J.: The Skein Hash Function Family (2010). http://www.skein-hash.info/sites/default/files/skein1.1.pdf

41. FIPS PUB 46: Data Encryption Standard. National Bureau of Standards (1977)

42. FIPS PUB 46-1: Data Encryption Standard. National Bureau of Standards (1988)

43. FIPS PUB 46-2: Data Encryption Standard. National Institute of Standards and Technology (NIST) (1993)

44. FIPS PUB 46-3: Data Encryption Standard (DES). Federal Information Processing Standards Publications (1999). http://csrc.nist.gov/publications/fips/fips46-3/fips46-3.pdf

45. FIPS PUB 180-4: Secure Hash Standard. National Institute of Standards and Technology (NIST) (2012)

46. FIPS PUB 197: Announcing the Advanced Encryption Standard (AES). National Institute of Standards and Technology (NIST) (2001)
47. Goutam, P., Subhamóy, M.: RC4 Stream Cipher and Its Variants. CRC Press, Boca Raton (2011)
48. Grajek, M.: Enigma. Bliżej Prawdy. Wydawnictwo Rebis, Poznań (2007). ISBN 978-83-7510-103-4
49. Hodges, A.: Alan Turing: The Enigma. Burnett Books, London (1992)
50. Homsirikamol, E., Morawiecki, P., Rogawski, M., Srebrny, M.: Security margin evaluation of SHA-3 contest finalists through SAT-based attacks (2013). Submitted for publication
51. http://www.interhack.net/projects/deschall/
52. https://www.enigmail.net/documentation/index.php
53. Internet key exchange protocol. In: RFC 2408 (1998)
54. Kahn, D.: The Codebreakers: The Comprehensive History of Secret Communication from Ancient Times to the Internet. Scribner's, New York (1996)
55. Khovratovich, D.: Bicliques for permutations: collision and preimage attacks in stronger settings. Cryptology ePrint Archive, Report 2012/141 (2012). http://eprint.iacr.org/2012/141.pdf
56. Khovratovich, D., Rechberger, C., Savelieva, A.: Bicliques for preimages: attacks on Skein-512 and the SHA-2 family. In: Fast Software Encryption (FSE). Lecture Notes in Computer Science Springer, Berlin (2012)
57. Kleinjung, T., et al.: Discrete logarithms in $GF(p)$—160 digits (2007). https://listserv.nodak.edu/cgibin/wa.exe?A2=ind0702
58. Kleinjung, T., Aoki, K., Franke, J., Lenstra, A.K., Thome, E., Bos, J.W., Gaudry, P., Kruppa, A., Montgomery, P.L., Osvik, D.A., te Riele, H., Timofeev, A., Zimmermann, P.: Factorization of a 768-bit RSA modulus. In: Advances in cryptology—Crypto 2010, vol. 6223, pp. 333–350 (2010)
59. Kumar, S., Paar, C., Pelzl, J., Pfeiffer, G., Rupp, A., Schimmler, M.: How to break DES for Euro 8980. In: 2nd Workshop on Special-Purpose Hardware for Attacking Cryptographic Systems, SHARCS 2006, Cologne, Germany (2006)
60. Kurkowski, M.: Deduction methods of verification of correctness of authentication protocols. Ph.D. Thesis. ICS PAS, Warsaw, Poland (2003)
61. Lai, X., Massey, J.L., Murphy, S.: Markov ciphers and differential cryptanalysis. In: Advances in Cryptology—Eurocrypt'91. Lecture Notes in Computer Science, vol. 576, pp. 17–38. Springer, Berlin (1992)
62. Lenstra, H.W. Jr., Pomerance, C.: Primality testing with Gaussian periods (2011). http://www.math.dartmouth.edu/~carlp/aks041411.pdf
63. Liangyu, X., Ji, L.: Attacks on Round-Reduced BLAKE. Cryptology ePrint Archive, Report 2009/238 (2009). http://eprint.iacr.org/2009/238.pdf
64. Lowe, G.: Breaking and fixing the Needham-Schroeder public-key protocol using FDR. In: Proceedings of TACAS, pp. 147–166 (1996)
65. Mason, S. (ed.): International Electronic Evidence. British Institute of International and Comparative Law (2008)
66. Mason, S. (ed.): Electronic Evidence, 2nd edn. LexisNexis, Butterworths (2010)
67. Matsui, M.: Linear cryptanalysis of DES cipher. In: Advances in Cryptology—Eurocrypt'93, pp. 386–397 (1994)
68. Menezes, A.J., van Oorschot, P.C., Vanstone, S.A.: Handbook of Applied Cryptography. CRC Press, Boca Raton (2001). Fifth printing with Errata: http://www.cacr.math.uwaterloo.ca/hac/errata/errata.html
69. Needham, R., Schroeder, M.: Using encryption for authentication in large networks of computers. Commun. ACM **21**(12), 993–999 (1978)
70. NIST Special Publication 800-67 Revision 1 Recommendation for the Triple Data Encryption Algorithm (TDEA) Block Cipher. National Institute of Standards and Technology (NIST) (2012)
71. NIST: NIST's Policy on Hash Functions. National Institute of Standards and Technology Computer Security Resource Center. http://csrc.nist.gov/groups/ST/hash/policy.html
72. NIST: Tentative SHA-3 standard (FIPS XXX) development timeline. National Institute of Standards and Technology. http://csrc.nist.gov/groups/ST/hash/sha-3/timeline_fips.html

73. NIST: SHA-3 Winner. http://csrc.nist.gov/groups/ST/hash/sha-3/winner_sha-3.html
74. Odlyzko, A.: Discrete logarithms: the past and the future. Des. Codes Cryptogr. **19**(2–3), 129–145 (2000)
75. Odlyzko, A.: Discrete logarithms over finite fields. In: Mullen, G., Panario, D. (eds.): Handbook of Finite Fields. CRC Press, Boca Raton (2013, to appear)
76. Palmgren, K.: Diffie-Hellman key exchange—a non-mathematician's explanation. ISSA J.
77. Papadimitriou, Ch.: Computational Complexity. Addison-Wesley, Reading (1994)
78. Paulson, L.C.: Inductive analysis of the internet protocol TLS. ACM Trans. Inf. Syst. Secur. **2**(3), 332–351 (1999)
79. Pieprzyk, J., Hardjono, T., Seberry, J.: Fundamentals of Computer Security. Springer, Berlin (2003)
80. Pinch, R.: The Carmichael numbers up to 10^{21} (2007). http://s369624816.websitehome.co.uk/rgep/p82.pdf
81. PKCS#1. PKCS, RSA Public Key Cryptography Standard #1 v2.1, RSA Laboratories (2002)
82. Recommendation for Key Management. Special Publication 800-57, Revision 3, Part 1, NIST, USA (2012)
83. Recommendation x.509: The directory—authentication framework. In: ITU-T (1997)
84. Rejewski, M.: How Polish mathematicians deciphered the Enigma. Ann. Hist. Comput. **3**(3), 213–234 (1981)
85. Ribenboim, P.: Cryptography and Data Security. Springer, Berlin (1991)
86. Rivest, R.L., Robshaw, M.J., Sidney, R., Yin, Y.L.: The RC6 Block Cipher. v1.1 (1998). http://people.csail.mit.edu/rivest/pubs/RRSY98.pdf
87. Ross, K.A., Wright, C.: Discrete Mathematics. Pearson Education, Upper Saddle River (2012)
88. RSA numbers. http://en.wikipedia.org/wiki/RSA_numbers (formerly on http://www.rsa.com/rsalabs/node.asp?id=2093)
89. Ryan, D.: Enigma: The Caldwell Series. AuthorHouse, Bloomington (2011)
90. Schläffer, M.: Updated Differential Analysis of Grøstl. Groestl website (2011). http://groestl.info/groestl-analysis.pdf
91. Schneier, B.: E-mail Security. Wiley, New York (1995)
92. Schneier, B.: Applied Cryptography: Protocols, Algorithms, and Source Code in C, 2nd edn. Wiley, New York (2004)
93. Set secure electronic transaction LLC. In: The SET Standard Specification (1997)
94. Shannon, C.E.: The communication theory of secrecy systems. Bell Syst. Tech. J. **28**(4), 656–715 (1949)
95. Singh, S.: The Code Book: The Science of Secrecy from Ancient Egypt to Quantum Cryptography. Random House, New York (2000)
96. Stengers, J.: Enigma, the French, the Poles and the British 1931–1940. Rev. Belge Philol. Hist. **82**(1–2), 449–466 (2004)
97. Stevens, M.: New collision attacks on SHA-1 based on optimal joint local-collision analysis. In: EUROCRYPT 2013. Lecture Notes in Computer Science, vol. 7881, pp. 245–261. Springer, Berlin (2013)
98. Stevens, M., Lenstra, A.K., de Weger, B.: Chosen-prefix collisions for MD5 and applications. Int. J. Appl. Cryptogr. **2**, 4 (2012)
99. The MD5 message-digest algorithm. In: RFC 1321 (1992)
100. Wang, X., Yin, Y.L., Yu, H.: Finding collisions in the full SHA-1. In: Crypto 2005. LNCS, vol. 3621, pp. 17–36. Springer, Berlin (2005)
101. Wenger, J.N., Engstrom, J.N., Meader, R.I.: History of the Bombe Project. OP-20-G, Memorandum dated 30 May 1944
102. What is digital timestamping. RSA Laboratories (2012). http://www.rsa.com/rsalabs/node.asp?id=2347
103. Wilcox, J.E.: About the Enigma, Solving the Enigma: History of the Cryptanalytic Bombe, a NSA pamphlet. Center for Cryptologic History, National Security Agency. http://edthelen.org/comp-hist/NSA-Enigma.html
104. Wobst, R.: Cryptology Unlocked. Wiley, New York (2007)
105. Woo, T., Lam, S.: A lesson on authentication protocol design. In: Operating Systems Review, pp. 24–37 (1994)

Index

C. Kościelny et al., *Modern Cryptography Primer*,
DOI 10.1007/978-3-642-41386-5, © Springer-Verlag Berlin Heidelberg 2013

Printed in the United States
By Bookmasters